The Edinburgh Companion to Irvine Welsh

Edinburgh Companions to Scottish Literature

Series Editors: Ian Brown and Thomas Owen Clancy

Titles in the series include:

The Edinburgh Companion to Robert Burns
Edited by Gerard Carruthers
978 0 7486 3648 8 (hardback)
978 0 7486 3649 5 (paperback)

The Edinburgh Companion to Twentieth-Century Scottish Literature
Edited by Ian Brown and Alan Riach
978 0 7486 3693 8 (hardback)
978 0 7486 3694 5 (paperback)

The Edinburgh Companion to Contemporary Scottish Poetry
Edited by Matt McGuire and Colin Nicholson
978 0 7486 3625 9 (hardback)
978 0 7486 3626 6 (paperback)

The Edinburgh Companion to Muriel Spark
Edited by Michael Gardiner and Willy Maley
978 0 7486 3768 3 (hardback)
978 0 7486 3769 0 (paperback)

The Edinburgh Companion to Robert Louis Stevenson
Edited by Penny Fielding
978 0 7486 3554 2 (hardback)
978 0 7486 3555 9 (paperback)

The Edinburgh Companion to Irvine Welsh
Edited by Berthold Schoene
978 0 7486 3917 5 (hardback)
978 0 7486 3918 2 (paperback)

The Edinburgh Companion to James Kelman
Edited by Scott Hames
978 0 7486 3963 2 (hardback)
978 0 7486 3964 9 (paperback)

Forthcoming volumes:

The Edinburgh Companion to Scottish Romanticism
Edited by Murray Pittock
978 0 7486 3845 1 (hardback)
978 0 7486 3846 8 (paperback)

The Edinburgh Companion to Scottish Drama
Edited by Ian Brown
978 0 7486 4108 6 (hardback)
978 0 7486 4107 9 (paperback)

The Edinburgh Companion to James Hogg
Edited by Ian Duncan and Douglas Mack
978 0 7486 4124 6 (hardback)
978 0 7486 4123 9 (paperback)

The Edinburgh Companion to Irvine Welsh

Edited by Berthold Schoene

Edinburgh University Press

Für Gerlinde

Edinburgh University Press Ltd
22 George Square, Edinburgh

www.euppublishing.com

Typeset in 10.5 on 12.5pt Goudy
by Servis Filmsetting Limited, Stockport, Cheshire, and
printed and bound in Great Britain by
CPI Antony Rowe Ltd, Chippenham and Eastbourne

A CIP record for this book is available from the British Library

ISBN 978 0 7486 3917 5 (hardback)
ISBN 978 0 7486 3918 2 (paperback)

Contents

Abbreviations vi
Series Editors' Preface vii
Brief Biography of Irvine Welsh viii

Introduction 1
Berthold Schoene
1 Welsh and Tradition 9
Alice Ferrebe
2 Welsh's Novels 19
Matt McGuire
3 Welsh's Shorter Fiction 31
David Borthwick
4 *Trainspotting*, the Film 42
Duncan Petrie
5 Welsh and Gender 54
Carole Jones
6 Welsh, Drugs and Subculture 65
Berthold Schoene
7 Welsh and the Theatre 77
Adrienne Scullion
8 Welsh and Identity Politics 89
Gavin Miller
9 Welsh and Edinburgh 100
Peter Clandfield and Christian Lloyd
10 Welsh in Translation 113
Katherine Ashley

Endnotes 126
Further Reading 141
Notes on Contributors 143
Index 145

Abbreviations

AH	*The Acid House*
BS	*The Bedroom Secrets of the Master Chefs*
C	*Crime*
E	*Ecstasy*
F	*Filth*
G	*Glue*
IY	*If You Liked School, You'll Love Work*
MSN	*Marabou Stork Nightmares*
P	*Porno*
T	*Trainspotting*

Series Editors' Preface

The preface to this series' initial tranche of volumes recognised that some literary canons can conceive of a single 'Great Tradition'. The series editors consider that there is no such simple way of conceiving of Scottish literature's variousness. This arises from a multilingual and multivalent culture. It also arises from a culture that includes authors who move for many different reasons beyond Scotland's physical boundaries, sometimes to return, sometimes not. The late Iain Wright in *The Edinburgh History of Scottish Literature* talked of the Scots as a 'semi-nomadic people'. Robert Louis Stevenson travelled in stages across the world; Muriel Spark settled in Southern Africa, England and then Italy; James Kelman, while remaining close to his roots in Glasgow, has spent important periods in the United States; Irvine Welsh has moved from Leith, in Edinburgh, to a series of domestic bases on both sides of the Atlantic.

All four writers at one time and in one way or another have been underappreciated. Stevenson – most notoriously perhaps – for a time was seen as simply an adventure writer for the young. Yet Stevenson is now recognised not for simplicity, but his wonderful complexity, an international writer whose admirers included Borges and Nabokov. Similarly, the other three have firm international reputations based on innovation, literary experiment and pushing formal boundaries. All have grown out of the rich interrelationship of English and Scots in the literature to which they contribute; they embody its intercultural richness, hybridity and cosmopolitan potential. Some of their subject matter is far-flung: often they are situated not only physically but also in literary terms well beyond Scotland. Yet they are all important contributors to Scottish literature, a fact which problematises in the most positive and creative way any easy notion of what Scottish literature is.

Ian Brown
Thomas Owen Clancy

Brief Biography of Irvine Welsh

Irvine Welsh was born on 27 September 1958 in Leith, the son of Peter Welsh, a dock worker, and his wife, Jean. The family relocated to Muirhouse, a new housing scheme on the outskirts of Edinburgh. On leaving school Welsh initially worked as a TV repairman. In 1978 he moved to London, where he became immersed in the punk music scene. He then spent time as a property entrepreneur before temping as a clerk for Hackney Council. In the late 1980s, newly married, Welsh returned to Edinburgh and became a training officer in Edinburgh District Council's housing department. From 1988 to 1990 he studied for an MBA at Heriot-Watt University. In the early 1990s short stories by Welsh began to appear in small, independent literary magazines. *Trainspotting* was published in 1993. The novel was among the final ten titles long-listed for the Booker Prize, but two judges were so offended by it that they threatened to resign should it make the shortlist. To date *Trainspotting* has sold over one million copies in the United Kingdom alone. Danny Boyle's film adaptation was released on 23 February 1996. The film took £11 million at the UK box office and became the most successful independent release of the year in the United States.

Following publication of four more novels and two collections of short stories, Welsh became a regular columnist for the *Daily Telegraph* in 2003. He also spent some time teaching creative writing at Columbia College, Chicago, where he met his second wife, Beth Quinn, whom he married in July 2005. (His first marriage had ended in divorce.) After living in Amsterdam for several years, since 2004 Welsh has been based mainly in Dublin. While continuing to produce fiction – *The Bedroom Secrets of the Masterchefs* (2006), *If You Liked School, You'll Love Work* (2007) and *Crime* (2008) – Welsh has begun to develop a strong interest in film. Welsh is a partner in two burgeoning film company projects: Four Ways and Jawbone Films. His enduring popularity and cultural import are documented by the recent publication of *Reheated Cabbage* (2009), a collection of some of his pre-*Trainspotting* work, most of which had been out of print since the early 1990s.

Introduction

Berthold Schoene

To fully appreciate the impact of Irvine Welsh's work on contemporary British culture and the Scottish literary imagination, one must begin with a quick look at the Scottish literary scene in 1993, the year that *Trainspotting*, Welsh's first and most successful novel, was published. As far as impact and iconic stature are concerned, *Trainspotting* joined Alasdair Gray's (b. 1934) *Lanark* (1981) as one of the two watershed texts that heralded a new heyday in Scottish writing. Both novels captured the mood of devolutionary uncertainty that simultaneously burdened and inspired the nation between the two home rule referenda of 1979 and 1997. *Trainspotting*'s greatest achievement resides in its re-authentication of the Scottish tradition, paradoxically achieved by breaking with it, by asserting a local rootedness marred by deracination, and by distilling a sense of flux and mobility from claustrophobic stagnation. Unselfconscious, unapologetic and seemingly unencumbered by generic conventions or any definite ideological agenda, Welsh's early work makes a perfect match for Hamish White and Janice Galloway's identikit of 'the vital and volatile brat that is [Scottish] literature in the making'.[1] By contrast, Welsh's more recent, post-devolution work has been received far less enthusiastically and is often read as insufferably formulaic and anodyne, signalling the apparent decline of this literary *enfant terrible*-turned-'master chef', who seems increasingly incapacitated by the branding of his notoriety.

In 1989 Craig Beveridge and Ronald Turnbull described Scotland as 'a land of no gods or heroes',[2] and in 1993 Gavin Wallace and Randall Stevenson represented the country as stifled by 'old dreams' and starved of 'new visions'.[3] It is within this atmosphere that *Trainspotting* burst onto the scene, transforming Scotland's image by contemptuously 'turn[ing] its back on Tartanry and Balmorality'[4] and celebrating an aggressively antinationalist stance of defiant deviancy, displayed previously only in the occasional television sit-com, such as BBC Scotland's *Rab C. Nesbitt* (1988–99). Welsh's novel imagined Scotland in a new, radically contemporary way, paying little heed to the academically nurtured chimera of a malaise-stricken nation. Symptomatically, in his analysis of the early 1990s, even a critic as forward-looking and shrewd as Wallace could not escape the representational tropes of Scotland's alleged inferiorism. Urging writers 'to find the cracked and strangled voice and lend it healing speech', Wallace couched his critique of Scotland's 'novel of damaged identity' in the same lachrymose style that he regarded as so detrimental to Scottish cultural autonomy. Wallace's conclusion that 'the sound of that new-found voice will always be recognised as unmistakably ours'[5] seems equally problematic in that it compounds the tension between a fixed sense of national authenticity on the one hand and genuine innovation on the other. What if the fixtures of Scotland were to be subjected to a radical transformation, and suddenly new and hitherto alien 'Scotlands' emerged, and as a result Scottishness began to voice itself in a previously inconceivable, unheard-of way?

Unprecedented and unforeseeable, *Trainspotting* exploded the mix of nostalgia and wishful utopian projection that informed Wallace and Stevenson's collection of critical essays. Welsh's novel at once thwarted and fulfilled Wallace's hope for the rise of a new, curative voice capable of re-authenticating 'our' literary and cultural self-portrayal. Though firmly rooted in Scottish culture, *Trainspotting* set out not so much to heal as to expose the Scottish malaise, and the malaise it exposed had little to do with the dignified, aestheticised inferiorism suffered by certain middle-class intellectuals. Rather, its representational power was dedicated to the despair and ferocious needs of an underclass previously without voice or visibility in Scottish literature. Derek Paget's comment on Danny Boyle's film adaptation – namely, that 'the *Trainspotting* moment signalled the rejection, at least temporarily, of one kind of Britishness – the kind that routinely looked away from, and denied, anything with which it was not comfortable'[6] – applies equally to the idea of a common Scottishness unperturbed by class or multicultural difference. *Trainspotting* could become such an influential phenomenon only because at the same time as it perpetrated a radical break with twentieth-century Scottish literature, spearheaded by writers such as Hugh MacDiarmid (1892–1978) and James Kelman (b. 1946), it also revived what have traditionally been Scottish literature's chief preoccupations: identity, class, language and fantasy. The main difference is that in *Trainspotting* nothing is ever clear-cut; Scottishness can signify cultural paralysis, rootedness and mobility, identity as well as difference. Like MacDiarmid's, Welsh's use of language could be described as 'synthetic' in that it is stylised and strategically crafted, but rather than superimposing a code of his own making and speaking through, or for, his characters, Welsh accentuates his protagonists' idiomatic diversity by rendering himself a mere mouthpiece. Unlike in other, perhaps more typical working-class writing, in *Trainspotting* class is a complex and complicated thing as each social category is shown to splinter endlessly into multitudinous sub-strata, so that ultimately what Welsh's readers are left with are groups of individuals marked by various degrees of ostracism. In terms of genre *Trainspotting* bears a number of traits traditionally associated with fantasy literature. However, the novel's surreal magic and horror never have an alienating effect on the reader. The opposite is the case as they transcend realist representation, yet retain a strong sense of experiential verisimilitude.

In an interview with Jenifer Berman, Welsh tried to explain the success of *Trainspotting* by pointing to its otherness: 'The book was so different and so obviously from another culture. They [the critics] weren't used to it.'[7] *Trainspotting* is not 'literary' in the conventional sense. One of its most prominent features is its detachment not only from mainstream culture, but also from the cultural 'fringe'. The latter's lack of meaning for people like Welsh is expressed in the protagonist Mark Renton's throw-away comment that 'somebody sais that it wis the first day ay the Festival. Well, they certainly got the weather fir it' (*T*, 27). Welsh's work takes us beyond the fringe, pushing the limits of what has been deemed representable. Yet at the same time as marginality manifests in his work as a nasty, at times barely stomachable beyond, his characters' daily lives are shown to run more or less parallel to our own. The majority of Welsh's characters hail from Leith or Edinburgh's dilapidated council estates, but Welsh does not leave them there to form neatly segregated communities of the oppressed. He insists on subculture's ubiquity; roaming and infiltrating the centre of the city, his characters successfully resist municipal ghettoisation. No doubt Alan Freeman is right when he writes that 'for all its swagger, Welsh's work exhibits lavish qualities of the spiritual despair and fractured identity so frequently found in Scottish fiction'.[8] However, Welsh will not let his characters wallow in their suffering, which thus never becomes wholly debilitating. *Trainspotting* can, and must, be read as a document of subcultural despondency, but Welsh portrays this despondency as a corrosive epidemic instead of an enfeebling, strictly localised disease. In Welsh's work despair is channelled into self-empowering gestures of defiance, creating an atmosphere in which even self-destructive behaviour can at times be forged into subcultural resistance.

While some fans of Welsh's work may welcome the fact that it took *Trainspotting* less than five years to become a classic course text in Scottish schools, others may regard this canonisation as a deliberate attempt to neuter a radically subversive text by absorbing it into the mainstream. *Trainspotting* itself refuses all conventional categories of belonging. Marked by a celebration of cultural dislocation which, according to Patricia Horton, derives from 'an inability to locate forms of identity through class, region or nationhood',[9] the novel vociferously militates against its own Scottishness. Disgusted by Scotland's collusion in its own subjugation, Renton, *Trainspotting*'s anti-hero, vents his anger and frustration by calling his home country:

> A place ay dispossessed white trash in a trash country fill ay dispossessed white trash. Some say that the Irish are the trash ay Europe. That's shite. It's the Scots. The Irish hud the bottle tae win thir country back, or at least maist ay it. Ah remember getting wound up when Nicksy's brar, down in London, described the Scots as 'porridge wogs'. Now ah realise that the only thing offensive about that statement was its racism against black people. Otherwise it's spot-on. Anybody will tell you; the Scots make good soldiers. Like ma brar, Billy. (*T*, 190)

Far removed from the nationalist imageries of contemporaneous Hollywood blockbusters such as Michael Caton-Jones's *Rob Roy* (1995) or Mel Gibson's *Braveheart* (1995), Renton's outburst is no cry to arms but a manifesto of national dissociation, underscored by Renton's departure from Scotland at the end of the novel. Fiona Oliver reads Renton's escape as 'a tentative but hopeful metaphor for Scotland in insisting on a national renewal once it has rid itself of the self-debasing and self-destructive notions of failure in its own identity',[10] but what does it really say about Welsh's view of Scotland if in his opinion it can only achieve regeneration whilst outside itself? In *Porno*, his twenty-first-century sequel to *Trainspotting*, Welsh repeats the gesture of saying farewell to Scotland: Renton returns to Edinburgh only to set off again as soon as he can, this time not to nearby Amsterdam but to San Francisco. Possibly to indicate the finality of his desertion, he is shown to emigrate not on his own but in the company of two nubile young women, one Scottish, the other English.

If Welsh's break with Scottishness is iconoclastic, the same is true of his remoulding of class as a hallmark of Scottish self-representation. Unlike writers of the urban Glasgow novel and most prominently Kelman, Welsh repudiates the fixity of class by problematising class-bound identities and showing working-class identity not only as heterogeneous, but as profoundly troubled and contradictory. As Welsh explains, 'there are two kinds of working-class philosophies, a radical or revolutionary one that sees the middle and upper classes as enemies; and another more individualistic desire to escape from the working class and assimilate into the upper classes'.[11] Welsh's characters do not always know where they are coming from or what they want; often they do not identify or recognise themselves as working-class, and with good reason. Much of Welsh's work introduces us to an under-class ostracised from hereditary forms of belonging. As Willy Maley puts it, Welsh 'takes us a step lower on the social ladder, to the bottom rung [. . .] sometimes he takes the ladder away altogether'.[12] Welsh depicts the lowest and most obscure substrata of society, but he does so without subscribing to a project of proletarian liberation. True to his intention 'to create characters who speak for themselves',[13] Welsh circumnavigates the social-realist tradition, which frequently 'was not merely on the side of the working class, but stood in their way, portraying them, representing them, speaking for them'.[14] Welsh's characters are left to *be* rather than represent, even if as a result his work appears at times to be without morality.

Only Welsh's refusal to set himself up 'as this great liberal who approves or disapproves of the characters'[15] could have resulted in the creation of Renton, a protagonist who is a hero and not a hero, who is not even always a protagonist, as on more than one occasion his prominence is called into question by the rise of other voices. Identified by some as Welsh's *alter ego*, Renton incorporates heterogeneity and hybridity: he is of working-class origin yet displays upward mobility by having been to university, if only for a term. Other features adding to his ambivalence include having a Protestant father and Catholic mother, being vegetarian but no animal lover, speaking both Scots and Standard English, being a lad happy to experiment with gay sex, a thinker desperate for oblivion, a lover wary of commitment, a junkie seemingly incapable of an addiction and, last but not least, an unpatriotic Scotsman. A perfect embodiment of Welsh's dismissal of fixed identities, Renton *is* undeniably Scottish, working-class and a drug user at the same time as he remains a shape-shifting borrower of identities, successfully mimicking both Anglo-Britishness and yuppie professionalism. In Sick Boy's view he is 'a traitor' (*P*, 170) and in his own 'a hypocrite, a winner who played at being a loser' (*P*, 382). Renton cannot be identified as unequivocally subversive either: his is not the voice of the proletariat or the subnation clamouring for enfranchisement. If Renton is a rebel, he is a rebel without a programme or plot, a rebel even without hope. Renton's is a boldly apolitical stance; he refuses to partake of anything larger or more abstract than his own individual self. Notably, rather than criticising Welsh for the hedonism of his characters, Maley picks up on the inarticulacy of their 'unspeakable hatred and violence',[16] suggesting that Renton and his associates' lack of politics might ultimately be explained by the absence of a suitable language in which they could adequately articulate their condition and state of mind.

Welsh's writing lacks the integrity of communal self-expression that is so characteristic of Kelman's work. Welsh's language is of course quite recognisably the east coast variant of vernacular Scots, but primarily it presents itself to us as idiolectal speech owned by individual speakers. Instead of listening in to emergent communal harmonies, readers are inundated by a cacophony of voices, an unwieldy orchestration of randomly assembled tales. In *Trainspotting* there are eight narrating voices, not including the omniscient narrator, and the timbre of the individual voice invariably sets the tone of the novel. In other words, 'idiolect becomes character in *Trainspotting* [. . .] all the principal first-person characters (Renton, Begbie, Sick Boy, Spud) have traits of speech which become a kind of recognizable signature tune of their character'.[17] Inevitably Welsh's writing is implicated in what Drew Milne has called 'the politics of accent', meaning that 'contemporary Scottish writers are [. . .] forced to negotiate the relation between English as a literary language and Englishness as a political formation'.[18] As Cairns Craig has explained in *The Modern Scottish Novel*, 'the existence of two or more distinct linguistic contexts within the text presumes the existence of alternative value systems which those linguistic systems express'.[19] Thus returning us to Maley's proposition that Welsh's characters' lack of agency is a corollary of their inarticulacy, Welsh's use of linguistic styles and registers shows that even if his characters appear to have embraced their political disenfranchisement, Welsh himself most certainly has not.

The chief characteristics of Welsh's work are also found in *Headstate*, not so much a play as a pre-club performance piece, which was premièred in 1994, one year after the publication of *Trainspotting*. The improvised nature of *Headstate* defies conclusive interpretation, and even producing a coherent summary proves difficult. Yet the play does merit attention, deriving from the same creative impulse that also delivered Welsh's debut novel, whose hybridity and structural openness it shares. Without a definite script, *Headstate* is no straightforward acting job; each time it has to be devised anew, opening up and exploring new interactive connections, or modifying the play's focus and perspective altogether. The play looks at the grand themes of love and life, as well as people's specific plights and pleasures with the former's manifold artificially induced replacements. Welsh's preoccupation with human desire for love and self-fulfilment, and how this desire collides with its own consumerist reification, can at times render his vision of the human extremely bleak, even nihilistic. At the same time, however, it infuses his work with great deconstructive power. To agree fully with Robert Morace's conclusion that 'the world according to Welsh is a place of unemployment, giro schemes, scruffiness, violence, drugs, prostitution, and the God of "Granton Star Cause" [in *The Acid House*], a mean-spirited old drunk'[20] would mean to ignore the unruly resourcefulness of Welsh's characters. As Mickey asserts in *Headstate* with regard to her fellow characters:

> They still care enough to feel strongly about things. This is where I get my fucking kicks. It proves that something's still going on inside there. It's still there; some sort of passion. It's warped, it's twisted and it's perverted, but it's still there. As long as it is there are possibilities that it can become something else. Something better.[21]

'Some sort of passion' – however directionless and inoperative, selfish or sordid – fuels all of Welsh's early work. Only following the publication of *Filth* in 1998 does his writing become more conventional in literary terms, as illustrated by *Glue* (2001), and more commercially aware, as documented a year later by *Porno*, *Trainspotting*'s sequel. What we subsequently encounter in Welsh's even more recent post-devolution work, however, ought not simply to be seen as the result of an authorial crisis triggered by Welsh's sudden wealth and celebrity status, but perhaps more poignantly as a literary reflection of the neoliberalist spirit of the post-Thatcher era, its relentless commodification of traditional values, radical atomisation of the individual and large-scale dismantling of society. I cannot entirely agree with Morace who, in deploring the disappearance of 'the filth and fury of his early work', appears to blame only Welsh himself for it, 'his drifting into hollow celebrity, the hedonism promoted by *Loaded* and *The Face* fuelled now by his *Daily Telegraph* column'.[22] Though relatively flaccid and dull in comparison to the earlier work's transgressiveness, Welsh's recent work still provides an accurate record of the changing cultural and socio-economic contexts of its production. The anodyne inconsequentiality of *The Bedroom Secrets of the Master Chefs* (2006) and *If You Liked School, You'll Love Work* (2007), which make it look as if Welsh finds himself creatively at a loose end or has quite simply run out of things worth saying, can easily be read as symptomatic of contemporary Britain's cultural status quo. Most indicative in this context perhaps is also an observation inserted by Welsh in the Afterword to *If You Liked School*, where he explains that 'when you write about places such as Cowdenbeath, and you come from a physically wee (but spiritually vast) country like Scotland, you have the responsibility to emphasise that this is not meant to depict the "real" place, but rather the "Cowdenbeath" of my imagination at the particular time of writing' (*IY*, 391). Pre-emptively marking his work as mere fiction to apologise for any possible offence caused, this is a far cry from the early Welsh's unconditional, 'in-yer-face' realism. It evacuates these later stories of the subversive bite and countercultural clout that motivated and propelled, for example, *The Acid House* (1994).

Morace makes a valid point when he writes that 'the earlier Welsh gave way to one less vernacular and impassioned, more refined and restrained, less like the poet laureate of the chemical generation and more like the grand old man of youth culture and member in good standing of the literary establishment'.[23] In this respect, however, Welsh's trajectory parallels that of post-devolution Scotland as a whole, which has similarly lost much of its explosiveness. Formerly an anti-hegemonic counter-discourse, in the post-devolution age Scottish nationalism's self-authenticating coalitional affinity with other minoritarian movements can no longer be taken for granted. Even though full statehood remains pending, equipped with a parliament of its own Scottishness must now be seen as an institutionalised force. It has lost its sub-national deviancy and hence, as a political strategy, pure and simple defiance must in future appear wholly inappropriate. No longer unproblematically oppositional, post-devolution Scottishness now stands for an established, politically enfranchised, general culture. It would seem not only anachronistic but deeply disingenuous to continue speaking in the same voice as before, a fact that applies to post-devolution Scotland as much as it does to post-devolution Irvine Welsh. The very timbre and texture of Scottishness have changed and, as a result, so must Scottish literature's. Devolution has brought about a fundamental shift in the imbrication of Scottish culture's tectonic plates, considerably compounding the question of who is now speaking for whom, or in contradiction of what. In this light Welsh's particular challenge, it would seem, is currently to learn how to speak meaningfully from an established rather than subaltern position.

Crime (2008), Welsh's most recent novel, looks like a step in the right direction. The novel features policeman Ray Lennox, whom we originally encountered as the reluctant sidekick of Detective Sergeant Bruce Robertson in *Filth*. Lennox makes a first-class literary *semblable* not only for Welsh as a post-devolution writer, but also for Scotland as a newly enfranchised nation. Institutionally empowered and well intentioned, if encumbered by personal flaws, Lennox is a Scottish everyman keen to do his best, yet often framed and not always succeeding. Notably, he is left to do battle entirely by himself, at once besieged by remorse and burdened with new responsibilities. Lennox finds himself embroiled in an unpredictable, treacherous world of crime, which leaves him permanently exposed to indictments of complicity and corruption. Despite *Crime*'s great promise, however, Welsh's future career might yet come to be thwarted by what looks like an oddly defeatist lack of confidence in his own work – either that or extremely poor marketing. How else – unless one sees it as a tongue-in-cheek stab at the *kailyard* tradition in Scottish literature – might one read the unfortunate title of Welsh's latest book, *Reheated Cabbage* (2009), a collection of long out-of-print stories from various subcultural magazines and anthologies? Can Welsh still provide fresh food for thought? While not always in perfect agreement about the taste or quality of his work, the contributors to this volume certainly believe so.

CHAPTER ONE

Welsh and Tradition

Alice Ferrebe

In *The Scottish Tradition in Literature* (1958) Kurt Wittig was certain about one aspect of the work of students of Scottish literature: texts had always to be read in the context of the national tradition that influenced them. 'For as long as even a few Scottish writers are conscious of having inherited a Scottish tradition', Wittig writes, 'we shall not do justice to their work unless we study it in relation to that Scottish tradition which they themselves are conscious of having inherited.' [1] Yet contemporary Scottish writers can be very prickly about their literary inheritance. A. L. Kennedy (b. 1965) believes that Scottish traditions of writing 'really are an irrelevance with most Scottish writers', and Alan Warner (b. 1964) is 'very fed up with being bunched with that whole Scottish thing'.[2]

Early in his career Irvine Welsh had a tendency to present himself as a kind of literary 'feral child', raised outwith any particular intellectual tradition or allegiance. 'I don't have any literary heroes at all,' he told John Walsh around the time *Marabou Stork Nightmares* was published in 1995. 'I don't take references from other writers, but from music lyrics, from videos and soap operas and stuff. I try and keep as far away from "the classics" [. . .] as possible.' [3] Significantly, the narrator of that other Scottish cult novel of heroin use, Alexander Trocchi's (1925–84) semi-autobiographical *Cain's Book* (1966), is acutely aware of the way in which literary traditions can hamper the process of authentic artistic creation. 'It is all very difficult, the past', Joe tells his reader, 'even more than the future, for the latter is at least probable, calculable, while the former is beyond the range of experiment. The past is always a lie, clung to by an odour of ancestors.' [4] One might, of course, construe the past more charitably, as a fiction rather than a 'lie', leaving us to trace how Welsh's own story of his literary influences has altered and developed over time. By 2003, in Channel 4's *The Story of the Novel*, his admiration is pledged to the indisputable 'classics' of Sir Walter Scott and to 'the greatest books ever written by English novelists' such as Jane Austen, Charlotte Brontë and George Eliot.[5] Yet as with many of Welsh's professions about his work, this stated allegiance needs to be inflected, in part, with devilment. Welsh claimed afterwards, in conversation with Aaron Kelly, that the producers of the programme had tried to steer him to talk about his debt to Trocchi and William Burroughs (1914–97), presumably because such an admission would have allowed the neat classification of a literary sub-genre of 'drugs novels'.[6] But Welsh is adamant that he only discovered this particular (anti-)canon of narcotic literature *after* launching his writing career.

In his interview with Kelly, Welsh outlines a less outlandish, more distinctly Scottish literary genealogy for his writing, citing the influence of Lewis Grassic Gibbon (1901–35), Alasdair Gray (b. 1934), James Hogg (1770–1835), James Kelman (b. 1946) and William McIlvanney (b. 1936). Spanning nearly 200 years of literary production, these writers share a dedication to the literary development of the Scottish vernacular, understood to be the register of the indigenous, 'natural' speech of the nation's people. The demotic style has been dominant in the Scottish novel, but it has been equally important in poetry (Robert Garioch, 1909–81, Kathleen Jamie, b. 1962 and Tom Leonard, b. 1944) and the theatre (John Byrne, b. 1940 and Tom McGrath, 1940–2009). Welsh's early work in particular slots easily into this genealogy of writing and is thus freighted with a particular ideological, intellectual and nationalist value which in itself constitutes a longstanding tradition. In his Preface to *Scottish Vernacular Literature* (1898) T. F. Henderson attempts to rally a cultural revival for vernacular literature after it had been 'blasted with so undeserved and mournful a fate'. 'Once its language is mastered', he explains, 'its native charm can hardly fail to disclose itself, especially to the Scot; for the bulk of it is exceptionally graphic and sincere, and its accent, its temper, its genius is Scottish to the core.'[7] Over a century later, this sense of a vital link between vernacular literature and Scottishness has by no means diminished. Cairns Craig claims that 'the dialect novel is one of the foundations of the philosophical orientation of Scottish fiction',[8] and his analysis places Welsh's debut novel, *Trainspotting*, precisely within that inherited philosophy of a radical, politicised realism.

Alan Riach goes still further in claiming an intimate kinship between a self-consciously demotic literary style and Scottish cultural identity, arguing that the 'central importance of the language of written texts and the speech of characters is much greater in Scottish literature than in English – much more important in Burns, Scott, Hogg, Galt, Stevenson, Lewis Grassic Gibbon, Neil Gunn and Irvine Welsh, than in Jane Austen, George Eliot, Martin Amis or Anita Brookner'.[9] Writing from an English perspective, Alan Sinfield has emphasised another purpose of Welsh's use of Scots and Scottish settings. In *Trainspotting*, he claims:

> The writing in dialect and the violence of language and action are not just realism: they are designed as an impediment to the middle-class and non-

> Scottish reader [. . .] What is accomplished specifically is that English people and other literary readers are prevented from supposing that they can readily assimilate Scotland, as if it were merely an extension of Englishness, or merely a tourist theme park.[10]

Welsh is clearly interested in upholding this rebarbative and rebellious power of the Scottish vernacular, on screen as well as on the page. In his view, Paul McGuigan's film version of *The Acid House*, to a far greater extent than Danny Boyle's adaptation of *Trainspotting*, sends the cultural tourist 'homewards tae think again'. 'It will be more inaccessible, more hard-core', Welsh asserted in anticipation of the film's release. 'The accents will be harder, so spoiled middle-class brats who want to shop around for their next culture fix will find it more impenetrable.'[11] In the Scottish context, literary use of the vernacular has come to signify political agency in its assertion of alternative kinds of authority – artistic, linguistic, political and philosophical – in rebellion against the single-voiced literary standard of Standard English.

Welsh's first novel, *Trainspotting*, in particular, is frequently cited to exemplify the culturally (and spiritually) regenerative power of literature in demotic Scots. Bonnie Blackwell reads it as an 'intricate proposal for the resacralization of language outside exhausted narrative templates'.[12] Such contemporary claims recall an earlier investment in the expressive and political value of the vernacular as a means of accessing and representing national authenticity, namely that of Hugh MacDiarmid (1892–1978) and the Scottish Literary Renaissance of the first half of the twentieth century. MacDiarmid intended to rectify what he considered to be the over-anglicised condition of British literary culture and criticism by resurrecting a distinct Scottish identity, manifesting in a 'renaissance' of Scottish letters. MacDiarmid was an active and contentious propagandist for the revival of the Scots language or, rather, a version of it that he had synthesised from various local dialects mixed with more traditionally literary registers. His own most prominent contribution to Scottish vernacular literature is his long poem, *A Drunk Man Looks at the Thistle* (1926). As already noted, Welsh's self-professed literary allegiances can change both rapidly and radically, but his vehement opposition to MacDiarmid's work has been a conspicuous constant throughout his career, highlighting his fundamental support for Alan Warner's objection to being 'bunched with that whole Scottish thing'. Commenting on the place of Trocchi's work in the Scottish tradition, Welsh casts MacDiarmid as a dogged parochialist, dubbing him 'a symbol of all that's horrific and hideous about Scotland and Scottish culture'.[13] Notably also, in *The Bedroom Secrets of the Master Chefs* the central hero Daniel Skinner's bookshelf is described as containing 'copious volumes of poetry by Byron, Shelley, Verlaine, Rimbaud, Baudelaire and Burns, and a big, obviously unleafed one of MacDiarmid'

(*BS*, 333). For all his alleged indifference to the Scottish literary tradition, Welsh's pointed opposition to MacDiarmid as the figurehead of a particular model of Scottish culture alerts us to an enduring schism in the nation's self-understanding and image, one which also allows greater insight into the place of Welsh's work within its literary tradition.

When Edwin Muir (1887–1959) published *Scott and Scotland* (1936), it fractured his friendship with MacDiarmid forever. This study of Sir Walter Scott's work professed strong doubt that modern Scottish writers could ever achieve an unfailingly independent cultural and linguistic identity. Craig, developing Muir's thesis in 1999, notes the way in which Scottish culture has frequently been understood as what he calls a 'culture of erasure'.[14] Within this paradigm, each cultural-historical manifestation of Scotland – already fractured by expressing itself in three languages (Scots, Gaelic and English) – is abolished by its usurper. As a result, Scotland seems doomed to a series of dislocated renaissances accompanied by a reflex veneration of the new at the expense of fusty (or, to use Trocchi's image, 'odorous') literary ancestors. Welsh's determination to deny the influence of Trocchi on his own writing, when the latter seems so much his thematic and stylistic precursor, only serves to perpetuate this 'tradition of newness'. If indeed Welsh had never read Trocchi before *Trainspotting*, the prestige of spontaneously producing a superior contemporary version of the cult but patchy *Cain's Book* would be all his.

Yet Welsh is by no means alone in accruing capital, cultural or otherwise, from this sense of a Scottish 'culture of erasure'. The Irvine Welsh phenomenon has been dedicatedly promoted amidst what Robert Morace describes as 'a highly commercialized atmosphere of cultural transgression'[15] in British publishing during the 1990s, which proliferated and thrived on daring gestures of defiance of and deviance from established literary conventions. During this decade cultural critics began to cite Scotland's multiple credentials as a model for new understandings of identity and allegiance. In their interpretations Scotland became designated as a 'post-colonial', 'post-industrial', 'post-devolution' and even 'post-national' configuration – in other words, 'a society that has discarded the notion of a homogeneous nation state with singular forms of belonging'.[16] Muir's pessimistic picture of an atomised, interrupted Scottish tradition underwent resignification into an exemplary postmodern paradigm of plurality, matching the intellectual tenets, values and convictions celebrated as paramount in current Western criticism. Working within this paradigm, the editors of the collection of essays *Beyond Scotland* (2004) have recently attested to the way in which 'Scots themselves have shown a greater gift for interdependence than independence – a value that eludes and obviates the kinds of false opposition created out of a yearning for wholeness that we have located at the heart of Scotland's critical self-consciousness'.[17]

MacDiarmid's and Muir's visions of a cultural tradition obviously oppose one another, yet at the core of each is the sense of a national identity, once whole, but now lost. By contrast, newer images of Scottishness, like that envisaged in *Beyond Scotland*, embrace and promote the fact that the nation's identity has always been complex, dynamic and productively diverse in its influences and inheritance.

Matters of literary style can also be used to disclose a satisfying match between Welsh's writing and the current ideal among Scottish critics of national culture as plural and non-hierarchical. Willy Maley makes the claim that:

> Welsh's style – sampling, streetwise, synthesizing – is implicitly anti-colonial. Welsh is more inclined than his predecessors to sift through the junk and pulp of Scottish culture, hence his cult status. Welsh's influences, or effluences, range across contemporary film, music and television rather than resting on the canon. He excels at that potent blend of the excremental and existential, 'keech and Kierkegaard', that is all the rage in new Scottish writing, a social surrealism that takes its cue from cinema and dance as much as literature. The pop video, the club and the fanzine are its archives.[18]

According to Trocchi's narrator, Joe, in *Cain's Book*, an unpleasant 'odour of ancestors' inevitably clings to every new generation of writers as they strive to produce innovative work. The American critic Harold Bloom famously identified what he called, rather more prosaically, an 'anxiety of influence' within poetic traditions, as younger poets invariably strive to 'clear imaginative space for themselves'.[19] Defying Bloom's diagnosis of an intimidating legacy of tradition and debt, one of the (few) reliable standards of Welsh's writing to date has been a kind of glee of influence. His often rampantly experimental intertextuality refuses to discriminate between established hierarchies of cultural forms that tend to place a sliding scale of value from High Art to lowly Pop Culture. Citing – like Maley's riff – the author's artistic method of serial celebratory appropriation of a wide range of heterogeneous source materials, Welsh's work can be upheld as the paradoxical example of a non-traditional traditionality. Welsh's preferred style of writing, then, undermines any hidebound sense of tradition by playfully, and often defiantly, manipulating and synthesising any influences that take his fancy.

Riach provides a rousing description of this literary method, urging artists to:

> Abandon any sense of 'Tradition' completely, when or if it becomes constricting or defined by uniformity or stultifying continuity and especially if it acts as a constraint on creativity – what is needed is not 'Tradition' but 'Precedents' – by which one might assume anything that might be put to creative use, from

> wherever in the world one might find it, models not to be imitated but used as points of departure for new creative work in a world the past could not have predicted.[20]

In fact, Riach is paraphrasing the slogan that appeared on the cover of the first edition of MacDiarmid's periodical *The Scottish Chapbook*: 'Not Traditions: Precedents'.[21] Riach's summary implicitly defends MacDiarmid against the kind of accusations of a blinkered parochialism routinely levelled against him by Welsh, suggesting instead that the poet's modernist strategy for national cultural rejuvenation might be just as relevant today. Notably, the second Scottish Literary Renaissance saw the emergence of a multi-vocal literature that demanded to be reviewed in international contexts while maintaining a clear sense of national identity, however non-prescriptive. Seamus Heaney cites the work of Gray, Leonard, Liz Lochhead (b. 1947) and Kelman from the 1970s onwards as 'an affirmation of MacDiarmid's stand for a plurality of voices and political self-consciousness'.[22] MacDiarmid's and Muir's dispute over the limits and potential of Scottish culture past and present is then still, it would seem, a live one.

Although absent from Heaney's list, Welsh has undeniably been an important figure in the ongoing rejuvenation of Scottish literature, garnering both international critical acclaim and phenomenal commercial success. Welsh himself is now being hailed as the literary ancestor of a variety of younger novelists. Starting around the turn of the new century, his name has been repeatedly invoked to market the latest generation of Scottish authors, including figures as diverse as Laura Hird (b. 1966, the 'female Welsh') and Suhayl Saadi (b. 1961, the 'Muslim Welsh'). Though Warner's first novel, *Morvern Caller*, was published in 1995, the same year as *Marabou Stork Nightmares*, seven years on the BBC still begins its review of Warner's fourth novel *The Man Who Walks* (2002) with the tag: 'He's heralded as the new Irvine Welsh. So who is he?' [23] Reviewers tend to use the Irvine Welsh literary brand transnationally, though it is applied almost exclusively to British authors, and most often to those with a certain Celtic tinge. Thus, reviewers for the *Independent* newspaper have noted how Niall Griffiths is being 'branded "the Welsh Irvine Welsh"' and Helen Walsh 'the Scouse Irvine Welsh'.[24] While this promotion is of course driven for the most part by canny marketing strategies rather than detailed critical judgement, it is clear the Welshian brand can increase sales and significantly widen the readership of new vernacular voices in contemporary British writing.

Much postmodern theorising on literature revels in the subversive potential of multiple meanings engendered in the interplay of words and texts. Some critics have discovered examples of such Derridean *différance* in Welsh's work, and in his literary rendering of the Leith demotic in particular.

Thus, according to Kelly, Welsh's phonetic rendering of 'I' as 'Ah' also signifies, 'variously, a pause or hesitation, the postponement of meaning and significance rather than its usual assertion with the annunciation of the first person singular, and also an expression of pain, or of disapproval'.[25] In his reading of *Trainspotting* Craig teases out the sterile mental monotony conveyed in the last two words of Begbie's dissolute dad's parting injunction to 'keep up the trainspottin mind' (*T*, 309), as he shuffles away from Leith's derelict railway station.[26] Readings such as these hint at a more complex relationship in Welsh's writing between the demotic and the political than the simple equation of writing in dialect with access to authentic national culture. The political agency of the vernacular, which has been so important to the Scottish literary tradition, is characteristically used by Welsh not to create the image of a reassuringly cohesive working-class community, but to demonstrate the failure and disintegration of that community under contemporary social conditions. Time and again his characters' Scots fails as a means of shared communication, leaving them in a state of isolation rather than solidarity. In their analysis of multiple meanings, critics like Kelly and Craig discover this political message inscribed at the level of the word. Postmodernism has been berated (by critics such as Fredric Jameson and Terry Eagleton, for example) for its apolitical nature and failure to engage with the reality of lived experience and real oppression. As an intellectual model, then, it might be thought to stand in opposition to a Scottish literary tradition defined on the grounds of nationhood and shared political history. However, Kelly's and Craig's postmodern analyses show a way that demotic language use can be read simultaneously as playfully ephemeral and meaningfully material, as spellings and sounds work to reveal deeper truths about the speakers' experience.

As both Welsh's literary precursor and immediate contemporary, Kelman provides a particularly instructive case for comparison with regard to the politics of literary language. Going further than Drew Milne's observation that 'Kelman's work created some of the critical context for Welsh's work', Morace draws 'a direct line in the minds of readers and critics linking Welsh to Kelman'.[27] This critical affiliation, of course, hinges on the use by both authors of the demotic. As is well known, Kelman has striven to excise Standard English from his narration, and so to exorcise its oppressive ideology and attendant class and national hierarchies. This, he has claimed, is part of a quest for a more authentic realism: 'Getting rid of the narrative voice is trying to get down to that level of pure objectivity. This is *the* reality here, within this culture. Facticity, or something like that.'[28] Kelman's formidable cultural reputation depends in part on the way in which his work can be read within both postmodernist and more traditional models of Scottish nationhood. His work is informed by a cosmopolitan, poststructuralist literary understanding and lends itself productively to such theorising. However, critics see it simultaneously as deeply rooted in the 'facticity' of an unwavering political, national and aesthetic integrity, which, once again, is understood as integral within an allegiance to the Scottish vernacular.

It is this combination that prompts Morace to describe Kelman as having a 'heightened literary style'.[29] Intriguingly, the increasingly negative assessment of Welsh's writing often seems to stem from disapproval of the aspirational, overtly 'literary' nature of his more recent work. His fourth novel, *Glue*, was widely derided for its attempt at a grander narrative scale tracing the faltering progress of its cast of characters from 1970 to the immediate present. The widened scope of the narrative, with its thirty-year timescale and its abundance of central characters, was judged to be a failure. It was deemed too arrogant and too bourgeois, an anachronistic, badly executed work with a Victorianist structure of little contemporary relevance. On BBC2's *Newsnight Review*, broadcast in April 2001, Philip Hensher described the novel as: '*The Old Curiosity Shop* with chemicals. It's really quite badly written in lots of ways'. Kelly takes particular issue with Welsh's positioning of the character of the American pop star Kathryn Joyner, in whose portrayal he sees 'a danger [. . .] of repeating a common bourgeois trope – and it is a trait for which Welsh often criticizes writers such as Martin Amis'.[30] The trait highlighted by Kelly is the implied inferiority of a language (in this case, working-class Scots) that maintains its emotional and experiential authenticity by the dubious virtue of excluding itself from cultural and capitalist privilege, however reified and debilitating this privilege might be. Coinciding with the publication of *Glue*, Elspeth Findlay produced an elegant critical rant accusing Welsh's work of harbouring an underlying 'traditional bourgeois vision', which allows its middle-class readership to luxuriate in the vices of the lower classes before primly appreciating the strictness of their deserved punishment. Findlay urges readers to fracture the automatic association of 'schemie subject matter and the use of dialect with a working-class aesthetic'.[31] Use of the Scottish vernacular and the setting of a fictional Scottish scheme, she is emphasising, do not guarantee cultural, moral or national authenticity. Findlay's view finds corroboration in Eagleton's argument in *The Idea of Culture* that postmodern culture's 'demotic disdain for elitism can sit easily enough with an endorsement of conservative values'.[32] Welsh's writing is increasingly being read as displaying not just demotic disdain, but a growing bourgeois conservatism too.

Welsh has responded to these accusations of class betrayal and bourgeois tendencies with characteristic belligerence. His most recent novels, from *Glue* to *Crime*, make increasing use of narration in Standard English, defying the critical (and nationalist) investment in his deployment of the demotic. He has also claimed a provocatively canonical pedigree for his sixth novel,

Bedroom Secrets of the Master Chefs. As well as *Macbeth*, this encompasses two undisputed Scottish classics: James Hogg's *The Private Memoirs and Confessions of a Justified Sinner* (1824) and Robert Louis Stevenson's *Dr Jekyll and Mr Hyde* (1886). The idea of the split self has been an enduringly influential trope in the academic analysis of Scottish literature as a distinct artistic field. The division of the self, and the resulting schism of personal morality, have frequently been upheld as characteristically Scottish – a literary representation of the nation's long-divided political loyalties and experiences. Back in 1919, in his book *Scottish Literature: Character and Influence*, Gregory Smith coined the phrase 'Caledonian Antisyzygy' to describe precisely this experience.[33] Yet by emphasising another literary debt, to the Anglo-Irishman Oscar Wilde's *The Picture of Dorian Gray*, Welsh covertly undermines the phenomenon of the divided self as particularly Scottish, rebelling once again against what he has called 'Scottish parochialism and the tedious nationalistic issues which every Scots writer is supposed to engage in'.[34]

All this high-cultural intertextuality prompts Morace to a now familiar judgement on Welsh's work – he condemns *Bedroom Secrets* for what he calls its '*faux* literary style'.[35] The novel features a punk band known as 'The Old Boys', who are described (by the Standard English voice of the third-person co-narrator) as 'a band ahead of their time: postmodern piss-takers in a more deadpan, serious, political era. Perhaps due to the frustration that nobody really got them, they started to parody themselves, with attendant declining returns' (*BS*, 316). The high pitch of the commercial and media promotion of the Irvine Welsh brand, in relation to both his own work and that of his perceived (and often imitative) ingénues, has produced an increasingly jaded critical response to the author's themes and aesthetic. His work is increasingly being judged as some kind of distasteful marketing hoax rather than the authentic vernacular expression of an urgent subcultural or subnational agenda. Robert Crawford points out the way in which 'Irvine Welsh himself has seemed only too alert to the demands of the marketplace, and (perhaps inevitably) his book [*Trainspotting*] has been bound up with carefully arranged high-capitalist promotion, so that it seems complicit with what it attacks'.[36] Various accusations drive this escalating critical disenchantment. Just like the Old Boys, Welsh's characteristic register is now repeatedly read as blankly parodic of the tradition he was originally credited with reviving; the relentless seriality of his use of the vernacular is being seen as a 'postmodern piss-take' too far. His politics are understood as degraded, compromised and corrupted by commercial commodification, and his use of the demotic is regarded as increasingly staged. 'Stale language for equally stale ideas'[37] is Morace's curt verdict.

In the quotation which opened this chapter, Wittig asserts the importance of placing Scottish writers within the context of their inherited traditions.

This search for a meaningful literary genealogy for Welsh's work has illuminated a clash of competing traditions, as Scotland and its literary culture are caught up in an ongoing negotiation of what Paul Gilroy has called 'the weird post-colonial pageantries of national decline and national rebirth'.[38] The rival viewpoints of MacDiarmid's and Muir's famous falling-out remain contentious. The nation currently imagines its identity as grounded in both a continuous, vernacular tradition and a tradition that is, paradoxically, non-traditional. The latter is defined by its dynamic tendency to evolve through serial acts of cultural erasure. On the one hand, Welsh's stylistics place his texts within this latter, postmodern paradigm, gleefully pilfering cultural influences with no respect for hierarchies. However, his use of the demotic has ensured his writing is simultaneously also judged against more traditional measures of authenticity and national identity. It is to this ambiguous position that we might attribute the critical volatility surrounding his work.

'Scottish literature', claimed Welsh's nemesis MacDiarmid, 'like all other literatures, has been *written* almost exclusively by blasphemers, immoralists, dipsomaniacs and madmen, but, unlike most other literatures, has been *written about* almost exclusively by ministers'.[39] To this schism we can add another: the critical community might not currently be overstuffed with ministers, but it does demonstrate a further division in its competing orthodoxies regarding the politics of language in the Scottish tradition. An enduring critical belief in the redemptive identity of the demotic has influenced responses to Welsh's writing from the beginning of his career. This involves widespread devotion to the panacean 'facticity' of vernacular language as an antidote to the oppressive standard of Standard English. Against this one can set the poststructuralist sanctification of the linguistic play of *différance*. Both these orthodoxies affect the reception of Welsh's work as a heavily publicised package of blasphemy, immorality and dipsomania, sometimes provoking its celebration and sometimes its condemnation. Despite the contemporary literary project to rewrite Scotland as an exemplary post-nation, postmodernism still sits uneasily with the vernacular tradition and with wider established intellectual histories for Scotland. This chapter has suggested how Welsh's work might be reread as a site of friction between these different beliefs. As such, it provides us with a provocative context in which to examine competing contemporary ideas of the Scottish literary tradition.

CHAPTER TWO

Welsh's Novels

Matt McGuire

Since the publication of *Trainspotting* in 1993, Irvine Welsh has produced seven novels, three collections of short stories and a variety of works for stage and screen. This range of creativity, coupled with an exceptional level of commercial success, has transformed Welsh from a mere novelist into what Robert Morace terms 'a cultural phenomenon'.[1] While the major critical publications on Welsh to date (by Morace and Aaron Kelly) examine the author's work within this wider critical context, this chapter is an attempt to trace the development of the novels in particular: *Trainspotting*, *Marabou Stork Nightmares* (1995), *Filth* (1998), *Glue* (2001), *Porno* (2002), *The Bedroom Secrets of the Master Chefs* (2006) and *Crime* (2008). The chapter surveys thematic terrains and highlights key issues in Welsh's work that will be excavated more fully in subsequent chapters of the *Companion*. These issues include representations of class and the author's own contribution to the evolution of the working-class novel, the treatment of gender as well as drugs, violence and criminality. The formal experimentalism of Welsh's writing will also be addressed. His evolution, from the fragmented and episodic narratives of *Trainspotting* to the more predictable plots of later novels, will be placed within a broader discussion of the novel as a literary form. Welsh's interest in genre, and particularly the mass market fiction of the romance novel and the detective story, will also be discussed. Following the huge success of *Trainspotting* is Welsh now merely writing to order, reproducing his own highly stylised form of pulp fiction? And how has Welsh's own transformation, from unknown Scottish writer to bestselling global author, altered his perspective on the communities his work depicts?

Trainspotting barely needs an introduction. Nevertheless, it must seem ironic to begin examining Welsh's novels with a text that early critics were reluctant to describe as a novel at all. For Michael Brockington it was 'hard to call it a novel, more a ragged accretion of short stories', while Sarah Hemming referred to 'a series of unrelated episodes', and Lucy Hughes-Hallett described a work 'broken up into fragments'.[2] Such statements accord with Welsh's own views about the anti-literary qualities of his work, already noted by Alice Ferrebe in her contribution to the present volume: 'I don't have any literary heroes at all [. . .] I don't take references from other writers, but from lyrics, from videos and soap operas and stuff. I try and keep as far away from "the classics" [. . .] as possible.' [3] This anti-literary pose will be picked up in due course. For now we can agree that the episodic and fragmented nature of *Trainspotting* is crucial to the universe of experiences it is attempting to depict. The junkies, misfits and 'schemies' that populate the novel inhabit highly chaotic and unpredictable lives. Unlike the film, where Ewan MacGregor's voiceover provides a sense of narrative continuity, the novel eschews such fixed anchor points. Less than half of the novel's forty-four, largely unrelated episodes are told from Renton's point of view; the rest are narrated by Sick Boy, Spud, Begbie, Tommy, Renton's brother Billy, Nina and Kelly. Instead of the narrative progress of an individual character, *Trainspotting* presents us with a community of voices.

The notion of community itself came under acute attack with the rise of Thatcherism in the 1980s, the period in which *Trainspotting* is set. The decimation of heavy industry, the privatisation of public services and the liberalisation of the free market were regarded by many as an onslaught on working-class communities throughout Britain. As an ideology Thatcherism also sought to discredit notions of class, arguing that the goal of society was to maximise economic efficiency by freeing individuals to pursue their own interests. This change in social values, resulting in a wider sense of community breakdown, pervades *Trainspotting*. In the first chapter we learn that there are 'nae friends in this game. Jist associates' (*T*, 6), and when baby Dawn dies and Leslie needs a hit, Renton cooks up, admitting he will look after himself first – that 'goes without saying' (*T*, 56). Obviously, the heroin subculture of the 1980s – is also a world where sharing, as in the sharing of needles, could quite literally cost one one's life by spreading HIV infection. At the time, Edinburgh held the unenviable reputation of being Britain's AIDS capital. Welsh's fiction explores the vacuum left behind by the disappearance of more traditional notions of class and community. What little narrative trajectory there is in *Trainspotting* sees Renton perform acts of rampant individualism, and at the end of the novel he commits the ultimate act of betrayal: he steals from his friends, turns his back on his community and flees to Amsterdam. The novel's conclusion is deeply pessimistic, suggesting that in the post-Thatcherite world society cannot be improved by the actions of the individual. Instead, we live a kind of economic Darwinism where the fittest survive and the weak are interminably exploited.

The lack of a stable narrative vantage point mirrors the experience of many characters in *Trainspotting*. Displaced to the socio-economic margins of society, their lives cannot be rendered by the cosy and predictable plots of bourgeois life. Heroin utterly annihilates all other narratives – work, family, sexual relationships – replacing them with the terminal logic of drug addiction. The formal politics of the novel are intimately bound up with *Trainspotting*'s interrogation of class. Welsh is highly sceptical of the bourgeois nature of traditional literary fiction, describing it as a 'middle-class plaything'.[4] *Trainspotting* eschews many of the traits of the traditional realist novel, particularly its use of third-person narrative, thus aligning itself with the textual politics which, as Liam McIlvanney has shown, underpin much recent working-class Scottish fiction.[5] For James Kelman (b. 1946), for example, the formal politics of the realist novel are inherently elitist; the omniscient third-person narrator assumes a position of authority over the text, interpreting, explaining and ultimately conferring significance on the lives of individual characters, or poignantly withholding such a conferral. *Trainspotting* deliberately subverts such hierarchical organisation, with the characters themselves acting as guides within the world of the novel.

If Welsh's work continues to perpetuate certain traditions of working-class fiction, it also marks something of a radical departure. *Trainspotting* offered an important corrective to the Glasgow bias – embodied by writers such as George Friel (1910–75), Archie Hind (1928–2008), Alasdair Gray (b. 1934), William McIlvanney (b. 1936) and Kelman – that had existed within Scottish working-class fiction. As at one stage Renton wryly comments, 'Ah've never met one Weedjie whae didnae think that they are the only genuinely suffering proletarians in Scotland' (*T*, 191). Welsh's fiction also signals a shift away from the depiction of lonely artists, bus conductors and disaffected school teachers as exemplars of working-class Scotland. Instead, his work focuses on a younger generation composed of characters that have never worked and in all likelihood never will. It is their leisure time rather than their experience of work that Welsh's writing explores. As such, *Trainspotting* implicitly questions the viability of such terms as 'working-class' when describing these characters and their experience of the world. There is also a generational shift at work: whereas Kelman and his fellow writers had been publishing since the 1970s, Welsh did not make his literary debut until the early 1990s. As a result, his work deals with a decidedly post-Thatcherite world, a place where, as the arrival of New Labour in the 1990s would soon demonstrate, there were no longer any viable alternatives to capitalism.

The novel takes its title from an episode set in Leith's disused Central Station, a place that gestures towards an industrial past that has all but disappeared. A largely labour-based society has been replaced by the ethics of mass consumerism. As already indicated, *Trainspotting* rarely depicts people working. Instead, through their use of heroin, Welsh's characters are in thrall to an abject form of conspicuous consumption, caught in a cycle of behaviour that will eventually destroy them. While the heroin hit short-circuits the endless deferment of pleasure that sustains contemporary culture, like all consumers the junkie can only ever be temporarily satisfied. Before long he must return for another hit, another purchase, another moment of ever-diminishing self-fulfilment. Renton's infamous rant – 'Choose life. Choose mortgage payments; choose washing machines [. . .]' (*T*, 187) – satirises the vacuous freedoms of modern consumer culture. Happiness lies in the freedom to choose anything one wants, a notion that masks the fact that one must be able to afford to make such choices in the first place. Ironically, of course, heroin addiction represents the nullification of choice, with addicts highly compromised in their ability to exercise free will or choose alternative forms of behaviour.

The depiction of drugs in *Trainspotting* is part of a general fascination with popular culture in Welsh's writing. According to Willy Maley, 'Welsh's influences, or effluences, range across contemporary film, music and television rather than resting on the [literary] canon.'[6] This predilection for the popular over the literary pervades *Trainspotting*, which opens with Renton entranced by a Jean-Claude Van Damme video. Sick Boy spends half his time talking to and impersonating an imaginary Sean Connery, and the novel is peppered with references to pop music (Iggy Pop, The Smiths and The Clash) and football, particularly the emotional highs and lows of being a Hibs fan. On a train journey to London, Begbie illustrates the divide between high and low culture, between the literary and the non-literary, in his own inimitable style: 'Wir supposed tae be doon here fir a fuckin laugh, no tae talk aboot fuckin books n aw that fuckin shite. See if it wis up tae me, ah'd git ivray fuckin book n pit thum on a great big fuckin pile n burn the fuckin loat' (*T*, 116). Is it Welsh's aim to define his book as some kind of anti-novel? One might seriously question the author's attempts to downplay the literary qualities of his work here. Episodic and fragmented narratives, a variety of perspectives and the use indirect discourse to access characters' inner worlds – are these not also the hallmarks of much high-modernist fiction, including such canonical works as James Joyce's (1882–1941) *Ulysses* (1922) or Virginia Woolf's (1882–1941) *Mrs Dalloway* (1925)?

Against his own pretensions to the contrary, Welsh's fiction can be productively read alongside Ian Watt's classic critical study *The Rise of the Novel* (1957), which explores the emergence of the form in the early eighteenth century.[7] In the works of Daniel Defoe (1660–1731), Samuel Richardson (1689–1761) and Henry Fielding (1707–54) the strict formal requirements of neo-classicist poetry gave way to more casual prose forms. Highly ornate poetic expression was replaced by a mode of writing that pursued a much closer approximation to actual speech. As is well known, these early fictions were decried as signalling a lowering of literary standards, a radical democratisation of literature and a worrying intrusion of commercial life into the artistic domain of writing – criticisms that could be said equally to pertain to

Trainspotting. Denying any literary pretence, the author Irvine Welsh mimics the wiliness of his character Mark Renton, who readily ventriloquises different voices and plays to different galleries throughout the novel, including a job interview panel and a High Court judge.

The artistic versatility of Welsh's fiction also shows in its ability to entice both the world of urban youth culture and that of the literary critic. Whenever Welsh focuses on taboo subject matters, such as drugs, football violence or pornography, he attempts to situate these phenomena within their broader sociological contexts. As noted above, heroin addiction is presented as highly anti-social, an all-consuming, annihilative way of life. It is 'a potent floating signifier of social pathology, political dependence, and consumer capitalism'.[8] When Welsh's subsequent novels feature drugs it is always as an issue hotly contested within highly politicised, ideological debates. In 1996 Welsh published *Ecstasy* in one of whose three novellas he compares the ecstasy dependency of club culture to the wilful escapism of romance fiction. Both getting 'loved up' and living for the weekend are read in terms of a desire for temporary reprieve from the everyday tedium of working life. Later, in *Porno*, it is cocaine which is used to dissect the unmitigated, aggressive selfishness of capitalist Britain, and of course pornography, which opens up another Pandora's box of 'addiction'.

Whereas Danny Boyle's adaptation of *Trainspotting* focuses primarily on the issue of drugs, the novel offers a more nuanced and expansive interrogation of Scottish working-class culture. The themes of sectarianism and racism, central to the book, barely feature in the film. In the novel the characters sing Irish rebel songs at Begbie's New Year's party, while Renton's brother is killed serving with the British Army in Northern Ireland. *Trainspotting* also demonstrates the ambiguous relationship between Scottish history and narratives of colonialism. An understanding of Scotland's complicity in the British imperial project exists alongside a wider sense of solidarity with other marginalised groups. Renton's infamous tirade that 'it's shite being Scottish' openly appropriates the rhetoric of postcolonial theory: 'It's nae good blamin it oan the English fir colonising us [. . .] They're just wankers. We are colonised by wankers. We can't even pick a decent, vibrant, healthy culture to be colonised by' (*T*, 78). Scotland's dual status, as both victim and perpetrator in the British imperial adventure, is most fully developed in Welsh's second novel, *Marabou Stork Nightmares*, which centres on Roy Strang, an Edinburgh scheme-dweller who lies in a comatose state in hospital following an attempted suicide. The suicide attempt was Roy's response to the unbearable guilt he suffered after participating in the brutal gang rape of a friend of his, Kirsty Chalmers.

The narrative of *Marabou Stork Nightmares* oscillates between the fantasy world of Roy's imagination and memories of his childhood in Muirhouse, his temporary emigration to South Africa and his life as a football casual back in Edinburgh. The emigration episode of the novel juxtaposes the class politics of modern Scotland with the racial segregation of apartheid South Africa. Disempowered and marginalised at home, the Strangs learn that as whites in South Africa they immediately assume a higher social status. Their life of privilege, however, is short-lived. The alcohol-fuelled temper of Roy's father eventually gets him arrested and the family is deported back to Muirhouse. In a much-cited and highly controversial passage Roy draws a comparison between his own experience of the scheme and the life of black South Africans under apartheid: 'Edinburgh to me represented serfdom. I realised that it was exactly the same situation as Johannesburg; the only difference was that the Kaffirs were white and called schemies' (*MSN*, 80). In separate articles Alan Freeman and Ellen-Raïssa Jackson, along with Willy Maley, question the suspicious ease with which Welsh's fiction attempts to appropriate the suffering of one group to accentuate the persecution suffered by another.[9] Welsh's deliberate identification of class with race evokes James Kelman's 1994 Booker Prize speech in which he described his own working-class fiction as belonging to 'a literature of decolonization'.[10] It also echoes Roddy Doyle's novel *The Commitments* (1989) in which a group of impoverished kids from a Dublin estate form an American soul band, claiming that the working class are 'the niggers of Ireland'.[11] As addressed by Gavin Miller in his contribution to the present volume, one might also read Welsh's conflation of race and class in terms of a more general crisis within the Left. By the end of the twentieth century the language of class, at least in its traditional form, had come to be regarded in many quarters as theoretically bankrupt.[12]

If Welsh's work deploys the discourse of race as a way of reconceptualising class, it is also interested in how racism and other kinds of discrimination operate within working-class culture. Begbie, for example, is denigrated as someone who is 'intae baseball-batting every fucker that's different: pakis, poof, n what huv ye' (*T*, 78). He represents the prototypical hard man who, whilst openly castigating his friend's heroin use, is himself addicted to violence. *Trainspotting* deconstructs the myth of the working-class hard man, depicting Begbie as a bullying wife-beater, fearfully indulged by his friends, whose reputation is born out of a psychotic disregard for others rather than any special skill or courage as a fighter. *Marabou Stork Nightmares* develops Welsh's interest in male violence by locating it within a broader sociological critique. As a child Roy is forced by his father to beat up his effeminate half-brother, Bernard. It is then that Roy's sense of masculinity becomes intimately tied to notions of physical aggression, exacerbated further by the sexual abuse he suffers at the hands of his uncle in South Africa. Welsh presents the link between masculinity and violence as a learned form of behaviour, one that is legitimated by a particular set of socio-cultural values.

In adult life the monotony of Roy's working life as a computer analyst is offset by the adrenalin rush of organised violence at the weekends. In its exploration of why young men participate in such behaviour, *Marabou Stork Nightmares* candidly reminds us of the entertainment value of such recreational violence. As we recall, *Trainspotting* opens with Renton watching a Jean-Claude Van Damme video in anticipation of 'some serious swedging' (*T*, 3). In terms of a wider cultural context the action movies of the 1980s would be superseded in the 1990s by a number of highly stylised cinematic renditions of violence, most influentially perhaps the films of Quentin Tarantino. *Marabou Stork Nightmares* might also be read in terms of the more specific questions posed about masculinity and violence in novels like Chuck Palahniuk's (b. 1962) *Fight Club* (1996). Welsh's novel portrays football violence primarily as a mere displacement activity, a misdirected, random form of retaliation, the reaction of a generation of working-class men to the demeaning experience of post-industrial society. Only at the very end of the novel, on coming face to face with his employer, does Roy realise who the real target of his aggression *should* be: 'No the boys wi knock fuck oot ay at the footba, no the birds we fuck aboot [. . .] [but] These cunts' (*MSN*, 201).

If racism and homophobia constitute the dark underbelly of working-class culture, so too does the misogyny that Welsh finds within this world. Begbie's penchant for violence extends to his wife, June, who, like his friends, lives in fear of his fists. Towards the end of *Trainspotting* Sick Boy and Renton play a practical joke on their friend Kelly, telephoning the bar where she works and asking, for 'Mark Hunt'. Kelly's subsequent cries of 'ANYBODY SEEN MARK HUNT?' are met with uproar from the all-male clientele and Renton realises, too late, that this is 'lynch mob laughter' (*T*, 279). In *Marabou Stork Nightmares* this misogynist tension is graphically played out in the rape of Kirsty Chalmers, and characteristic of Welsh's fiction, the novel does not spare us the explicit details. Unsurprisingly perhaps, Welsh has been accused not only of colluding with the patriarchal violence his work purports to condemn, but also of reinscribing the classist elitism it ostensibly critiques. According to Elspeth Findlay, Welsh's novels provide an essentially bourgeois readership with the opportunity to holiday safely in other people's misery.[13] Similarly, even though *Marabou Stork Nightmares* exposes the patriarchal bias of the British justice system (Kirsty is forced publicly to recount her ordeal, only to find her own sexual conduct interrogated in court, which effectively rapes her a second time), Welsh's feminist credentials have been questioned by a number of critics. When Kirsty is denied justice at the trial she visits the comatose Roy in hospital and exacts her own revenge by cutting off his penis. Female empowerment is thus represented in masculinist terms, through the exercise of violence and the reciprocal violation of the male body, arguably preventing Kirsty from escaping the codes of a male-dominated society.[14]

While *Marabou Stork Nightmares* diagnoses the ineffectiveness of the justice system, Welsh's third novel, *Filth*, turns its gaze on another state institution: the police. In contrast to the decentred nature of Welsh's earlier novels, *Filth* mimics the narrative logic of crime fiction in which the plot traditionally revolves around an outspoken detective figure and his attempts to solve a murder. In this case Detective Sergeant Bruce Robertson is on the hunt for the killer of Efan Wurie, a Ghanaian journalist. As is often the case in crime writing, in *Filth* the plot serves as a loose framework in which to characterise the figure of the detective. As John Scagg explains, the 'Private I' of detective fiction often works as a 'Private Eye', granting the reader a unique perspective on the world of the text.[15] Even more so than the quixotic Philip Marlowe of Raymond Chandler's fiction or Ian Rankin's stubbornly righteous Rebus, Robertson is an anti-hero, an accumulation of all that is most loathsome in Welsh's earlier creations. Far from being the enigmatic justice-seeker, Robertson is a racist misogynist and homophobe, who combines a misanthropic personality with heavy drinking, drug-taking and ruthless careerism. Similar to Roy Strang in *Marabou Stork Nightmares*, Robertson is a character that it is difficult to spend much time with. As the novel progresses we learn that, far from hunting Wurie's killer, the detective is actually attempting a cover-up as he himself is the murderer he purports to be looking for. The novel ends with Robertson committing suicide.

Filth not only sees the development of more extravagant story-lines, it also shows Welsh attempting to develop – arguably, with limited success – the kind of narrative experimentalism that defines his earlier fiction. Robertson's first-person narrative is sporadically interrupted by that of a tapeworm which, supported by its host's unhealthy lifestyle, is slowly gestating in the police officer's stomach. The worm's voice appears in speech bubbles which at times partially eclipse the main narrative, gradually taking up more space as the novel progresses. The tapeworm features as the voice of Robertson's conscience which, by the end of the novel, reveals his personal history and the events that moulded his detestable character. Welsh's venture into crime writing does not represent such a radical departure from his earlier fiction as it may initially seem. Throughout the novel he remains preoccupied with the sociological implications opened up by the genre. As Kelly argues, 'Welsh makes subversive use of the detective thriller in *Filth* to turn the genre's formal logic of pursuing crime towards a questioning of the very legitimacy of the police and the state'.[16]

In *Glue*, his forth novel, Welsh returns to themes and motifs familiar from his debut *Trainspotting*. Like its predecessor *Glue* focuses on the lives of several characters (Billy Birrel, Andrew Galloway a.k.a. Gally, Carl Ewart and Terry Lawson), sharing out narrative duties while refusing to present a singular or coherent perspective on the world. The title of the novel also revisits familiar terrain, alluding to the question of social bonds and what it is that fashions individuals into communities. *Glue* does, however, mark a significant departure in terms of its historical scale. Whereas Welsh's earlier novels introduce their characters *in medias res*, as thrown into existence, *Glue* locates its characters' origins in the 1970s and then traces their lives over a period of four decades from childhood into adolescence and early manhood. For Kelly this change of narrative perspective is born out of the author's increasing estrangement from the experiences of the community he attempts to write about.[17] In contrast to the total immersion of *Trainspotting*, *Glue* holds its characters at a distance, elaborating on a greater historical context against which to read their lives.

Glue is followed by *Porno*, a novel which sees the return of the *Trainspotting* cast, including Renton, Sick Boy, Begbie, Spud and Diane. Sick Boy and Renton, enemies since the latter's betrayal, return to Leith after several years of working in London and Amsterdam respectively. *Porno* might be read as a homecoming for both Welsh and his two most memorable protagonists. However, the Leith to which Sick Boy and Renton return is markedly different from the one they left. Like so many post-industrial urban areas, it has become subject to a process of gentrification. As Sick Boy puts it, the place has turned 'from Jakey Central to new Leith café society' (*P*, 45). Notably, the characters in *Porno* show varying degrees of adaptability to the changing nature of their beloved port. As we recall, in the court scene in *Trainspotting* Renton's adaptability, which resulted in his suspended sentence, by far surpassed that of Spud, who, unable to act convincingly the part of the contrite defendant, received a custodial sentence. Similarly, in *Porno* it is Renton and Sick Boy who are most adept at turning the post-industrial landscape to their advantage. Spud, battling to stay clean, and Begbie, newly released from prison, regard the changes as just another form of the world's inherent instability. One might also read the heightened commercialism of the new Leith in terms of Welsh's decision to return to his original cast of characters in the first place. In interview the author has commented frankly on the potential to make 'mega-bucks' from his own 'minor Harry Potter franchise'.[18] This quite outspoken willingness to resuscitate characters, scenarios and settings for financial gain might also reflect on Welsh's recent experimentation with more popular fictional genres, such as the detective story, the romance and the thriller.

His decision in *Porno* to write about the sex industry shows Welsh's continual readiness to take contemporary fiction into new territory. Pornography as such is heavily implicated in notions of male voyeurism and spectator pleasure, a fact that only serves to rekindle older debates about the exploitative nature of Welsh's fiction. Without doubt *Porno* diagnoses a wider cultural shift in the 1990s regarding mainstream representations of women. The emergence of men's magazines such as *Loaded* (to which, notably, Welsh was a regular contributor) and *FHM* during this period saw highly sexualised images of women become an increasingly integral part of everyday culture. In keeping with the critical engagement of his earlier novels, Welsh sets out to examine pornography as the apotheosis of late capitalism's commodification of all aspects of human experience. In *Porno* Nikki Fuller-Smith, a middle-class English student jaded by the perceived empty pretentiousness of university life, becomes a sex worker and, subsequently, an actor in Sick Boy's film. Initially, Nikki is presented as the kind of liberated, confident and sexually permissive woman who believes she can single-handedly redefine female sexuality and its relationship to something as politically problematic as pornography. Eventually, however, she concedes that it is impossible for a woman to secure a meaningful form of socio-economic empowerment from prostitution which panders to the sexual pleasures of men.

Welsh's sixth novel, *The Bedroom Secrets of the Master Chefs*, tells the story of Danny Skinner and Brian Kibby, two young men who work as restaurant inspectors for Edinburgh Council. Playing with concepts of the double and duality familiar to readers of Scottish fiction as far back as James Hogg's (1770–1835) *The Private Memoirs and Confessions of a Justified Sinner* (1824) and Robert Louis Stevenson's (1850–94) *The Strange Case of Dr Jekyll and Mr Hyde* (1886), Skinner and Kibby are polar opposites in almost every way. Skinner is an alcoholic binge drinker from Leith, who takes cocaine and spends his weekends running with the local Hibs casuals. By contrast Kibby is a nerd who does not drink and spends his spare time hill-walking with a local rambling club. Skinner's broken background (he never knew his father) is juxtaposed with Kibby's own domestic stability. Early in the novel the death of Kibby's father sets up the novel's climactic revelation that Skinner and Kibby are in fact half-brothers. Like Welsh's earlier novels, *The Bedroom Secrets of the Master Chefs* is interested in the portrayal of extreme behaviour. Taking its cue from the contemporary media cult of the celebrity chef as well as, without doubt, the bestselling works of writer-chefs such as Anthony Bourdain, the title refers to a book that in the novel becomes Skinner's hedonist's bible. Full of overblown accounts of culinary and sexual excesses, this book acts as a guide to the gluttonous overindulgence of contemporary society.

Echoing the magical-realist presence of an eloquent tapeworm in *Filth*, *Bedroom Secrets* likewise documents Welsh's penchant for the surreal and the fantastic. Spurred by personal jealousy and professional competitiveness, Skinner is somehow able to wish all his hangovers onto Kibby who, as a result, begins to suffer the consequences of his rival's excesses. The novel interrogates contemporary hedonism and its false promise of limitless licentiousness without negative repercussions. A warning of the long-term implications of our current lifestyles, in terms of the environment and of public health, underpins the novel's surreal narrative. While Skinner attacks life with reckless abandon, Kibby is eventually hospitalised and has to have emergency liver surgery. In contrast to the largely episodic nature of Welsh's earlier novels, *Bedroom Secrets* offers a consistently linear narrative, as the book's fantastic story-line is propelled by Skinner's search for his father. He believes that finding his father will explain why he has become the person he is today. Notably, when his journey takes him to San Francisco, Skinner realises that the environment at home is heavily implicated in his alcoholism: 'But the pull, oh my God the fucking pull, aye, much stronger in dingy auld Edina than in sunny Cal-i-for-nigh-ay [. . .] Every bar I pass containing a face: a memory, a story, and the fabric of a life. More than the alcohol I'm addicted to that way of life, that culture, those social relationships' (*BS*, 319). The novel deconstructs notions of place, probing their specific effect in fostering self-destructive behaviours. Allegedly, the bad weather and ubiquity of bars make Edinburgh predisposed to the kind of terminal excess that we see Skinner pursue.

Like *Porno*, *Crime*, Welsh's latest novel to date, returns to fleshing out a character that featured in an earlier novel, in this case Ray Lennox, who first appeared alongside Detective Sergeant Bruce Robertson in *Filth*. The novel shows Lennox and his fiancée, Trudi, in Miami on a recuperative holiday designed to alleviate Lennox's stress following his involvement in the case of a young Edinburgh girl who had been abducted, sexually assaulted and murdered. Never one to shun controversy, Welsh's most recent novel tackles the issue of paedophilia and quite clearly also draws on the huge media interest surrounding the real-life abduction of three-year-old Madeleine McCann in the holiday resort of Praia da Luz in Portugal in May 2007. In Miami, following a row with Trudi, Lennox, a recovering cocaine addict, embarks on a solitary drinking spree during which he meets a couple of women who take him home. At the party that follows, Lennox witnesses a man attempt to sexually assault Tianna, the ten-year-old daughter of one of the women. The next morning Lennox finds himself alone with Tianna and responsible for her safety, a situation that escalates as the girl's attacker turns out to be not only on very amiable terms with the local police, but also involved in the organisation of a nationwide paedophile ring.

As the lone individual battling to restore social order, Lennox situates Welsh in a radically different terrain from where he began with *Trainspotting*. For nationalist critics the use of various genres might locate Welsh in a tradition of popular Scottish writing, one that includes the adventure stories of Robert Louis Stevenson, the detective fiction of Sir Arthur Conan Doyle and the international thrillers of John Buchan. But Welsh's generic turn could also be seen to reflect a wider democratic shift within contemporary literature, as the gap between literary and more popular modes of fiction continues to narrow. In this context, Welsh's work provides a useful barometer with which to measure present-day literary values. The international phenomenon that Welsh has become is also mirrored in the cosmopolitan locations (Amsterdam, San Francisco, Miami) of his more recent work. While such moves echo the increased globalisation of twenty-first-century culture in general, there is also a sense in which the further Welsh departs from Leith, as well as his original literary experimentalism, the less powerful his fiction becomes. Recent rumours about a prequel to *Trainspotting* may augur something of a spiritual and artistic homecoming for the author. At the same time, however, one cannot but wonder about Welsh's commercial instincts and whether this latest venture might merely represent yet another attempt to cash in on the *Trainspotting* brand.

CHAPTER THREE

Welsh's Shorter Fiction

David Borthwick

According to Frank O'Connor, 'the short story has never had a hero. What it has instead is a submerged population group [. . .] whatever these may be at any given time – tramps, artists, lonely idealists, dreamers, and spoiled priests.' [1] In O'Connor's view the short story deals with a very different territory from the novel. Whereas 'the novel can still adhere to the classical concept of civilized society [. . .] the short story remains by its very nature remote from the community – romantic, individualistic, and intransigent'. The short story embraces incoherence and otherness; its characters often appear as the cast-offs from more successful, central national narratives, 'outlawed figures wandering about the fringes of society'. This is the territory charted by Welsh since the beginning of his career across several genres. While the bulk of his output has come in the form of novels, the latter tend to evade the reader's expectations of what a novel should offer or be. Eschewing linearity and coherent progression, many of Welsh's writings unfold outside 'essential form'. As O'Connor puts it, 'because [the short story writer's] frame of reference can never be the totality of a human life, he must be forever selecting the point at which he can approach it, and each selection he makes contains the possibility of a new form as well as the possibility of a complete fiasco'.

Welsh deploys in his work a 'diffuse arsenal of representational modes',[2] including typographical experimentation, fragmentary accounts of drug-induced hallucination, regional dialects, as well as interludes of magical realism and Kafkaesque metamorphosis. The lives of Welsh's characters cannot be represented as aspiring to anything as grand as narrative totality. His work is the antithesis of measured order and balance, challenging the uses of literary fiction by embracing a 'sensationalist mode of narrative, intimate with genres such as pulp fiction, pornography and popular music'.[3] The critical reception of Welsh's early work has often suffered owing to its departure from the novelistic standards of coherence and linearity 'by which a society is adjudged to be normal, healthy and historically mature'. As Aaron Kelly points out, 'nations, peoples, individuals or classes which do not produce novels in this normative form are not merely different but abnormal, aberrant and, according to the bourgeois narrative of historical development, immature or not fully formed social subjects for constituencies'.[4] Welsh's cultivation of short story techniques can therefore be seen as a radical challenge to normative literary expression. More often than not quite deliberately courting critical outrage and rejection, it identifies his work as a crucial cultural intervention, especially in the 1990s when the stability of received social structures and hierarchies was coming under attack by the new youth movement of rave culture's 'chemical generation'. Concerned with Welsh's body of short stories, this chapter pays particular attention to his collections of the mid-1990s, *The Acid House* (1994) and *Ecstasy* (1996), which speak most directly to, and of, the lifestyles and attitudes of the social milieu with which Welsh has become predominantly associated.

Traditionally, the short story as we now know it evolved at precisely the same time as the novel, yet its origin and demographic affiliation have always been significantly different. As William Boyd notes, 'the short story had always existed as an informal oral tradition, but until the mass middle-class literacy of the 19th century arrived in the west, and the magazine and periodical market was invented to service the new reading public's desires and preferences, there had been no real publishing forum for a piece of short fiction'.[5] The short story's origins are in the mouths of the people; it is a more democratic and inclusive genre than the novel, catering to popular needs and tastes outside the elitist strongholds of literary culture. Retaining this edginess the genre has grown into a more spontaneous, open and politically subversive alternative to the centripetally inclined novel, 'representing precisely the substrata of people and places which the imagined unity of that dominant form seeks to suppress'.[6] It seems apt, then, that the short story became the most pertinent form for representing the new youth culture movements of the 1990s. In Scotland in particular the genre was embraced by a younger generation of writers who wished to respond to contemporary changes in society and culture, publishing in magazines and periodicals such as Duncan McLean's *Clocktower Press* or Kevin Williamson's *Rebel Inc.* The latter consciously emulated the 1970s punk ethos of 'DIY. One man and his photocopier', following in both attitude and layout, design and scope the example of football fanzines such as *When Saturday Comes* and *Not the View*, as well as the Scottish music magazine *Cut*. As Williamson concludes his account of the press's genesis, 'if anyone didn't like the fictional content of sex, drugs, language, politics, violence and attitude they could go fuck themselves as far as I was concerned'.[7]

Williamson demonstrates vividly the ways in which *Rebel Inc.* refused to recognise the benchmarks of literary value, instead appealing to the values of its target readership: a new generation whose sensibilities had been formed by the visual and attitudinal thrust of pop-cultural magazines rather than the established tradition of literary periodicals and chapbooks. While somewhat less dismissive of the latter, McLean shared Williamson's DIY spirit, mainly due to his vexation at the established presses' ponderous, procedural pace of publication: 'There'd be a gap of at least six months – and often eighteen months or two *years* – before the stories actually appeared in print [. . .] This was frustrating, as we were both trying to write new stories, written in the language of the day, about the ideas and problems that confronted us here and now.' [8] Between them, *Rebel Inc.* and *Clocktower* published works by a broad range of new writers, including Laura Hird (b. 1966), Alison Kermack (b. 1965, now Alison Flett), Gordon Legge (b.1961), James Meek (b.1962), Alan Warner (b. 1964) and, indeed, Irvine Welsh. Even as the writers involved in Williamson's and McLean's projects began to come to the attention of mainstream publishers, they maintained their commitment to the depiction of the lives of the young and often marginalised, as well as the lifestyles and popular culture references that their readership would recognise.

One of *Rebel Inc.*'s first publications after becoming an imprint of the Edinburgh publisher Canongate was a collection of stories entitled *Children of Albion Rovers* (1996). Named after a low-division Lanarkshire football team, the collection keeps up fanzine associations, with authors pictured in the team's colours and Williamson's introduction assigning each of them a tactical position. At first glance little more than a flippant football reference, the title of the volume alludes to Michael Horowitz's *Children of Albion: Poetry of the Underground in Britain* (1969), which – inspired by the visionary Romantic mythology of William Blake – sought to challenge mainstream British poetry in the light of the cultural upheavals of the 1960s, offering an alternative canon of sixty-three writers (including Edwin Morgan and Alexander Trocchi) whose techniques and themes were, in the broad sense of the word, countercultural. *Children of Albion Rovers* demonstrates the mixture of irreverence and tradition-consciousness of young Scottish writers in the 1990s: at once dismissive of and attached to the literary culture out of which they emerged. There can be little doubt that *Children of Albion Rovers* was meant to capture the rebellious spirit of Horowitz's counter-canonical collection of 'altered states' writing, or that the writers of the *Clocktower* and *Rebel Inc.* initiatives envisaged their work as a countercultural response to an epoch of similarly enormous change. The individualist ethos of the 1980s, of Thatcherism and rising consumer materialism, combined with the destruction of traditional working-class life, expresses itself in their fiction through an alienated, if dynamic, popular culture which is at once symptom and cause of their protagonists' plights.

Welsh's *The Acid House* and *Ecstasy* were published as the rave culture of the late 1980s found itself at the crucial tipping point of divorcing its countercultural, underground scene origins to undergo increasing mainstream commodification, while retaining illegal drug use as a central part of its cultural make-up. As Robert Morace reports, 'rave, especially tartan techno, was at or near its height [. . .] media panic over drugs (especially Ecstasy) was high [and] government efforts to control youth culture resulted in the passage of the Criminal Justice Act of 1994'.[9] Rave's new illegality ironically conferred upon those allied to its movement of dance, music and designer drugs a strong sense of countercultural legitimacy. The Criminal Justice and Public Order Act of 1994, which defined an unlicensed rave as a gathering of more than 100 people to the soundtrack of music characterised 'by the emission of a succession of repetitive beats', served to enforce rather than disperse a sense of community. Jürgen Neubauer has talked about 'a symbolic border' between users and non-users of drugs, whereby those 'outside the mainstream' employ drug use as 'an escape from the dominant logic of normalcy in a catalogue world'; meanwhile, 'those "inside" the mainstream criminalise users as a particular threat to their version of the normal'.[10]

Welsh's work has consistently advertised its transgression beyond various kinds of symbolic borders, not only marking out his often youthful characters as living in a world fundamentally different from that of their parents, but also extending to a demarcation between the values of literary critics and the values of the readership that is Welsh's intended audience. Employing techniques originating in the short-story form, Welsh moves beyond territories considered 'normal' by the bourgeois reader and instead maps a rather different landscape. Welsh's first collection of stories, *The Acid House*, is an eclectic work comprising twenty-one short stories and a concluding novella. The stories in *The Acid House* capture in tone and content the universe Welsh established in *Trainspotting* (indeed, Spud reappears in the closing novella), yet the collection also takes in a much wider scope than Welsh's debut, both stylistically and in terms of class and characterisation. There is, for example, 'Vat '96', in which a middle-class woman's dinner party has as its centrepiece the decapitated head of her husband, kept alive following a car accident by a machine which cost 'four hundred and thirty-two thousand pounds' (*AH*, 43). The couple's material wealth staves off mortality, but the husband must suffer watching his wife's extramarital affairs from the confines of his tank. 'The Last Resort on the Adriatic' follows another (equally tedious) middle-class character as he prepares to commit suicide on the anniversary of his wife's death.

'Where the Debris Meets the Sea' is notable on account of its focus on four Hollywood and/or pop-cultural celebrities – Kim Basinger, Kylie Minogue, Madonna and Victoria Principal – who compare magazine articles in their opulent apartment in Santa Monica, discussing the relative merits of, among others, 'Deek Prentice fae Gilmerton' and 'Dode Chalmers' resplendent with 'shaved head, Castlemaine XXXX t-shirt and levis'. The story's comic inversion of the consumption of celebrity tittle-tattle and popular concern with female sex appeal also sees the four Americans speak in the Leith demotic: 'Kylie inspected the image clinically [. . .] "No a bad arse on it like, bit ah'm no really intae flat-toaps"' (*AH*, 88). These stories serve to establish Welsh's output as a brand of alternative fiction, produced, as Morace has noted astutely, for a readership familiar with a range of postmodern media, such as 'sci-fi, porn and video games, covers for albums [. . .] graphic novels and dark comics',[11] rather than traditional literary fiction with its emphasis on verisimilitude and adherence to genre conventions. More than this, however, *The Acid House* serves to illustrate where Welsh's sympathies lie. Middle-class characters are stumbling fools or self-congratulatory grotesques. Celebrities are decrowned and made to adhere to the values of those who, on a final analysis, actually provide the wealth and status they unthinkingly enjoy. Those who possess established roles and secure financial circumstances, and ontological certainty, are mocked and derided from a variety of vantage points. By contrast, many of the other stories in the collection express, if often indirectly, empathy with and understanding of those characters who serve to illuminate, even if they cannot account for, the world in which they live.

In 'The House of John Deaf' a young man describes the home of a profoundly deaf boy he knew as an adolescent, a house which 'had fuck all in it; nae furniture or nowt like that' (*AH*, 99); instead, the house is swarming with white mice purchased from a local pet shop. On discovering his sister and John engaged in a sexual act, the narrator is savagely beaten by John and, in revenge, kills his favourite mouse: 'one thit eh had kicked thit had baith ay its back legs broken. It used to drag itsel acroass the floor wi its front legs' (*AH*, 99). Following the death of his grandfather, John Deaf is 'taken away', never to return to the scheme. The narrator can find no closure on his relationship with John Deaf, as expressed through the central image of the white mouse, which remains similarly ambiguous, capable of symbolising at once John Deaf and the narrator, both limited and severely damaged by their experiences, simultaneously victims and perpetrators of violence and (self-) destructiveness: 'Ah've nivir been the same since that doin eh gied ays, ah kin tell ye' (*AH*, 102). This unresolved ambiguity and lack of clarity of events and experiences characterise several of the stories in *The Acid House*. Welsh's protagonists across a wide range of the stories seem unable to locate a sense of order or coherence in their lives which would allow a deeper sense of understanding to emerge. Living beyond the symbolic border of normalcy in terms of lifestyles, identities and morals, Welsh's characters can find no metanarrative framework in which to operate or account for themselves.

Welsh has always been fully aware that his fiction documents the lives of those who lack stability and definition in relation to wider society.

'Nowadays', Welsh asserts, 'younger working-class people grow up in a society in which the main institutions of socialisation, where kids learn morality – the family, the community, the trade unions and the churches – have been emasculated by the promotion of consumerism and the market economy.' [12] Deprived of the stable traditions of working-class life, Welsh's youth inhabit a landscape very different from their parents': a consumerist landscape which encourages investment in leisure rather than self-definition through work, a landscape symbolised by the raves and acid-house parties, as well as the use of drugs and alcohol to which Welsh's fiction continually returns. The corollary of this dislocated and fractured sense of class and familial identity is a more serious crisis in personal identification, perhaps best summed up by the sociologist and cultural critic Zygmunt Bauman. In a consumer society, Bauman argues, 'taking risks replaces the stubborn pursuit of goals [. . .] there is little in the world which one could consider solid and reliable, nothing reminiscent of a tough canvas in which one could weave one's own life itinerary'.[13] Traditional working-class narratives of a cohesive community, of aspirational self-improvement, are no longer relevant. Reflecting the generic properties of the short story, there is no essential form one's life must take, no sense of progression that will result in a life made wholly coherent or meaningful.

Yet the fractured narrative forms Welsh is renowned for mark an ironically neat dovetailing of subject and form: the partial and fragmentary experiences of his characters are mirrored in the narrative styles employed, and the short story crystallises as an apt vehicle for the lifestyles thus documented. The social milieu that holds Welsh's attention concerns characters propelled by a sense of immediacy and living for instant gratification. These characters find limited freedom in the unexamined life, avoiding the constraints and responsibilities of a stable identity in favour of moral relativity and ceaseless mobility. In 'Eurotrash', for example, Euan arrives in Amsterdam to stay with a friend from Scotland, but he finds Rab (now 'Robbie') much changed from the person he knew at home. Euan succumbs to a ubiquitous deconstruction of identity, exacerbated by drug consumption and metropolitan displacement. In the street, drug dealers attempt to engage him by inviting a choice of nationality: 'French? American? English?' Euan also meets Chrissie, who is not quite what s/he seems, flaunting 'a Liverpool affectation to what generally seemed to be a hybrid of middle-class English and French, although I was sure it was all a pose' (*AH*, 18). 'Eurotrash' documents an increasing contingency of identity, coupled with possibilities for adopting ever new personas and practising continual self-reinvention without closure or final responsibility. Welsh's characters inhabit ways of being that correspond to what Bauman has described as 'liquid life', capturing 'a society in which the conditions under which its members act changes faster than it takes the ways of acting to consolidate into habits and routines'.[14] The frenetic currents of unrestrained free market capitalism have come to determine the very behaviour of people, as each individual effectively acts not as a stable agent, or even citizen, but ultimately as a human consumable, subject to the ephemerality of brands and the fickleness of supply and demand. Mobility and constant self-reinvention are necessary to retain and bolster one's own currency. 'Life in a liquid modern society cannot stand still', Bauman writes. 'The need here is to run with all one's strength just to stay in the same place and away from the rubbish bin where the hindmost are doomed to land.' [15]

In 'A Smart Cunt', with which *The Acid House* concludes, Brian's acquaintances exemplify Bauman's prognosis. Denise appears 'in a state of transformation from one queen stereotype into another', entering a bar 'with a pair of young queens who look exactly like Denise used to look' (*AH*, 241). Another character – 'enough like her friends to want to be like someone else, someone they wanted to be like' (*AH*, 273) – is known interchangeably as Olly or Livvy. These are not simply cases of youthful reinvention, of the adolescent process of finding one's place within society; rather, they signal an imperative striving to remain relevant, 'nudged from behind by the horror of expiry',[16] which manifests itself in Welsh's work as the failure of sexual prowess, notoriety or social desirability. In 'The Undefeated', the third of the 'chemical romances' that comprise *Ecstasy*, we witness Lloyd worrying about his social decrepitude, while Ally salves his concerns: 'Ye have got it, ya daft cunt, just like you had punk, just ye'll have the next thing that comes along' (*E*, 161). In Welsh's social universe 'identities, just like consumer goods, are to be appropriated and possessed, but only in order to be consumed, and so to disappear again'.[17] This sense of a 'liquid' self is central to Welsh's work. Unable to conceive of progress, his characters inhabit life as an erratic process, replacing settled societal and personal coordinates – a coherent positioning of self in relation to others – with radical mobility. This mobility has been a hallmark of Welsh's work since *Trainspotting*, whose ending sees Renton heading for Amsterdam, free to 'be what he wanted to be' and newly empowered to cast a fresh Renton franchise, liberated from Leith. Similarly, Brian in 'A Smart Cunt' reflects that 'London had been starting to feel like Edinburgh had before I'd left it [. . .] a set of expectations which snapped around me like a sprung trap. You can only be free for so long, then the chains start to bind you. The answer is to keep moving' (*AH*, 274). Divorced from past and future, Welsh's characters are left chafing against perceived impediments to individual freedom, afflicted by a sense of alienation or exclusion, yet unable to quantify these dissatisfactions into coherent resistance. These characters may be described in Bauman's terms as a 'spiritual lumpenproletariat', a grouping whose priorities are limited to the present and for whom 'the world is not their home ground and not their property (having relieved themselves of the burdens of heritage, they feel free but somehow disinherited – robbed of something, betrayed by someone), they see nothing wrong with exploiting it at will'.[18]

In *Ecstasy*, Welsh's second collection, whose stories all feature rave and dance culture to varying degrees, the sentiments of a selection of clubbers demonstrate the accuracy of Bauman's observation. In 'Lorraine Goes to Livingston' Glen, a mortuary assistant who has hours earlier accepted a bribe from a necrophiliac, feels that rave music (accompanied by ecstasy) enables him to see 'all the bad things in Britain [. . .] this twentieth-century urban blues music defined and illustrated them more sharply than ever' (*E*, 26). As Glen sees it, 'political sloganeering and posturing meant nothing; you had to celebrate the joy of life in the face of all those grey forces and dead spirits who controlled everything, who fucked with your head and livelihood anyway, if you weren't one of them' (*E*, 27). Another character, Lloyd, feels similarly aggrieved, describing himself as 'fucking emotional wreckage, the waste product of a shitey world a bunch of cunts have set up for themselves at our expense' (*E*, 272–3). In each case, citizenship and political accountability are identified as belonging to faceless powerbrokers, inflicting on Welsh's characters a strong yet undefined sense of emotional damage. In Glen's as well as Lloyd's view, the liquid(is)ation of identity offered by mind-altering substances affords the only possible escape, to such a degree that social functioning becomes almost wholly dependent on the use of drugs. Lloyd's love life is fuelled by ecstasy and amyl nitrate, the latter being 'no really an optional extra, now really as essential as a cock or a fanny' (*E*, 160). As the effect of the chemicals abates, the intensity of intimate relationships subsides: 'Ah could feel the distance growing between us with the MDMA running down in our bodies' (*E*, 163). As Lloyd meets his new girlfriend, Heather, she calls for him to moderate his drug intake, a prospect which scares him precisely because 'when I'm E'd up it's like ah want to be. It's no like anything's been added to me, it's like it's been taken away fae me; aw the shite in the world that gets intae your heid. When I'm E'd up I'm my real self' (*E*, 272).

However, drugs are never quite that reliable. At one point we hear Lloyd complain about a batch of ecstasy pills that 'you had to neck them two at a time for any buzz at aw' (*E*, 220), while another batch he purchases later 'were different again, like Ketamine or something' (*E*, 225). Altered states are not subject to any kind of guarantee: purchasing a particular drug may result in a mind-altering experience quite different from what is expected. Identities are as uncertain and unreliable as the drugs that supposedly work to transcend them. In Welsh's world, nothing is certain, no position constant or identity negotiated securely. Life's liquidity results in the reeling off of a never-ending slideshow of new identities, disabling any enduring construction of identity within a fixed range of discourses of nation or class. 'Consigned to an endless present, a sequence of discrete, divided moments of experience',[19] the lives of

Welsh's characters remain inconclusive and, as such, are suited perfectly for representation in the short-story form, maintaining, as they do, the inherent individualism and intransigence which O'Connor identifies as so essential to the genre's view of the world.

Indeed, Welsh makes a stylistic virtue out of his characters' experience of life as a series of discrete episodes. Whenever more than one character is invoked, as is the case in each of the three stories in *Ecstasy*, Welsh tends to present us with alternating segments of narration that enable the reader to be privy to a range of different points of view. 'Lorraine Goes to Livingston', for example, contains six separate focalisers as well as extracts from one character's novel in progress. Welsh's novels, too, largely feature ensemble casts whose lives are conveyed in isolated monologic fragments, frequently manoeuvring the reader into a position of 'linguistic, moral and social complicity'.[20] Thrust into such intimate engagement with a particular set of priorities, or an obsessive, highly eccentric worldview, the reader cannot but perceive the world through whichever character's lens happens to be used for focalisation. As Alan Riach has noted, Welsh's particular brand of realism 'is constructed by the language of his characters'.[21] What emerges from these hyperbolically individualised narratives is 'a series of dramatically self-deconstructing narrator-characters'[22] who, in revealing their particular dispositions via eclectic, and at times random, citation and intertextual referencing, disclose the utter contingency of their psychological make-up. When in 'Fortune's Always Hiding' Dave contemplates exchanging life with his football hooligan friends for a relationship with Samantha, his deepest emotional insights draw upon 'that ABC song [. . .] when they go on about the past being your bleedin' sacred cow, and how we all gotta fucking change' (*E*, 123). While Welsh's technique allows us to understand and even sympathise with profoundly dislikeable characters, ultimately it opens up a rather cynical worldview in which any given statement or behaviour can be justified, however spuriously, by subjective contextualisation. It is a powerfully consumerist worldview in which everything is a matter of off-the-peg choice, burdening the individual with only limited responsibility for his or her decision-making. In Welsh's work, then, individualism and individual agency follow a consumerist blueprint of virtually infinitely free choice unfettered by communal responsibility. Indeed, as Kelly deplores, in Welsh's fiction 'interpersonal friendships, familial bonds and codes of sociality seem irreparably sundered by the enveloping late capitalist system'.[23]

On the face of it Welsh's narrative universe, while filled with black humour and extraordinary energy, presents the reader with a hostile and nihilistic vision of contemporary popular culture and, by extension, modern Scotland. As Gerard Carruthers has remarked of *Trainspotting* (though the sentiment applies equally to Welsh's short stories), 'that it is sceptical towards the notion of a "real Scotland" or a "real Britain" or a "real world" marks perhaps either the bleakest or most liberated point in the literature of the nation'.[24] In rejecting any stable viewpoint or coherent sense of personal identity, Welsh's fiction may indeed appear bleak. However, an alternative view is possible. According to Morace, 'what the literary culture (or subculture) sees as a limitation [. . .] strikes those steeped in visual culture quite differently'.[25] Taking their cue from pornography, graphic novels and videogames, Welsh's stories revel in hyperbole. Welsh's characters – from psychopathic Begbie in *Trainspotting* to necrophiliac television presenter Freddie Royle in 'Lorraine goes to Livingston' – have always tended to be overdrawn, presenting extreme behaviours and viewpoints.[26] Morace argues that if Welsh's characters at times appear monstrous, this is because 'the outsize is the *lingua franca* of a postliterate generation, for whom "fine writing" and psychological realism are passé'.[27] In effect, Welsh's short stories evade conventional expectations about literary verisimilitude as much as his novels do, appealing instead to the more visually inclined, media-fuelled imagination of his core audience of younger readers. Throughout his career Welsh has sought to retain the early edginess and transgressive stance cultivated by Williamson's Rebel Inc. enterprise, at once working within and against mainstream literary culture. His work may be documenting the lives of those unable as well as unwilling to account for the nature of their existence, but this ontological uncertainty is accompanied by other, liberating possibilities, which Welsh's fiction – and particularly his short stories – explores by formally enacting the lack of order and balance that informs his characters' lives.

The development of Welsh's writing of short stories traces a movement away from conventional realism towards a heightened, multidimensional mode of representation in which bold, primary colours and sweeping imageries are employed in a carnivalesque celebration of people from a variety of submerged population groups, people who are at once assaulted by, enmeshed in, yet still claiming resistance to an overbearing consumerist culture. Willy Maley highlights Welsh's penchant for 'cartoon violence',[28] an apposite description of the author's highly visual graphic style, exemplified perhaps most memorably by two stories of transformation in *The Acid House*: 'The Acid House', in which Coco Bryce's soul transmigrates into the body of a newborn child, and 'The Granton Star Cause', in which Boab undergoes transformation into a fly. Both stories take the liquidity of identity to its extreme, providing allegories of a fundamental estrangement from both self and other, as both Boab's and Coco's new lives crystallise as mocking ripostes to their previous social and personal circumstances. Kelly reads Boab's metamorphosis as 'an allegory of the estrangements of human identity under late capitalism and our seeming incapacity to comprehend the profound and bewildering systemic changes taking place under globalisation'.[29]

Welsh's story employs a comic scenario and improbable events to express Boab's profound problems of identification and self-actualisation, but Welsh's departures into such magical realism also emphasise the lack of consistency in the lives of characters whose liquid identities obstruct a deeper sense of understanding.

Such technicolor depictions of listless liquidity continue to dominate Welsh's most recent collection, *If You Liked School, You'll Love Work* (2007), whose title story introduces cockney ex-pat Mickey, the owner of a tourist bar in Fuerteventura and an unreconstructed womaniser, who views himself as 'squelching through a swamp of moral relativism every day' (*IY*, 84). 'Kingdom of Fife', another story, ends with Jason King, ex-jockey and table football champion, leaving Cowdenbeath with Jenni for a new life in Spain. Their mobility echoes that of many of Welsh's other characters, as does Jason's cultivation of personal relationships that provide financial reward or mere physical pleasure. At one stage he admits to going along with Jenni's suggestions because 'she's the one with the tits n fanny, n it'll be a long time afore ah'm satiated enough tae turn ma nose up at thon currency!' (*IY*, 377). Welsh's recent stories continue to display a concern with supply and demand, consumption and waste. As with his earlier work, his latest batch of hyperbolic parables rejects stability and order in favour of relativity and fluidity.

Welsh's short stories engage a narrative universe that eschews realist depiction of a conventional sort in order to mobilise contradiction, deviancy, discontinuity and transgression. The grittily real and wilfully fantastic coexist within fractured tales of excess and liquidity, prioritising stylistic largesse and graphic exuberance over a formal essentialism. Welsh's use of multiple focalisation answers O'Connor's claim that the short story is a genre that denies the existence of a hero – the epitome of order and established values – to make room for a multitudinous submerged populace that, in Welsh's work, often struggles to assert itself as a stable community. Welsh's short fiction is fundamentally concerned with infinite variation and the creation of alternatives. This is likely to be motivated by the fact that the social milieu Welsh most sympathises with has suffered irremediable cultural dislocation and a loss of values that it does not have the power or will to substitute satisfactorily. The short story is the most suitable narrative form to represent the fractious and frenetic lives of Welsh's characters; as a genre it requires no final resolution, no arrival at or return to unity and equilibrium. Welsh's characters must suffer to live life beyond closure, from moment to moment, always on the move, without satisfactory progress.

CHAPTER FOUR

Trainspotting, the Film

Duncan Petrie

By the end of 1995 Irvine Welsh was firmly established as the *enfant terrible* of a vibrant new wave of Scottish writing and an emerging figure on the wider British cultural scene. But it was to be the enormous impact of the cinematic adaptation of *Trainspotting*, directed by Danny Boyle and released in the UK in February 1996, that would elevate both the author and his fictional creations from the arcane marginality of a hip but niche market novel to the mainstream familiarity of a hugely successful commercial product. The film version of *Trainspotting* also served to confirm the vibrancy of contemporary Scottish culture by bridging the considerable achievements of a national literary scene reinvigorated in the 1980s by Alasdair Gray (b. 1934) and James Kelman (b. 1946) and subsequently consolidated by Welsh and his peers on the one hand, and on the other, a newly emergent Scottish cinema underpinned by new sources of institutional support.[1]

A key landmark in the latter cultural movement had been the stylish low-budget thriller *Shallow Grave* (1994), the debut feature of a creative team comprising Boyle (b. 1956), producer Andrew MacDonald (b. 1965) and writer John Hodge (b. 1964). This tale of three self-obsessed Edinburgh yuppies who, on finding their new flatmate dead in his room with a suitcase full of money, decide to erase all traces of him in order to keep the cash, earned an astonishing £5 million at the British box office, making *Shallow Grave* the first truly popular Scottish film since Bill Forsyth's *Local Hero* (1983). With all manner of possibilities opened up for their next production, including the inevitable interest from Hollywood, Boyle, MacDonald and Hodge decided instead to turn their attention to *Trainspotting*. The film proved nothing less than a sensation, confounding MacDonald's expectation that the subject matter of Welsh's novel would considerably limit its box-office success. *Trainspotting* quickly became one of the most successful British productions of all time, grossing in excess of £12 million in the UK, where it was the top-grossing, wholly UK-financed production for 1996, and more than $72 million world-wide, including $16.5 million in the United States alone. By virtue of its low budget of £1.7 million, *Trainspotting* earned the distinction of being by far the most profitable film of the year. In addition to its commercial success, *Trainspotting* garnered substantial critical acclaim, including a number of prestigious awards and an Oscar nomination for Best Adapted Screenplay.[2] In addition to confirming the talent of its core creative team, the film launched the careers of its ensemble cast of young actors, including Ewan McGregor (who had previously appeared in *Shallow Grave*), Robert Carlyle, Jonny Lee Miller, Ewen Bremner, Kelly MacDonald and Kevin McKidd, fuelling a growing interest in Scottish cinematic creativity.

Of course, the other major beneficiary of the *Trainspotting* phenomenon was Irvine Welsh himself. Not only did the film bring his name and face (by virtue of his cameo appearance as drug dealer Mikey Forrester) to a wide international public, it also had an immediate effect on sales of his original novel. As part of the wider marketing campaign for the film in the UK, *Trainspottting* had been republished with a new cover featuring the iconic image of Ewan McGregor in the central role of Mark Renton. At the point of the film's release the novel had sold almost 150,000 copies in Britain. But a mere five months later this had jumped to half a million. In the United States the effect was even more fundamental. As Robert Morace notes, the release of the film in July 1996 'in effect introduced Welsh to an audience for whom the publication of *Trainspotting, Marabou Stork Nightmares* and *Ecstasy* more or less coincided with the film's release'.[3] *Trainspotting* became an international cultural phenomenon on the back of which Welsh was well and truly catapulted out of the 'underground'. Yet the transformation and repackaging of reputedly 'the most shoplifted novel in British publishing history'[4] into a product intended for widespread international consumption also raises a host of questions concerning the cultural status and discursive significance of the different versions. Whereas Welsh's own creative vision cast an angry backward glance at the social exclusion, stagnation and decay that characterised great swathes of Thatcher's divided Britain, the mid-1990s moment of the film anticipated the dawn of a feel-good, socially inclusive optimism that was to herald the advent of Tony Blair's New Labour in 1997. As a popular and highly influential cultural product, the film version of *Trainspotting* came to be regarded as emblematic of that moment. Its complex and at times harrowing subject matter seemed displaced or transcended by the clever exuberance of its form, providing an example of the kind of triumph of style over substance that was to characterise and ultimately tarnish the legacy of the Blairite revolution.

The enormous success of a feature film about the experiences of Edinburgh heroin addicts, made on a low budget and featuring no A-list stars, was primarily testament to the skill and inventiveness of Boyle and his team. The intrinsic qualities of the production prompted Murray Smith to opine that '*Trainspotting* justifies and rewards sustained consideration not only in terms of its cultural impact in general and its significance for Scottish and British film culture in particular, but above all for its accomplishment as a work of art', asserting that '*Trainspotting* really is a "modern classic"'.[5] The creative transformation of Welsh's vision began with Hodge's screenplay. Overcoming an initial reaction that the novel's fragmented structure and array of internal monologues made it unadaptable, Hodge succeeded in reworking the material into a screenplay for a 90-minute feature film that crucially managed to retain and convey 'at least some of the spirit and content of the book'.[6] As with all adaptations this involved not only a robust process of compression (via the amalgamation of characters, the omission of scenes, the transferring of incident and dialogue from one character to another), but also of invention, for example, the inclusion of entirely original scenes, some inspired by minor details from the novel or, quite possibly also, Harry Gibson's stage adaptation of 1994.

While retaining the core of Welsh's ensemble of characters, Hodge followed Hollywood rather than art-house orthodoxy in placing Renton much more firmly at the centre of the narrative and making his character's trajectory the primary driving force behind the plot. His central point of view is further enhanced by the liberal use of voiceovers throughout the film, offering a key site of access and identification for the audience. The prospective appeal to viewers is also ensured by the casting of Ewan McGregor, his good looks and charisma making Renton a far more attractive protagonist than the acne-scarred redhead of the novel. From the very outset it is clear that the filmmakers were interested in creating an emotional rather than intellectual response from the audience, drawing them into the story rather than keeping them at a more contemplative distance. The choice of other key cast members also functions effectively to capture the essence of the characters within the repertoire of familiar cinematic types. So we have pretty-boy Jonny Lee Miller portraying the suave but ruthless Sick Boy, Ewen Bremner as the geeky, hapless but gentle Spud, Kevin McKidd as the fit and healthy 'regular guy' Tommy, and moustachioed Robert Carlyle as Begbie, an essay in pure malevolence and a new manifestation of the diminutive Scottish 'hard man'. In addition, fresh-faced newcomer Kelly MacDonald provided the appropriate naïve sassiness of Diane, Renton's love interest.

In addition to being motivated by the central protagonist, the narrative trajectory of *Trainspotting* also falls into the classic three-act structure of mainstream cinema. The first act sets the scene in a resolutely up-beat fashion, establishing the characters and focusing on the pleasures of heroin before giving way to Renton's rather comical attempts to quit, involving various distractions and adventures with the other members of the gang. Cleaning up his act also restores Renton's libido, which leads to a sexual encounter with Diane. The first act culminates in the humorous, but poignant trip to 'the great outdoors', where Renton bemoans the national condition and delivers his much-cited 'it's shite being Scottish' rant, leading him, Sick Boy and Spud to decide to go back on heroin. This action motivates the second act, which becomes progressively darker in tone as Renton and his gang descend into a self-serving rush of cheating, scamming and thieving to finance their habit. The downward slide culminates in the death of Alison's baby in the shooting gallery, Spud being sent to prison for stealing, Renton's near-fatal overdose and his protracted nightmare of withdrawal, and finally the revelation that Tommy, who only started using heroin after his girlfriend Lizzy left him, is now dying of AIDS.

Encouraged by Diane to recognise that the world is changing, Renton is propelled into a third decisive action. The final act commences with his move to London where he becomes involved in the world of real estate, an environment in which his skills of scamming prove highly useful. But when first Begbie and then Sick Boy turn up, Renton realises that his past cannot be discarded so easily. On a return visit to Edinburgh for Tommy's funeral, the three (along with Spud) embark on a major drug deal that takes them back to London where they sell the stash for £16,000. When the subsequent celebrations are ruined once again by Begbie's senseless violence, Renton is propelled towards his final action, making off with the money, presumably into a new, brighter future.

While this structure serves to simplify and render palatable the novel's fragmented and impressionistic narrative, Boyle's visual style brings about a direct cinematic translation of the vitality of Welsh's writing. Boyle's starting point was an absolute rejection of the kind of realist orthodoxy in British films dealing with gritty contemporary subject matter. This approach met with approval all round, with Welsh claiming it was a key factor in persuading him to sell the rights of *Trainspotting* to MacDonald in the first place:

> I would have been disappointed if it had been a kind of worthy piece of social realism. I think there's more to it than that. It's about the culture and the lifestyle in a non-judgemental way. It's about how people live their lives and how people interact. To see it as just a kind of reaction to social oppression, to social circumstances, is to rip some of the soul out of it and to make the characters into victims.[7]

The creative constraints imposed by the low budget further enhanced the creative direction of the production. The seven-week shoot included three weeks in a makeshift studio in Glasgow (the former Wills' cigarette factory), where several highly stylised sets were built by production designer Kave Quinn. These included Mother Superior's flat where Renton and his associates go to get wasted, constructed as an expressionistic cavern bathed in strong reds, greens, oranges and blues rather than a naturalistic squalid and cramped drug den. Quinn's designs are augmented throughout by the cinematography of Brian Tufano, whose predilection for 'noir lighting in colour' was equally central to the look of *Shallow Grave*. Such creative licence was absolutely central to Boyle's vision for the film:

> If we had a chance to go back to *Trainspotting* we'd make even more of it in the studio. Realism is Britain's trademark in terms of television drama and film. We've made this choice to dampen ourselves down so that sex and colours are not something to be celebrated. And if you go out into the street, we're such a small country architecturally and geographically that it's very difficult to create a sense of myth. It's very difficult actually to expand – to create a space big enough for the cinema screen [. . .] Unless, of course, if you can do it in the studio and build your own world [. . .] and you can use colours, space and movement that is not natural in British flats and houses and streets.[8]

Boyle had screened a number of films for the crew and cast prior to shooting, including Stanley Kubrick's *A Clockwork Orange* (1971), Kathryn Bigelow's *Near Dark* (1987) and Martin Scorsese's *Goodfellas* (1990) which, along with the paintings of Francis Bacon, clearly inspired the film's dominant neo-expressionist aesthetic. But just as Welsh had struck a delicate balance in his depiction of the drug scene as caught between pain and pleasure, despair and euphoria, communality and isolation, so the moody, noirish tendency in the film is leavened by the life-affirming zest and breakneck narrative propulsion inspired by Richard Lester's Beatles films *A Hard Day's Night* (1964) and *Help!* (1965), which in themselves constitute a British appropriation of the pioneering, self-reflexive experimentation of the French *nouvelle vague*. This is manifest in the playful manipulations of time and space, the stories-within-stories, the use of elliptical and intrusive editing, freeze-frames, split screens and subtitles that create a *mise en scène* characterised by pleasurable excess. The opening sequence is a case in point, exploding into life with Renton and Spud racing down Princes Street accompanied on the soundtrack by Renton's 'Choose Life' monologue and Iggy Pop's 'Lust for Life', which provide a sonic bridge to the subsequent images intercut between Swanney's shooting gallery and a five-a-side football match. The sequence also introduces the main characters via freeze-frames and on-screen titles, recalling the opening of Martin Scorsese's *Mean Streets* (1973).

Another characteristically playful scene features the intercut couplings of Renton and Diane, Tommy and Lizzie, and the unconscious Spud and Gail, which are given an additional *frisson* with the inclusion of the footage of Archie Gemmill's celebrated goal against Holland in the 1978 World Cup finals. Elsewhere Boyle pushes anti-naturalism even further, most audaciously in the 'worst toilet in Scotland' scene when Renton literally disappears into a filthy toilet bowl to retrieve his opium suppositories before swimming through clear-blue water as if diving for pearls. While John Orr has suggested that the supercharged hyper-real quality of the film constructs a mythic Edinburgh environment in which the real is substituted by 'the burning intensity of the copy',[9] Smith describes *Trainspotting*'s aesthetic as 'black magic realism', distinguished by 'a concentration on the most dismal aspects of realist *mise en scène*, in order both to draw a kind of gallows humour from them and to lay the groundwork for a miraculous transformation of them'.[10] The image of Mark diving for his suppositories may be motivated in part by the mind-altering effects of the drugs. But Smith notes that it also reinforces an inclination in the film towards what he calls 'aesthetic redemption', which depicts poverty realistically, but in a way that draws a kind of vitality from adverse conditions, encompassing 'possibilities of escape as well as entrapment'.[11]

The kinetic-visual energy of the film, which places Boyle alongside other popular contemporary cinema stylists such as Quentin Tarantino, Baz Luhrmann and Jean Paul Jeunet, is matched by the innovative use of music. The *Trainspotting* soundtrack features an impressive array: from luminaries of the 1970s counterculture, such as Lou Reed and Iggy Pop, to a roll-call of some of the hippest bands associated with the Britpop and techno-dance scenes of the mid-1990s, such as Blur, Pulp, Elastica, Sleeper, Primal Scream, Underworld and Leftfield, augmented, as Smith points out, by 1980s tracks from bands like New Order and Heaven 17 and even Bizet's *Carmen*. In addition to providing an appropriate sonic augmentation to the visual pyrotechnics, this eclectic aural mix considerably broadens the appeal of the film by expanding the cultural frame of reference beyond Leith, Edinburgh, Scotland or even the UK. Smith identifies important transatlantic links via Iggy Pop and Lou Reed, the influence of American independent cinema and the pop art of Andy Warhol and Barnett Newman, as well as an abundance of other cultural references which he describes in terms of 'the call and response between the regional and "Hollywood International"' [12] – a relationship that equally applies to the Australian Luhrmann, the Frenchman Jeunet and even the American Tarantino, whose own borrowings from world cinema are central to his work. The sheer slickness of this discursive negotiation helps not only to explain the widespread popularity of Boyle's film, but also its transcendence as an aesthetic work above and beyond Welsh's more confrontational, difficult and locally specific original.

The transformation of *Trainspotting* into an entertainment with considerable commercial potential is equally clear from a business perspective. Having reaped the benefits as the major financier of *Shallow Grave*, Channel 4 demonstrated its total confidence in both the creative team and the project by providing the entire £1.7 million budget for *Trainspotting*. Such faith in the film's potential appeal was shared by the distributor Polygram, which invested more than £850,000 in the UK marketing campaign. The key elements of this campaign included a teaser trailer directed by Boyle shown in cinemas and featured on the video release of *Shallow Grave* as well as an iconic poster campaign featuring images of the central characters, shot by Lorenzo Agius, whose own successful career as a celebrity portrait photographer was thus launched. Publicity for the film was further generated by the release of the soundtrack on the EMI label and the publication of the screenplay by Faber and Faber. *Trainspotting* received its world première at the Glasgow Odeon on 15 February 1996 before going on national release on 23 February, initially with thirteen prints in London and twenty-three in Scotland and selected sites in Oxford, Cambridge and Dublin showing at a total of fifty-seven screens. Two weeks on, the release was widened to 175 prints on 245 screens. The film's popularity was not only extensive, it also proved enduring: *Trainspotting* was to remain in cinemas for thirty-eight weeks, earning a massive £12,344,534 in the process (the ninth highest-grossing film at the UK box office that year).

Despite being turned down for the official competition, *Trainspotting* had a special midnight screening at the prestigious Cannes Film Festival, followed by a glitzy party featuring music from Leftfield, where cast, crew and, of course, Welsh mingled with celebrities such as Mick Jagger, Eric Clapton, Noel Gallagher and Damon Albarn. The Cannes showcase was subsequently used as a platform to launch the film internationally. In France it opened on 221 screens nationally, including forty-four in Paris and its suburbs. To make *Trainspotting* more accessible to American audiences, forty lines of dialogue were cut and redubbed from the first twenty minutes, and the US distributor Miramax followed Polygram's strategy by emphasising the hip aspects of the film rather than the problematic subject matter in their marketing campaign. Once again the simultaneous release of the soundtrack was to be a crucial aspect of the marketing and when presidential candidate Bob Dole criticised the film as dangerous, Capitol Records publicised the soundtrack with a 'mock' campaign poster featuring Dole wearing an 'Iggy Pop for President' lapel badge.[13]

Beyond its success in the cinema, *Trainspotting* has also enjoyed a high profile and extended commercial life on the small screen. Initially released on VHS in the UK in the summer of 1996, it became the sixth most popular rental title that year and the sixth highest-selling retail title. In September 1997 a new edition of the video featuring scenes deleted from the final version was released, followed a month later by a second soundtrack (both were packaged in green to distinguish them from the iconic orange of the original video and soundtrack). Within a year the video had sold more than 720,000 copies, breaking one million by the end of 1997. The release of a DVD version in October 1999 kept sales ticking over. The second major boost came with the appearance of the definitive edition DVD in June 2003, a double-disk set with deleted scenes, interviews and a host of additional extras timed to mark the tenth anniversary of the publication of the novel. Since then, almost 600,000 additional units have been sold, taking the combined total number of VHS/DVDs sold in the UK to an astonishing 1.9 million. At the time of writing new HD and Bluray versions have also recently appeared on the market, and so it may not be long before the two million mark is reached. *Trainspotting* has also been screened four times by Channel 4 on their UK terrestrial service – premièring on 26 November 1997 when it was watched by 4.6 million viewers, followed by further screenings in 1999, 2001 and 2004 – and multiple times also on the Film Four cable/satellite channel. The operation of this long tail of distribution and exhibition has ensured *Trainspotting*'s enduring popularity, as demonstrated by its consistently strong showing in various polls of best and favourite films from fourth Best British Film of all time in a 2004 poll for the populist magazine *Total Film* to tenth position in the 1999 British Film Institute poll of top British films.

The popularity of *Trainspotting* has much to do with its accessibility as both product and aesthetic object. Morace describes the film as 'one of the most free floating signifiers of the past decade'.[14] This openness has allowed it to be appropriated or consumed by a wide variety of audiences. While the contemporary transnational elements central to the film's production and consumption have been acknowledged, the retention of a specifically Scottish dimension remains central. Beyond the obvious elements including the Edinburgh setting and the accents, the film engages with complex questions of culture, identity and representation with a characteristic intelligence and lightness of touch. The construction of place is one such context, and John Hill has examined the ways in which *Trainspotting* plays with the inherited imagery of both England and Scotland in a creative and insightful way. The montage marking Renton's move to London features a melange of touristic clichés – famous landmarks, red buses, pearly kings and queens – which for Hill constitutes 'an ironic inversion of the touristic imagery which commonly accompanies the arrival of an English character in Scotland'.[15] Hill also assesses Renton's famous anti-nationalist monologue, which in the novel is directed against 'cunts like Begbie' and takes place in the pub, but in the film is relocated to 'the great outdoors', allowing a wryly humorous deconstruction of the long-established romanticisation of the Scottish landscape so central to contemporaneous Hollywood productions like *Rob Roy* (1995) and *Braveheart* (1995). For Hill, 'while *Trainspotting* may speak with a voice that is decidedly Scottish, it does so in a way that avoids simple pieties concerning "Scottish" or "British" identity'.[16]

Another example of the film's cultural knowingness is provided by the amusing inclusion of Archie Gemmill's celebrated 1978 World Cup goal against Holland in its compounded three-couple sex scene. Gemmill's goal marked the only bright spot in a campaign that otherwise proved to be a disaster for 'Ally's Army', the Scottish football team that had gone to Argentina with vastly inflated expectations. The combination of 'disappointment, betrayal and confusion', regarded by Hodge as 'an ideal emotional cocktail for Mark Renton',[17] places it alongside the 'stolen' referendum for a Scottish Assembly in 1979 as a key moment of symbolic national humiliation and consequently as further confirmation of Renton's gloomy assessment of the Scottish condition. But the irony here, of course, is that these elements are presented within a film and at a moment in history when Scottishness had come to assume a rather different sense of cultural and political worth, particularly within a wider British and international context. For by the mid-1990s the goal of political devolution was seriously back on the agenda, this time reinforced by a quantum leap in cultural self-confidence and supported by a revitalised and ideologically transformed Labour Party dominated by Scots.

Critics who locate *Trainspotting* within a broader British context make much of the advent of 'Cool Britannia', placing the film alongside the impact of Britpop and also the BritArt movement, led by the likes of Damien Hirst and Tracy Emin. This marketing exercise chimed with the aspirations of Blair's New Labour, which came to power in May 1997, to re-energise and rebrand Britain after eighteen years of Tory rule. Blairism set out its stall by distancing itself from 'Old Labour', most notably through an enthusiastic embrace of the market, consumption and entrepreneurialism as the primary drivers of the new society, principles that were also to influence cultural policy with its advocacy of the economic value of the creative industries. If the 'new' Britain aspired to be bold, confident and consumer-friendly while retaining a certain nonconformist edge, then *Trainspotting* can be regarded as a Blairite film *avant la lettre* in both form and content. The film captures the exuberance and irreverence of Welsh's novel by maximising audience pleasure and minimising dissonance and political critique. While Boyle's aesthetic may be innovative and dynamic, the film's 'subversive hip edge'[18] is more rhetorical than real, representing a mere flirtation with transgression which in the end does nothing to threaten the status quo of a youth-oriented, self-regarding and hedonistic consumer society. Indeed, on an ideological level the film can be regarded as endorsing the very values of neoliberal consumerism it initially seems to reject, and which are unquestionably contested by Welsh's novel.

Bert Cardullo notes that the relationship between Renton's opening and closing voiceovers presents the key to interpreting the film, as well as its departure from the novel.[19] The famous 'choose life' mantra that opens the film conveys Renton's assessment of mainstream culture:

> Choose life. Choose a job. Choose a family. Choose a fucking big television. Choose washing machines, cars, compact disk players and electrical tin openers. Choose good health, low cholesterol and dental insurance. Choose fixed interest mortgage repayments. Choose a starter home. Choose your friends. Choose leisurewear and matching luggage. Choose a three piece suite in a range of fucking fabrics. Choose DIY and wonder how you are on a fucking Sunday morning. Choose sitting on that couch watching mind numbing, spirit crushing game shows, stuffing fucking junk food into your mouth. Choose rotting away at the end of it all, pishing your last in a miserable home, nothing more than an embarrassment to the fucked up selfish brats you've spawned to replace yourself. Choose your future. Choose life . . . But why would I want to do a thing like that? I chose not to choose life. I chose something else. And the reasons? There are no reasons. Who needs reasons when you've got heroin?

Notably, this spirited rejection is recanted, just as emphatically, in the final scene in which, having absconded with the drug-deal money, Renton crosses Westminster Bridge, smiling to himself, bathed in the optimism of the morning light. This time he proclaims his decision to 'choose life' by 'cleaning up and moving on' and that he now 'wants to be just like you' after all. While maintaining a certain tongue-in-cheek – postmodern culture's cynical get-out gesture – it is difficult to read this symbolic embrace of mainstream values as anything other than a capitulation to the values of consumerism. The film provides no other appropriate social alternative. This interpretation is lent even greater force by *Trainspotting*'s own status within the logic of commodity capitalism, which continually spawns a network of interrelated commodities: the film begets the video/DVD, which begets the special edition video with deleted scenes and the definitive DVD augmented by the soundtrack, the second soundtrack, the published screenplay, the t-shirt, the poster, and so on, with consumers enticed into a series of multiple transactions.

Some of the more astute commentators on both the novel and film have drawn similar conclusions. Alan Sinfield, for example, bemoans the way in which the film effectively 'diminishes or removes most of the challenging aspects of the book'. While his enthusiasm for Welsh's original was fired by 'its repudiation of mainstream culture in the interest of a national, class and generational specificity',[20] capitalist society's ability to co-opt and neutralise is evinced by the film, which could have been set anywhere and in which the drug theme eclipses Welsh's broader interest in the lives of the marginalised and the excluded. Sinfield also identifies the way in which the film suppresses the contrast between Renton and Sick Boy, crediting the former with the latter's Thatcherite selfishness and making this, by way of the ending, the 'natural' way to live. This negative reading is shared by Aaron Kelly, who suggests that:

> Given that the decade in which the novel and the film are set witnessed a full-scale assault upon working-class resistance to the policies of the free market and commodity culture, then such a Thatcherite project surely finds affinity with a film that arrogates the living culture of the working class and then seeks to remarket it back to them as a commodity.[21]

Kelly also bemoans the positioning of the film within the above-noted wider currents of contemporary British culture as exacerbating not only the erasure of class, but also the novel's recognition of inequality and disadvantage, by reframing social difference as a depoliticised question of diversity, in this case the 'Cool Caledonia' element of the wider UK brand. Consequently, *Trainspotting* becomes the ideal Blairite product, conspicuously displaying its 'coolness' via a hip edginess masquerading as transgression, but ultimately affirming the self-conscious, self-regarding and starkly depoliticised state of contemporary British society.

To conclude, one may want to investigate the implications of all of this for the by now considerably enhanced reputation of Irvine Welsh. For all his public enthusiasm for the film it is perhaps instructive that when Welsh came to adapt three of the short stories from *The Acid House* (1995) for a portmanteau feature released in 1999, he chose an approach very different from Boyle's in *Trainspotting*. Welsh clearly felt the necessity to fashion a much harder and unforgiving portrait of the lives of the characters:

> I think after *Trainspotting*, which has become a bit of a reference point for just about every British film, that it's very difficult to do something a bit different, a bit less airbrushed, a bit less for the mass market. We wanted the actors to be rougher and to speak roughly. It's very difficult after that, to just do our own wee daft film.[22]

As detailed in Clandfield and Lloyd's contribution to the present volume, *The Acid House* is located firmly in real Edinburgh locations, particularly some of the grim housing schemes on the periphery of the city, a strategy that adds a certain gritty verisimilitude. Director Paul McGuigan adopts an even more excessive visual style than did Boyle, incorporating a dizzy array of hand-held camera, slow motion, distorting lenses, jump-cuts, stop-motion and extreme point-of-view shots. The effect is not only hallucinogenic, its frenzied excess leaves the spectator decidedly queasy – an effect reinforced by the misanthropy of Welsh's script, which renders the characters either pathetic losers or contemptible, self-centred exploiters. In their attempt to reject the crowd-pleasing compromises of Boyle's reworking of *Trainspotting*, Welsh and McGuigan end up responding with a dead-end cynicism combining shock, contempt and self-parody, arguably even further removed from the moral and social complexities that made Welsh's reputation in the first place. Even more regrettable, similar flaws were to be increasingly discernible in Welsh's fiction, perhaps most notably in *Ecstasy* and *Filth*. The contradictions between being simultaneously a genuinely transgressive writer in the tradition of Alexander Trocchi and James Kelman and 'the poet laureate of the Chemical Generation' – that is, a tabloid celebrity figure created in part by the impact of Boyle's film – had come to place too great a strain on Welsh's creative abilities. Or perhaps, at this high-profile moment in his career, Welsh had simply (if ironically) run out of ideas.

CHAPTER FIVE

Welsh and Gender

Carole Jones

Irvine Welsh is infamous for his representation of men and masculinity, most notoriously his 'hard men', such as *Trainspotting*'s Begbie and Roy Strang in *Marabou Stork Nightmares*. At times his work seems indeed best described as 'ladlit of a misogynistic kind for the *Loaded* crowd'.[1] Beyond the widely felt shock and awe of his engagement with such toxic masculinities, however, his work most effectively highlights and problematises our own contemporary anxieties regarding unstable gender roles in transition. Many critics would agree with Stefan Herbrechter who states that Welsh writes 'above all, about the dissolution of patriarchy and the de(con)struction of masculinity'.[2] There is also recognition that Welsh practises an 'unprogrammatic inclusion of a broad range of gender identities as a natural part of his fictional world'.[3] Yet, as this chapter will show, Welsh's portrayal of gender relations calls into question such potentially optimistic readings. In Welsh's narratives men and women usually only come together for sex, and the main focus is on depicting the dissonant pleasures of a rarely breachable gulf between them, while also often intimating the violent potential of male sexuality, shockingly realised in the lengthy depiction of a gang rape in *Marabou Stork Nightmares*. Welsh's obsession with the visceral existence of male and female bodies has encouraged commentators to employ such labels as 'the aesthetics of repulsion'[4] to describe his work. Within such a putatively dystopian gender context, this chapter will examine the trajectory of gender representation in Welsh's work, paying special attention to the increasing visibility and presence of women, which has culminated most recently in the co-authored television drama *Wedding Belles* (2007), Welsh's first major narrative to feature exclusively female protagonists.

This turn to femininity has prompted Morace to comment that in his later work Welsh seems 'to be trying to make amends and to prove that he can "do" women'.[5] But more significantly perhaps, the representation of women prompts the question whether these narratives, as is Welsh's professed desire,[6] succeed in exposing the sexist workings of a patriarchal society at the end of its legitimacy. Or do they, as some critics argue in relation to the earlier novels, reproduce what they are intended to critique, namely oppressive representations of women?[7] Put differently, do the later fictions promote a 'repositioning of traditional gender roles',[8] or are Welsh's women merely 'dragged up' men, 'XX-chromosome versions of the lads'?[9] The gender inversion of the latter image suggests that the Bakhtinian concept of the carnivalesque might be a useful tool for rethinking Welsh's engagement with gender. The carnivalesque is a prominent feature of Mikhail Bakhtin's dialogism – his theories regarding the relational nature of language and the novel form, which have been applied to much Scottish writing, and to Welsh's fiction in particular. Roderick Watson, for example, has commented that 'the Bakhtinian concepts of dialogical processes, Rabelaisian excess and heteroglossia have become very valuable models for defining and discussing the Scottish literary and cultural tradition'.[10] With regard to Welsh, these concepts are often employed in reference to his language, his use of the vernacular in particular, as 'the interplay of a multiplicity of voices [. . .] fully embodies Bakhtin's concept of *heteroglossia* [and] revels in [. . .] over-turnings of received meanings'.[11] However, it is primarily the piquant reversals of the 'scary carnival'[12] of Welsh's writing that so exuberantly evoke a Bakhtinian reading of his treatment of gender.

Carnival, Bakhtin's 'most popular and clichéd concept',[13] refers to a range of tendencies in literary representation which 'involve the temporary cessation, overturning or inversion of the world of monological authority and orthodoxy and the erupting of the liberating forces of lawless proliferation and renewal'.[14] This concept has its origins in medieval carnival, which 'temporarily suspended and upturned the orthodox hierarchy and allowed, quite literally, the people their "voices"'.[15] It is a parodic and relativising strategy, which subverts repressive authority and 'constructs a cynical linguistic distance between the two voices or perspectives [the parody and its source], causing them to interrogate each other's "truth", thereby refuting either's claim to unitary, uncontestable "Truth"'.[16] A major feature for Bakhtin is the 'grotesque realism' of the carnivalesque with, as Mary Russo points out, particular emphasis on the 'grotesque body':

> The open, protruding, extended, secreting body, the body of becoming, process, and change. The grotesque body is opposed to the classical body, which is monumental, static, closed, and sleek, corresponding to the aspirations of bourgeois individualism; the grotesque body is connected to the rest of the world.[17]

Welsh's writing is, of course, replete with images of such excess, not least in *Trainspotting*, which marked the beginning of his career. The 'First Day of the Edinburgh Festival' section with its notorious opium suppository episode – made more infamous, if less filthy, by Danny Boyle's film version

– is an obvious example, as Renton's rebellious, heroin-starved body seeks sudden and urgent relief: 'Ah empty my guts, feeling as if everything; bowel, stomach, intestines, spleen, liver, kidneys, heart, lungs and fucking brains are aw falling through ma arsehole intae the bowl' (*T*, 25). Traditionally associated with women, leaky bodies also feature prominently in a later episode, 'Eating Out', in which the waitress Kelly has her revenge on some obnoxious English 'white-settler type' (*T*, 301) customers by lacing their food with her own bodily excretions, including menstrual blood and urine.

The carnivalesque transgression of order may at first glance appear promising for representations of the feminine; the overturning of established hierarchies suggests an undermining of power relations which can be shown to benefit women in the struggle to resist their inferior social positioning. However, as Kate Webb points out, the appropriation of carnival for feminist purposes is not as straightforward a strategy as some would wish. 'Women and carnival', she writes, 'might, ultimately, be inimical because female biology and the fact of motherhood make women an essentially connecting force, while carnival is essentially the celebration of transgression and breakdown.' [18] Webb, intentionally or not, fixes women in a manner that Welsh resists, marginalising and often expelling from his texts mothers and the nurturing, connective power of mothering. Yet in Welsh the resistance to order manifests itself more often than not in a 'truly, frighteningly, carnivalesque' world of 'violence, homophobia, the most profound sexism, male rage and rape'.[19] According to Webb:

> When women become the object of this disorder – as they are in war, or in rape, or in 'kiddiporn' – then the idea of carnival becomes much more problematic for them, and their relation to it becomes an inevitably ambivalent one [. . .] carnival is as likely to defeat women as it is to bring down order.[20]

Does the carnival aspect of Welsh's writing therefore illustrate Webb's thesis that 'patriarchy relies upon such masculine transgression of order as a reminder and a symbol of the very force which shores it up'?[21] And does it ultimately serve to highlight what Jackson and Maley identify as 'a lacuna in Welsh's work, the question of female agency'?[22]

Certainly, Welsh's women are 'more strictly delimited by the directives of plot and their relationships with men than by their own character and motivation'.[23] In effect, their identities have a greater fixity in comparison with those of the men who often appear as more adaptable, versatile performers of their identities, as more effective ventriloquisers of multiple discourses and language registers. 'Growing up in Public', for instance, the first scene in *Trainspotting* to be viewed from a female standpoint, is rendered in a third-person Scottish Standard English, unlike most of the male-focused scenes, which are in the first person and in the vernacular. Renton in particular displays his 'skill in negotiating a subversive path through the implications of power in language'[24] as he frequently code-switches between the Leith vernacular and Standard English, most impressively in court when, to avoid a custodial sentence for shoplifting, he avers that he intended to read the stolen books and not to sell them, and gives an eloquent account of Kierkegaard's existential philosophy. Similar performance skills are demonstrated in the 'Equal Opportunities' section of *Filth* where Detective Sergeant Bruce Robertson intersperses the sexist, racist, expletive-laden language of his own thoughts with a perfect command of the discourse of political correctness in order to undermine the running of an anti-racism course he has been forced to attend. Women – albeit traditionally associated with a lack of authenticity and presence, with mimicry and performance – are denied this postmodern multiplicity. In *Trainspotting*, for instance, 'whilst the names of the female characters remain fixed [. . .] the male figures are subject to continually shifting designations', enabled by their colourful portfolio of nicknames.[25]

Though for Kelly this apparent multiplicity emphasises a sense of masculinity in crisis, the men's slippery identities may also be interpreted as appropriating characteristics traditionally associated with femininity: masquerade, performativity and a general lack of fixity. In Welsh's earlier fiction, where female characters are relatively sparse and marginalised, this appropriation can, in Abigail Soloman-Godeau's words, amount to a 'colonization of femininity [. . .] so that what has been rendered peripheral and marginal in the social and cultural realm, or actively devalued, is effectively incorporated within the compass of masculinity'.[26] This can result in the exclusion of women from representation and a more complicated designation of the feminine. For example, an expulsion of the feminine principle is most dramatically executed in *Marabou Stork Nightmares*, in which the rape victim, Kirsty, takes her personal revenge on her attackers, murdering them one by one. When at the end of the novel she tells Roy, the principal perpetrator of the crime, before killing him, that 'you've made me just like you' (*MSN*, 259), she is effectively masculinised, leaving him at the close of the narrative as the main, perhaps the only, victim. The 'lacuna' of female agency, then, becomes 'an eradication of sexual difference', a disappearance of the feminine.[27]

However, in line with Soloman-Godeau's ideas, it is possible also to detect an attempt at reconnection with the feminine in a significant number of Welsh's narratives. This reconnection often takes the form of an unhappy queering of the male body. A number of homosexuals, transsexuals, drag queens and transvestites populate the work, lacing the texts with a notion of feminised masculinity. In 'A Smart Cunt' in *The Acid House*, for instance, Welsh rightly discerns that there is a feminine aspect to the hysterical volatility of the 'hard man':

> One thing about hard cunts that I've never understood: why do they all have to be such big sensitive blouses? The Scottish Hardman ladders his tights so he rips open the face of a passer-by. The Scottish Hardman chips a nail, so he head-butts some poor fucker. Some other guy is wearing the same patterned dress as the Scottish Hardman, and gets a glass in his face for his troubles. (*AH*, 276)

The marginalisation of women itself promotes a proliferation of other(ed) femininities, part of Morace's 'broad range of gender identities', as masculinity invariably seeks to define itself in relation. These include 'the gorgeous young queen' Renton picks up, who 'looked like this lassie ah used tae fancy ages ago' (*T*, 233–4); Denise, the drag queen in 'A Smart Cunt', who 'embarrasses most homosexuals' and 'loves to be hated' (*AH*, 243) and Chrissie, the 'scarred' male-to-female transsexual in 'Eurotrash' (*AH*, 20); as well as Bernard, Roy's 'broken-spirited pansy half-brother' (*MSN*, 30), in *Marabou Stork Nightmares*.

The most extreme example, however, manifests in *Filth* where cross-dressing and female impersonation signal the limits of the male protagonist's psychotic dissociation. The novel enacts a vigorous exposure and humiliation of the sexist male, embodied in the corrupt policeman, Bruce Robertson. His relentless misanthropy expresses a desire to cause pain, which in itself is an attempt to offset his own shame instilled in him through childhood abuse and the circumstances of his birth as the illegitimate child of an infamous rapist. In *Filth* Welsh roguishly compounds the question of the origin of evil, whether it is produced through nature or nurture, as the novel frenetically spins out its carnivalesque narrative into disorder and misrule overturning the moral weightiness of any authority. The law enforcer is a hard-drinking, drug-taking, corrupt sociopath, which is, admittedly, not in itself an original strategy. The novel gets its special satirical rudeness and clout from assigning the voice of reason to the tapeworm in Bruce's gut: 'I know for sure that the complexity of my soul doesn't even start to approximate the basic organism that is my body,' says the worm, and, in a parody of Cartesian subjectivity, it continues: 'So what can I call myself then? Well, all I can call myself is the Self' (*F*, 70).

The celebratory chaos of the carnivalesque is certainly strained here, and indeed the malicious sexism and racism voiced in the novel appear as 'a sign of the resentment that is the inverse of carnival's joyous relativity [. . .] that results when carnival turns bitter'.[28] But 'joyous' does not quite capture the reconnection with the feminine attempted in *Filth* through Bruce's 'incorporation' of his wife, Carole. Rather, it is a sign of masculinity's complete disintegration – a psychic fragmenting of selfhood that parallels the breakdown of his body – which ultimately results in suicide. The sections of the novel which initially appear to be narrated by Bruce's estranged wife – titled

'Carole', 'Carole Again', etc. – gradually transpire to be projections of Bruce's own consciousness: 'We're remembering how this all started: that when Carole first left with the bairn we used to set the table for two and then we started wearing her clathes and it was like she was still with us but no really' (*F*, 343). Bruce's cross-dressing is a symptom of the sexist, all-male dystopia he inhabits where women are not subjects in their own right, but 'objects upon which male subjects project their fears and anxieties'.[29] Consequently, Bruce's apparent attempt at reconnection with the feminine is little more than the realisation of a 'sick' male fantasy which serves only to exacerbate the marginalisation of women in Welsh's fictional worlds.

Filth constitutes a turning point in Welsh's *oeuvre*, the point on the trajectory after which queered male characters largely disappear and women begin to become more prominent and significant. Such a development can perhaps be thought of as an endeavour, though a slowly realised one, to reverse the colonisation of femininity and give women a voice and an opportunity to be heard among Welsh's cacophonous heteroglossia, a form of reparation but also proof that he 'can "do" women'. Welsh's next novel, *Glue*, an expansive narrative about male friendship and bonding over the period of a generation, presents the novelty of a group of women characters, introduced late in Part IV, 'who have their own stories to tell and whose lives are, at least initially, perfectly unrelated to that of the men'.[30] Similarly, in *Porno*, a sequel to *Trainspotting*, which takes as its subject the 'do-it-yourself' dimension of the pornography industry, one of the four narrators, Nikki Fuller-Smith, is a young, middle-class English student at Edinburgh University who seeks fame in becoming a porn star. It is a cogent irony that female characters emerge as more vocal and visible at the point where, as critics have observed, Welsh's fiction starts to become more conventional. Thus, in *Glue*, he 'jettisons the radical typographical and technical experimentation' to write a 'proper book',[31] in which 'much of the writing seems canned or a combination of the inept and the inapt [. . .] stale language for equally stale ideas',[32] while *Porno* is a 'flaccid read'.[33] It seems quite as if the radically decentring formal initiatives of the earlier narratives have been tamed by Welsh's incorporation of the feminine.

However, the increased female visibility is also characteristically Welshian in many ways. Welsh's women are often irreverent and exuberant; they indulge in drink, drugs and sex with enthusiasm just like the men, and they speak the vernacular with equally colourful fervour. They are overturning the dominant scripts of femininity; like the women Maria Pini describes in her account of rave culture, these female characters explore 'a right to adventure' and insist on indulging in the same 'illegal adventures which have traditionally been primarily the preserve of men'.[34] Welsh promotes this radical egalitarianism throughout his fiction, but perhaps in a particularly parodic manner in an early short story, 'Where the Debris Meets the Sea' in *The Acid House*, in which four iconic female celebrities – Madonna, Kylie Minogue, Victoria Principal and Kim Basinger – languish in a luxurious Californian mansion entertaining themselves by fantasising over magazines and videos of sexy young Leith men. To complete the comic reversal, they speak in the Leith vernacular: '"We'll nivir go tae fuckin Leith!" Kim said, in a tone of scornful dismissal. "Yous ur fuckin dreamin"'(*AH*, 92). Such representations prompt the accusation that Welsh's women are simply loutish and laddish, who, by turning the tables on men, are merely mimicking them and not undermining the oppressive, objectifying system of interpersonal relations that frames male behaviour. Ultimately, they are 'dragged-up' men. Berthold Schoene disagrees with the generalised sweep of this critique, seeing Lisa and Charlene in *Glue*, for instance, 'as emancipated females, who categorically reject woman's inferior place':

> What seems more significant is that Welsh portrays his women characters as capable of forming strong homosocial bonds, without the mediation of men, and that their practices of resistance and self-assertion are presented to us as a true alternative to the men's [. . .] What ensues is a dramatic deconstruction of traditional gender polarity, and the tentative beginnings of a radical communal reassembling.[35]

Ending as the novel does on the death of the father of one of the four staunch male friends, signalling the passing of the traditional male values for which he stood, perhaps Schoene is justified in promoting such an optimistic reading.

Schoene's view can be put to a more stringent test with reference to a text that absolutely prioritises female experience. *Wedding Belles*, Welsh's television film for Channel 4, explores the friendship and bonding of four women protagonists in difficult circumstances. In this it follows the Welshian model of male bonding introduced in *Trainspotting* and *Glue*, and the dominant themes of drugs, violence, ribald humour, carnivalesque sexuality and grotesque corporeality do at first glance suggest that these women are simply female versions of Welsh's stock characters. This impression is strengthened by Welsh's assertion, published on his official website, that 'I liked the girls so much that I wanted to be one of them and so got dragged up'. (In the extras to the DVD edition of the film we see him in the process of accomplishing this, sitting in front of a dressing-room mirror being made up by a professional make-up artist, though we do not see the completed transformation.) Conscious of Welsh's penchant for irreverent anti-establishment male characterisation, our attention is thus drawn to the possibility that he may only be able to create characters from a masculinised point of view. It might also suggest that 'Welsh has lost his distinctive voice and, with it, the "bunch of voices shouting to be heard" that made his early fiction so urgent, unpretentious and compellingly local', and that the feminisation of his characters may be one way in which he is trying to refresh his 'jaded' literary corpus.[36] Obviously, the use of femininity as a kind of narrative injection to invigorate a supine masculine form can only exacerbate the colonisation and objectification of the feminine, thus undermining the subversive potential of literary carnival where women are concerned.

Certainly, *Wedding Belles* has enough of the carnivalesque about it to make us wary on this count. Interjected fantasy murder sequences, a 'saints and sinners' fancy-dress party, senior-citizen sexuality and an irreverent anti-political-correctness humour all contribute to a raucous upturning of established hierarchies. However, its sustained focus on female experience does foreground serious consideration of the particular material detail of female oppression: the sexual abuse of girl children and unwanted pregnancy, the effects of trauma, cosmetic surgery and its violent enactment of a fascistic conceptualisation of the female body all contribute to the specific oppressive timbre of the women's lives represented here. Indeed, the hairdresser Amanda's display of her labiaplasty (her 'designer vagina') to her cleaning woman, praising it as 'perfectly symmetrical', illustrates how cosmetic surgery engages with and promotes the image of the impossibly smooth, sleek, classical body. Of course, this scene is also a moment of carnivalesque unruliness as the public exposure of one's genitals upsets all standards of decorum and propriety. Welsh's allusion to Amanda's transfigured, mut(il)ated genitals evokes the countercultural forcefulness of the grotesque body, as we acknowledge at once the excess that is absent as well as the smoothness that is present.

The boundaries of femininity are pressurised in *Wedding Belles*. The opening of the narrative introduces a female revenge tale where the four women, in wedding dresses and a transit van, kidnap and execute four men who have betrayed them. Though this sequence turns out to be a fantasy – a crack-withdrawal dream of Rhona's – the relationships alluded to here are intimately connected to the women's lives. The four women are old mates, abrasively affectionate and aggressively supportive of each other. Amanda is a successful business woman, running her own beauty salon, and the narrative is framed by the preparations for her wedding to Joshua, an ostensibly clean-living pilot who in reality has been stealing money from her to fund his internet gambling addiction. Shaz is a care worker, who is having an affair with a priest, while Rhona is a former model, whose suicidal descent into drug addiction has been triggered by the death of her fiancé in a car crash caused by a joyrider. Kelly, the most tragic of the four, was abused by her father and gave birth to a son who has been brought up as her brother. These stories of loss and yearning give rise to the revenge fantasy in which the women's ritual execution of their oppressors signifies their rebellion against lives circumscribed by exploitation and betrayal.

There is, then, from the opening of the film, a carnivalised reversal of gender expectations. The women are costumed in wedding dresses, the stereotypical uniform of traditionally acceptable femininity, while behaving like a criminal gang, flaunting violent power over others and brandishing with expert style the masculine accessories of the gun and the transit van. However, this fantasy of female dominance is followed immediately by a nightmarish evocation, dreamt by Amanda, of her wedding reception, in which Joshua is a perverse master of ceremonies, lewdly exhibiting and manipulating her and inviting the serial killers Fred and Rosemary West on their honeymoon. This spontaneous combustion of the fantasy of female dominance constitutes a warning against celebrating too quickly the appropriation of male power by women. As such we can interpret it as a further problematisation of the close of *Marabou Stork Nightmares* with its recentring of the male as victim, and as a thought experiment which deliberately questions the possibilities of female power, whether masculinised or otherwise, in a misogynist culture. Significantly, the humiliation of Amanda in her nightmare is an equally tenable expression of the carnivalesque, demonstrating that so much of the effective overturning and undermining of social conventions and hierarchies revolves on improper behaviour within the context of which women are often not the subjects but the objects of disorder. As such they still present a danger, as well as being themselves at risk in the world. As carnivalesque misrule is by definition a temporary state, in many ways a licensed disorder, any empowerment of the marginalised, such as women, is a dangerous precedent not without effect when the status quo is restored. Yet even in its modes of disorder, there must be 'a reminder and a symbol', in Kate Webb's words, of patriarchy's power.[37]

Other questionable implications of hierarchical reversals are highlighted in *Wedding Belles*, particularly regarding Amanda's partners, her fiancé Joshua and her ex-fiancé Barney, an armed robber who has just been released from jail. Having rejected Barney because of his insincerity and criminal activity, Amanda is betrayed by Joshua's embezzlement of her business capital in a parodic overturning of the hero–villain coupling. Dressed in angelic wings for the 'saints and sinners' party, Joshua's aura of wholesome innocence is exposed as a performance, while Barney is recuperated into respectable society through his marriage to Amanda's 'nemesis' – a woman with a disability previously attacked by Amanda. Barney's rehabilitation from criminal to respectable citizen is initially enacted at his 'coming out' party – that is, his coming out of prison celebration – when, in a scene of soft-focused, sentimental sensuality, he dances solo, circled by admiring friends, to a love- and life-affirming soul soundtrack. This performance signals his reform from hard man to husband; it civilises him, disarming through choreographic synchronisation the threat of disorder he symbolises and, dancing being an activity traditionally associated with femininity, also signalling his access to a more feminine sphere. Witnessing Barney's wedding, the four female protagonists contemplate their own failure to find a place in mainstream society through the traditional female narrative closure of marriage. They are left to carry on as they were: Shaz with the priest, Rhona scoring drugs, and Amanda and Kelly chasing romance with new men. This lack of conclusion in their stories suggests their continued social marginalisation while simultaneously reinforcing their status as dangerous and transgressive.

At the end of *Wedding Belles*, then, the implication is that women as outsiders are really the only subversives left in the social scene, still willing and able to destabilise the dominant social hierarchies and relations. At the same time, the reincorporation of the criminal into society constitutes a re-establishment of the status quo and, in effect, a recentring of the disruptive marginalised male. His marriage to a woman with a disability signals the widening berth of the social mainstream, but also its maintenance in compliance with the norms and values of the patriarchal centre. This rush to embourgeoisement, suggested by Barney's running to the church, illustrates the ambivalence of Welsh's carnivalesque strategies and the stalling of their disruptive power. As with Renton's rush to individualism in the betrayal of his mates at the end of *Trainspotting* – 'Now, free from them all, for good, he could be what he wanted to be. He'd stand or fall alone' (*T*, 344) – Welsh's delinquent males are self-contradictory, at once anarchic and conventional, signalling the limitations of Welsh's carnivalesque subversion in an era in which 'the conflation of subcultural dissent and entrepreneurial capitalism holds no contradiction'.[38]

Yet viewed against the trajectory of his engagement with gender relations, as well as his more recent representation of seriously seditious women, might the revolutionary inconsistencies of Welsh's male characters be regarded as symptomatic of a masculine inability, except through colonisation, to connect with the feminine and its potential for invigorating and revitalising critical disruption? It appears significant, for instance, that in *Wedding Belles* the four protagonists are left marginalised as a continuing threat to order, but they are also given the moral upper hand in contrast to many of Welsh's men, as the worst of the women's violence remains confined to fantasies. Without doubt they are capable of aggression: in one scene an indifferent Amanda gives Shaz and Kelly permission to attack a man they believe to have stolen his mother's purse. Poignantly also, Kelly reveals that she was responsible for starting the fire which killed her father, but in which she herself also intended to die. This (sometimes passive) aggressive self-defence defines the women's capability for violence as controlled and even judicious, almost as if they were resigned to the imperative of occasionally deploying a male approach to conflict resolution, simply because misogynist society continues to be unable to dispense justice for women. Perhaps these aggressive acts could be identified, on Schoene's terms, as women's 'practices of resistance and self-assertion', even if they obviously do not constitute 'a true alternative to the men's'. Certainly, this (at times violent) female resistance to male exploitation and cruelty evokes Schoene's desire for 'a turbulent reshuffling' and 'communal reassembling' of gender roles and relations, a process of mobilisation and repositioning which is beginning to be imagined here.[39]

Such radical possibilities arguably spring from female resistance to the dominant images and scripts of hegemonic femininity, as shown in the raucous portrayal of the brides in *Wedding Belles*. Interestingly, Clair Wills writes of Klaus Theweleit's influential *Male Fantasies* (1987) that in presenting a 'different history of the creation of bourgeois identity [Theweleit] stresses the part played by a fantasy construction of womanhood in the evolution of a "civilised" ego', a construction that is distorted and arises from 'a historically repressed femaleness'.[40] Such constructions, as expressed in Bruce Robertson's mimicry of his wife Carole in *Filth*, are resolutely resisted by Amanda, Shaz, Rhona and Kelly, in both their fantasies and their waking lives. As agents of anti-bourgeois disaffection, they are Welsh's only potential subversives. Yet they also sound warning bells about the effectiveness of the carnivalesque for promoting social change, particularly where women are concerned. The film passes judgement on Welsh's use of carnival over the span of his *oeuvre*, impelling us to reread – from the point of view of the subversive feminine – his previous fictional attempts to contain, disarm and co-opt disruptive female power.

CHAPTER SIX

Welsh, Drugs and Subculture

Berthold Schoene

Readers and critics alike have been perplexed by the title of Welsh's debut novel, which refers to the solitary and rather pointless hobby of standing about on railway platforms to record the engine numbers of incoming and departing trains. Bert Cardullo has suggested that 'this activity is intended to be a metaphor for shooting heroin and the obsessional, senseless nature of the addict's life',[1] which would find support in Patricia Horton's explanation that the term 'trainspotting' is used 'to describe the process of finding a vein when injecting [heroin]'.[2] Yet it remains difficult to see what exactly trainspotters and Welsh's drug-users might have in common, the former being reticent, heavily anoraked, apparitional figures while the latter are alive-and-kicking hedonists flaunting an aggressively 'in-yer-face' attitude and lifestyle. The only context in which trainspotting finds mention in the novel itself is a scene set at Leith Central Station, closed in 1952 and 'now a barren, desolate hangar' (*T*, 308),[3] where Renton and Begbie are accosted by a homeless drunk who turns out to be Begbie's estranged father. The encounter is resonant of the derelict state of the Scottish working class which, like Begbie's father, has come down in the world and whose demise represents a key factor in the younger generation's despondency and lack of direction. There is no escape from their dilemma either since the last train that might be spotted left the station a long time ago. Their only means of transport into another, seemingly better world is drug consumption.

Danny Boyle's film version provides another interesting rendition of the trainspotting motif. When after an overdose Renton's parents force their son to withdraw, we find the walls of his room to be covered in images of trains and steam engines. Reinforced by the monotonous beat of the accompanying soundtrack, viewers are given the impression that locked into a hurtling railway carriage Renton is forcibly transported back to reality and made to confront his part in Tommy's contraction of HIV, Spud's jail sentence and, most intolerably, the cot death of baby Dawn. The experience of drug withdrawal becomes indistinguishable from the daily horror of life as an addict, suggesting that tripping and withdrawing prove in the end equally agonising.

As Cardullo puts it, in the eyes of Scotland's underprivileged, ghettoised youth, 'life without drugs is just as absurd, just as pointless in the end, as life *on* drugs [. . .] each is its own kind of inane trainspotting, and the sole issue becomes how much you can, or want to, take of either'.[4] However, as Welsh is hardly known for his desire to moralise, it seems far more likely that the true ingenuity of the title is nothing at all to do with its allegorical potential but instead with its complete detachment from the novel's thematic concerns. Although the title does allude to the randomness of human life and the brittle artifice of all meaning-making systems, it is also clear that any other, more immediately pertinent title would have jeopardised Welsh's project of open-ended, strictly anti-authorial and non-judgemental narration.

Even if the title of Welsh's novel is not intended as a commentary on postmodern life or the human condition, it remains tempting to read *Trainspotting* as a representation of the Scottish national experience before devolution. No matter how fervently the novel disavows its postcoloniality, it is of course deeply enmeshed in Scottish cultural politics and thus inevitably reflects on Scotland's subnational status within the United Kingdom. On the one hand, Welsh employs Renton to articulate his own passionate resistance to the allure of the postcolonial, underdog mentality and the nationalist complacency that tends to accompany it: 'It's nae good blamin it oan the English fir colonising us [. . .] Ah don't hate the English [. . .] Ah hate the Scots' (*T*, 78). Yet, on the other hand, Welsh encourages us to regard his characters' choice of drugs over drudgery as a nationalistically inspired strategy of 'psychic defence' (*T*, 71). The headings of the novel's seven sections could easily be construed as references to Scotland's fraught devolutionary struggle. The first four – 'Kicking', 'Relapsing', 'Kicking Again', 'Blowing It' – would articulate the subnational effort at political self-assertion, and how the subnation's resistance has repeatedly been compromised by moments of weakness, voluntary subjection and collusion. The nation advertises its desire for freedom and self-rule, but then not only allows itself to be shackled and disenfranchised, but also actively courts its annihilation. The final three headings – 'Exile', 'Home', 'Exit' – encapsulate the dislocation of the subnational mind, its state of being torn between two cultures, and the temptation to embrace departure or 'opting out' as an easy solution. As Horton explains, within the context of such a strictly postcolonial reading of *Trainspotting*, heroin addiction *per se* would become a metaphor signifying 'a disease of the body politic and of the civic body that is Edinburgh', as well as the political system of Great Britain as a whole.[5]

A number of critics have examined the relationship between heroin and heroism, the psychological triangulation between drug addiction, self-assertion and resistance, as well as the reasons for drug use and its personal, cultural and political implications. Kevin McCarron concludes his comparison of slave narratives to what he calls 'junk narratives' by denying the latter any enduring political import. 'The protagonists of junk narratives', McCarron writes, 'have no interest in politics, or at least no interest in political change; it is rare to encounter any addiction narrative which puts the blame for addiction on society.' [6] In contrast, approaching the subject from a radically different perspective, Kevin Williamson persuades us to see heroin first and foremost as 'a social painkiller'. Establishing a clear link between drug addiction and socio-economic status, in *Drugs and the Party Line* Williamson illustrates how 'heroin is frequently used to blot out the pain of unemployment, lack of a future, stress, relationship breakups and boredom'.[7] The most intriguing contribution on the subject, however, is by Neil McMillan, whose essay 'Junked Exiles, Exiled Junk' steers clear of a discussion of drug addiction as a symptom of political disenchantment or social deprivation – not interested in addiction at all, but in the use of drugs as a lifestyle choice and gesture of intellectual defiance. As McMillan demonstrates, contrary to the perception that 'to take drugs [. . .] is to put a whole, healthy self in exile',[8] some drug users argue that their habit should be seen as a self-protective manoeuvre, a means of not giving in to society's manifold anti-individualist pressures. This is certainly Renton's position:

> Society invents a spurious convoluted logic tae absorb and change people whae's behaviour is outside its mainstream. Suppose that ah ken aw the pros and cons [. . .] but still want tae use smack? [. . .] They won't let ye dae it, because it's seen as a sign ay thir ain failure. The fact that ye jist simply choose tae reject whit they huv tae offer. Choose us. Choose life. Choose mortgage payments; choose washing machines; choose cars; choose sitting oan a couch watching mind-numbing and spirit-crushing game shows, stuffing fuckin junk food intae yir mooth. Choose rotting away, pishing and shiteing yersel in a home, a total fuckin embarrassment tae the selfish, fucked-up brats ye've produced. Choose life. (*T*, 187)

This myth of heroin as an instrument of asserting and maintaining one's autonomy as an individual is of course easily unravelled. While heroin may promise freedom, a refuge, even orgasmic self-fulfilment, it is ultimately a trap resulting in enslavement and abject misery. Far from exempting the drug-user from the obligation to work, for example, his or her work is simply of a different order. As Ruth Helyer points out, Renton 'does not work in the accepted sense; however he has a fulltime "job", ensuring that he is always able to obtain drugs'.[9] In this light, then, McMillan's parodist retort to Renton's anti-Establishment rant is as excoriating as it is to the point: 'Chooses paying drug dealers; chooses sitting oan a couch watching Jean-Claude Van Damme videos, injecting junk intae his veins. Chooses rotting away, pishing and shiteing himself in a bookie's toilets, a total fucking embarrassment tae the doting, smothering parents who produced him. Chooses smack.' [10] Yet self-delusion prevails in *Trainspotting* as, in Renton's view, 'trying tae manage a junk problem is the ultimate challenge' (*T*, 90); it is an ongoing testing of his masculine stamina, strength of will and endurance. As portrayed so memorably in Boyle's film, even plunging head first into a filthy toilet bowl to retrieve a couple of painkillers is transformed by the junkie's imagination into a picture-book treasure hunt to 'the parallel universe of a blue lagoon, beautifully clean and clear, shot though with sunlight'.[11]

Trainspotting privileges subcultural perspectives. Not only did the novel succeed in reactivating public debates on drug consumption, it proved equally successful in asserting Scottish subnational awareness and giving voice to the attitudes, desires and concerns of a late capitalist urban underclass. Yet not once does the novel give in to a facile celebration of subcultural defiance, as Welsh repeatedly disrupts his apparent glamorisation of supposedly recreational drug-taking with scenes of abject horror and grim self-degradation. Renton's bravado and Sick Boy's 'take-it-or-leave-it' mastery over the drug ring hollow against the deaths of Tommy and baby Dawn, or Spud's inability to extricate himself from the stranglehold of drug addiction in *Porno*. More importantly, there is no communal solidarity among Welsh's drug-users. From the start we are given to understand that there are 'nae friends in this game. Jist associates' (*T*, 6). The very concept of community is marred by the threat of HIV infection. As Robert Morace explains, 'IV drug use, after AIDS, makes "positive" (as in HIV-positive) negative and "sharing" (and other forms of intimacy) dangerous to the user's health'.[12] Heroin addiction seriously impedes the formation of politically viable subcultural identities as death and destruction make rather self-defeating strategies of 'dropping out'. Confirming Willy Maley's observation that 'Welsh's work is not just cult fiction, but diffi-cult fiction',[13] one cannot avoid the impression that Welsh's subcultures require to be understood primarily not in terms of subversion or countercultural political agitation, but purely in terms of subjection and subjugation. Despite their rebellious aspirations, Welsh's characters are first and foremost 'the lowest of the low' who fail to rise or lift themselves up unless chemically aroused.

Whatever subversive potential *Trainspotting* possessed has been compromised by its popular appeal, as the novel's – and in particular the film's – commercial success quickly led to its assimilation into mainstream culture, its subcultural menace reduced to fixing up middle-class audiences with a vicarious shudder and thrill. Karen Lury's description of Boyle's film as 'a commodity which critiques but also takes part in a culture increasingly defined by the character and power of the brand'[14] seems apt. As Lury demonstrates, both the characters of *Trainspotting* and the actors that played them swiftly became celebrities advertising the wasted look of the junkie as subcultural chic. The iconoclastic imagery of *Trainspotting* became iconic, adorning t-shirts, CD covers and teenage bedroom walls. Yet even Welsh's novel can hardly be said to pursue a strictly anti-capitalist agenda, no matter how determinedly its characters appear to cultivate an anti-Establishment stance. As Horton points out, 'the actions of the characters in the novel are not diametrically opposed to consumer culture [. . .] Rather the characters are constructed by and implicated in that culture and reproduce it'.[15] Similarly, Ian Haywood insists that in *Trainspotting* 'drug addiction has become the demonic and demonised reflection of a commodified, fetishised and irresponsible capitalist system'.[16] Rather than enabling the junkies to extricate themselves from an oppressive general culture, heroin aggravates their subjection by luring them ever deeper into a culture of vending and purchasing. Welsh's awareness of the drug subculture's capitalist implication is beyond doubt. As Renton expresses it in *Porno*, 'it's naïve to expect drugs tae be exempt from the laws of modern consumer capitalism. Especially when, as a product, they best help define it' (*P*, 408).

In Welsh's representation, economic success itself often looks like an addiction, as both Renton in *Trainspotting*, temporarily working as an estate agent in London, and Sick Boy in *Porno*, as the landlord of a pub and director of a burgeoning porn film company, are yuppies and junkies at the same time, each identity mirroring – that is, simultaneously bolstering and undermining – its counterpart. As *Trainspotting* illustrates, no subculture – no matter how far removed and discrete from the general culture it appears to be positioned, or chooses to position itself – ought to be recognised simplistically in terms of a free subversive cell. Any distinctions made between exploiters and exploited, perpetrators and victims, remain blurred, as all find themselves enmeshed in a Foucauldian grid of complicity and mutual implication. Renton's credo to opt out of bourgeois consumerism and thus save himself from corruption seems just as fallacious as the deeply flawed reasoning of Alex, Anthony Burgess's (1917–93) hero in *A Clockwork Orange* (1962), on lodging a plea for his right to be 'bad', declaring that 'what I do I do because I like to do'.[17] No self exists outside its cultural context; hence, what selves choose to identify as their strategies of resistance to systems of oppression is culturally predictable and, for this very reason, quite easy to keep in check. Both Renton's resort to drugs and Alex's resort to 'badness' are really only to be expected of angry young men of their background and intelligence.

An analysis of Welsh's treatment of subculture and drugs would be incomplete without exploring the correlation between drug use and gender. *Trainspotting* as well as Welsh's other works are focused chiefly on how young men handle drug consumption, whereas women feature less prominently, leading for the most part obscured, ancillary lives. In his interview with Jenifer Berman, Welsh approves of Boyle's cinematic rendition of the novel, commending in particular 'the film's bias towards action, rather than reflection. Because that's one of the reasons people go on taking drugs . . . 'cause they don't reflect, they just keep moving'.[18] The tendency to champion action over introspection is of course traditionally a male characteristic, which has been identified as harmful to men by both feminist writers and proponents of masculinity studies. It definitely proves harmful to Welsh's protagonists who, throughout the novel, insist on walking a very fine line between mastering the drug and succumbing to it, that is, between asserting their masculinity by proving themselves capable of managing heroin and yielding to the abjectly emasculating experience of drug-induced debilitation, disease and death. With respect to the men's emotional disposition, the impact of heroin is twofold: like alcohol, it appears initially to remove the homophobic burden of masculinity, its relentless competitiveness, resulting in men becoming more overtly affectionate with each other. But this heroin-induced intensification of homosocial intimacy always turns out to have been little more than a hallucination of the irremediably solitary and emotionally autistic male mind. Boyle's film excels at depicting this masturbatory, endothermic loneliness of the junkie: in *Trainspotting* the 'friends' always start by joining each other to take heroin *together*, yet once the drug hits their bloodstream, they drop out of the circle one by one, literally lapsing from a deliberate effort at community into the abyss of their isolated selves.

Whereas Welsh's attitude towards drugs is sceptical rather than celebratory, and he is aware of the devastating impact of heroin on people's lives, he is also against bourgeois hypocrisy, determined to shed light on the sinister, yet so often irresistibly alluring ambivalence of drugs. As Derek Paget comments, on reading Welsh 'one is never in any doubt that drugs do you serious harm, as well as offering a pleasure better than orgasm'.[19] His portrayal of drug culture's ecstatic highs and abject lows has earned him the title of 'poet laureate of the chemical generation'; however, to fully deserve the label 'junkie bible' *Trainspotting* appears too pessimistic. Only Renton escapes to the golden city of Amsterdam, whose unrivalled status at the end of the twentieth century as European capital of drug-related HIV infection must surely detract from its apparent glamour, rendering Renton's triumphant walk into the sunset at the close of *Trainspotting* a rather dubious exit. But if Welsh demonstrates that drug cultures, however radical or anarchic, can never wholly detach themselves from the general culture, he also shows how the general culture remains profoundly implicated in what it purports to have successfully excised. Britain, 'like most Western societies, is a drug society; in so far as most social interaction outside work [. . .] is defined by drugs'.[20] Welsh's portrayal of drug culture is so controversial because, whilst in no doubt *that* people take drugs, he is keen to explore and explain *why*. Instead of worrying greatly about people's drug consumption, or the legality or illegality of certain drugs, Welsh is concerned with what he calls people's 'negative' – that is, their desperately escapist – reasons for resorting to drugs, the fact 'that so many people feel that straight life in this society has so little to offer them'.[21]

Particularly noteworthy in this context is Welsh's post-*Trainspotting* shift of focus from heroin addiction to 'rave' and ecstasy culture, which involves a much larger and predominantly mainstream demographic. Almost immediately the public debate reopened on whether Welsh should be seen as a reckless promoter of drug consumption whose work posed a serious threat to his mainly young adult readership. The occasion for the rekindling of this debate was *Ecstasy: Three Tales of Chemical Romance*, published in June 1996 in the aftermath of the widely publicised ecstasy-related death of an English teenager, Leah Betts, in November 1995. The book's provocative cover, showing somebody taking an ecstasy pill, was interpreted as a cynical and disrespectful response to the attempt of Leah's grieving parents to launch a nationwide awareness-raising campaign against the drug. Leah's cheerful, smiling face appeared on billboards across Britain, bearing the caption 'Sorted – Only One Ecstasy Tablet Killed Leah Betts'. Yet Welsh's decision to start writing about ecstasy was not motivated by a gratuitous urge to offend, but by a desire to record significant changes in attitude and behaviour within late twentieth-century youth culture. *Trainspotting* could be described as marking the end of an era, and one is tempted to commend Welsh for rising so swiftly to the challenge of representing a culture caught up in transition, a transition which also manifests in a scene in Boyle's film in which fourteen-year-old Diane challenges the lifestyle of her junkie boyfriend Renton by asserting that 'drugs are changing, music is changing . . . are you clean?' Renton himself elaborates on this by observing that 'even men and women are changing'. Indeed, the rise of ecstasy culture in the late 1980s is often seen as coinciding with a remarkable shift in young people's attitudes towards traditional gender formations. As Simon Reynolds argues, within this new youth culture feminine spontaneity, fluidity and openness began to be thought of and experienced as far more attractive than masculine self-composure, tumescence and closure. 'Particularly for men', Reynolds writes, rave culture's 'drug/music interface acts to dephallicise the body and open it to enraptured, abandoned, "effeminate" gestures.'[22]

There appears to be a consensus that heroin is a 'hard', addictive and self-destructive drug, whereas popular attitudes towards ecstasy continue to be more divergent and open, describing the drug as 'soft', recreational and even life-enhancing. Ecstasy also appears more subculture-friendly as it reinforces people's natural urge to relate and communicate. While heroin spawns small ostracised cells of outcasts with little more in common than their drug-induced misery, ecstasy is much more easily reconcilable with a normal bourgeois lifestyle. The consumption of ecstasy is generally confined to certain subcultural spaces and times of the working week rather than condemning its consumers to live their whole lives in certain subcultural spaces, as heroin does. The use of terms like 'hard' and 'soft' to distinguish between heroin and ecstasy highlights the inherent genderedness of the relevant discourses. Even if in *Trainspotting* 'a needle brings more pleasure than a penis'[23] and, as a result, the male anatomy suffers a radical devaluation within heroin culture, phallic imagery persists as the drug itself becomes a kind of *über*-phallus, symbolically represented by the syringe. Irrespective of their biological sex, the experience of heroin users is one of climax induced by penetrative sex or, as Alison pronounces it in the novel, heroin 'beats any meat injection' (*T*, 9). Ecstasy seems equally emasculating. As Reynolds points out, 'E is notorious for making erection difficult and male orgasm virtually impossible'.[24] In contrast to the phallic imagery traditionally associated with heroin, however, ecstasy-induced experience is commonly likened to the female orgasm, not a rushed climax followed by detumescence and post-coital *tristesse*, but rather a sensation comparable to that of soaring on music, an enduring emotional high that builds up and intensifies as gradually as it eventually subsides. However crassly stereotyping these descriptions of male and female sexual experience may be, they clearly play into the hands of a writer like Welsh, whose male protagonists (Renton in both *Trainspotting* and *Porno*, Roy in *Marabou Stork Nightmares*) are desperate to escape not only from the clutches of heroin addiction, but also from a certain type of Scottish working-class 'hard man' masculinity. Harrowingly epitomised by Begbie, this masculinity is 'like junk, a habit' (*T*, 83). At the end of *Porno* we witness Renton triumphantly shaking it off as, accompanied by two women, he leaves Edinburgh for San Francisco. Sick Boy, on the other hand, fails to achieve a similar liberation when in the final paragraph of the novel he is held back by Begbie – presumed dead but in fact very much alive – grabbing his hand and holding it 'like a vice' (*P*, 484).

Welsh's characters find in ecstasy what they also looked for in heroin, the difference being that ecstasy appears to provide escape from quotidian pressures without the threat of addiction and painful withdrawal. Ecstasy seems like the perfect drug for recreational self-fulfilment, enabling its users to feel at one with the world, to 'find love' and forget about their real-life alienation. But of course the kind of wholesome communal incorporation experienced by users of ecstasy is only another transient, drug-induced illusion. According to Reynolds, ecstasy culture fails dismally to initiate genuine *agape* and is much more aptly described as 'a collective autism'. What its members invoke as 'love' and 'community' in reality amounts to little more than each individual's frenzy of 'intransitive amorousness'. Like heroin culture, ecstasy culture fails to devise a viable subcultural politics for a new kind of social order that would make the use of artificially life-enhancing drugs redundant. As Reynolds concludes, 'rave culture has never really been about altering reality, merely exempting yourself from it for a while'.[25]

To return to Welsh's *Ecstasy*, one other possible reason why so many critics felt compelled to comment on the book's controversial cover, which seemed to be advertising the cool cultural chic of ecstasy consumption, might quite simply have been the poor quality of the three stories it comprised. In *The Observer* Tim Adams concluded that 'Welsh has never been a subtle writer, but this is satire as headbutt',[26] and Welsh himself has admitted that *Ecstasy* 'wasn't up to the standard of the first three [books]', adding that 'much of the writing is too sparse and cold'.[27] Yet despite its literary inferiority, the collection remains interesting, chiefly because, contrary to its reputation as a celebration of ecstasy culture, it testifies to Welsh's growing disenchantment with the drug as well as his disillusionment with rave culture's rapid decline into commercialised club culture, utterly devoid now of whatever subversive politics and attitude it once held and stood for. Whereas 'Lorraine Goes to Livingston', however listless and half-hearted, may still be seen as keen to show ecstasy's self-liberating potential, the final story, 'The Undefeated', provides a passionate critique of ecstasy consumption, illustrating how the drug comes between individuals and their happiness. Recounting the love story of Lloyd and Heather, 'The Undefeated' falls into two sections: 'The Overwhelming Love of Ecstasy' followed by 'The Overwhelming Ecstasy of Love', introducing a sense of mutual exclusivity between drug addiction on the one hand, and the unadulterated pleasures and delights of 'real' love on the other. The opening of the story, set at a rave, affords us a momentary glimpse into Lloyd's interior world, exposing some of the less glamorous effects of the drug in the process, such as its taker's voluntary subjection to the remote control of a 'leader' and its confusion of genuine erotic appeal with masturbatory commodification:

> Then it's ma main man [the DJ] on the decks, and he's on the form tonight, just pulling away at our collective psychic sex organs as they lay splayed out before us and ah get a big rose smile off this goddess in a Lycra top, who, with her tanned skin and veneer of sweat, looks as enticing as a bottle of Becks from the cold shelf on a hot, muggy day. (*E*, 155)

Rather than facilitating Lloyd's self-fulfilment, ecstasy inhibits and obstructs it. Before Lloyd can find happiness with Heather, he must emancipate himself from the drug. Dismantling Welsh's reputation as rave culture's poet laureate, the story reads like an anti-drugs leaflet, the romantic encounter of Heather and Lloyd serving as a kind of picture story illustrating the various stages of Lloyd's growing self-awareness. As Lloyd comes to realise, ecstasy is a great facilitator of sex between strangers but 'see in someone you love though, the barriers should be down anyway' (*E*, 269). When Heather sets her boyfriend an ultimatum, suggesting that in order to experience true ecstasy with her he must wean himself off the drug, Lloyd promptly complies. As Lloyd's best friend explains, Lloyd 'didnae want a pill, eh no . . . Didnae want ehs perspective damaged' (*E*, 276).

Disaffiliated from the general culture, the lives of many of Welsh's characters match the subcultural criteria provided by Ken Gelder, who lists among subcultures' most characteristic attributes their often negative 'relation to labour or work', their deviance in terms of 'disavowing class affiliations or even "transcending" class' [. . .] often constituting a kind of '*lumpenproletariat*: that is, groups of people *below* class-based identity and without class consciousness', as well as their incorporation of 'excess or exaggeration [. . .] through a range of excessive attributes – behaviour, styles and dress, noise, argot or language, consumption, and so on'. Yet Gelder's definition requires modification. As noted above, the apparent disaffiliation of Welsh's characters from mainstream culture is hardly ever perfectly deliberate, voluntary or total, let alone successfully strategic; rather, the way in which their 'subcultural identity is pitched against the conformist pressures of mass society and massification'[28] often reveals itself as mere pose, designed to assert a sense of pride and dignity by presenting one's abjection as a matter of informed choice instead of compulsion. Welsh is never interested in a one-sided championing or defence of subcultural life; what concerns him much more is the interplay between mainstream society and its multifarious offshoots, their manifold crossovers as well as their amalgamation, however occasional or momentary. Aware of the stratification of the world we live in, Welsh is certainly no advocate of social or cultural compartmentalisation. As his work demonstrates time and again, there is only one society. Subcultural life does not unfold and take its course safely sectioned away from us; whether we like it or not, the deprived and the depraved are in our midst, as our fellow citizens. Similarly, subcultural identity cannot be forged and cherished in isolation. Any attempt to disengage from society, while its global organisation becomes increasingly liquefying and all-absorbing, must inevitably prove futile.

While society's struggle to think of itself as one in communal terms continues, there is no doubt that all of its members are corralled into one and the same marketplace. *Porno* might indeed be aptly described as 'a sort of Junkies Reunited',[29] yet by far more striking than the apparent subcultural peculiarity of the novel's personnel is its plot, which is driven by the same neoliberal entrepreneurialism that appeals to – or should one say 'afflicts' – every one of us in equal measure as all of us aspire to very similar goals of success and profitable self-fulfilment. Definite frontiers between subcultural and mainstream life no longer exist, if ever they did. Subcultures are big business now, and drug use is rife among the bourgeoisie. What used to be elements of subculture have become constitutive and even defining, if as yet often concealed or hushed-up, traits of society as a whole. Like ecstasy and cocaine 'porn is mainstream now', asserts Sick Boy in *Porno* (*P*, 347). But pornography does not simply augment our recreational repertoire of leisurely addictions; its increasing popularity is emblematic of society's quotidian habit of self-commodification. The careless consumption and exploitation of ourselves and of our others has become a way of life. As Welsh recognises, a culture that sees nothing wrong in pornography is at risk of becoming pornographic itself. 'People want sex, violence, food, pets, DIY and humiliation,' Renton reckons. 'Look at humiliation television, look at the papers and the mags, look at the class system, the jealousy, the bitterness that oozes out of our culture: in Britain we want to see people get fucked' (*P*, 179). Critical accusations that Welsh might be selling out in his more recent work appear to be underestimating the author's intelligence, his insight into his own commercialisation as well as the almost spontaneous assimilation of anything even vaguely subcultural into the mainstream. Our escapist entertainment industries are a hardcore business operating beyond any reference to, let alone realisation of, countercultural subversion. Commercially produced fairy-tale magic is riddled by modes of media exploitation often as casual as they are unconscionable. This is the background against which one must read Welsh's vision of 'Sick Boy becoming a franchise. I worry that I may be turning him into a schemie, coke-fuelled Harry Potter [. . .] Stand by for *Sick Boy and the Goblet of Vomit* around 2005.' [30] Evidently, all it would take to desecrate one make-believe subcultural icon (Harry Potter) by using it to thoroughly de-authenticate another (Sick Boy) is one inspired coup of ruthless entrepreneurial genius.

In Welsh's latest novel, *Crime* (2008), there are no longer any clear-cut demarcations between a subcultural underground and society's mainstream, nor does the plot come reassuringly full circle by centring on victim-perpetrators or killer-policemen, as in *Marabou Stork Nightmares* or *Filth*. Genuine countercultural dissent has all but disappeared in our brave new globalised world while deviancy has become at once more sinister and less easily identifiable. The novel features at least one Miami police officer involved in running a nationwide paedophile ring, and it also exposes Scottish policemen as having engaged in sex with underaged girls whilst on a stag-do holiday in Thailand. Yet its true focus appears to be on western society's most common crime, that of not living up to its own equal opportunities agenda and failing to care for children like Britney and Tianna, two young girls from disadvantaged single-parent backgrounds whose welfare and indeed very lives are at risk. By selecting for the role of protagonist an everyman character displaying both heroic and anti-heroic traits, Welsh implies that this crime is ultimately our own, no matter how fervently committed we may be, or become, to its eradication. Shrewdly the novel sets the tone by choosing for the part Ray Lennox, whom we recognise from an earlier novel as somebody else's sidekick and circumstantial accomplice: as we remember, Lennox repeatedly turned a blind eye to his superior Robertson's manifold sordidly exploitative manoeuvres in *Filth*.

Welsh's recent move no longer to represent subculture as a reservoir of 'in-yer-face' rebellious resistance but a predatory underground of organised crime, bolstered, however obliquely or unwittingly, by the general culture, enables also an interesting new perspective on the opening scene of Boyle's *Trainspotting*. Caught shoplifting, we see Renton and a couple of his mates being chased down Edinburgh's Princes Street by police. The chase leads down some steps onto Calton Road near the huge gothic archway buttressing Waterloo Place. The intended impression is clearly that of some undesirable low-lifers returning to where they belong, which is definitely not in the picturesque commercial heart of Scotland's capital city. It is at the close of this scene that Renton is almost run over by a car coming out of a hidden back alley, and he stops to laugh in the face of the driver, effectively mocking us, the bourgeois-bohemian cinema audience, whose position and view are by default identical with the invisible, anonymous driver's. It would seem apt to interpret this moment as simply showing Renton's irreverent defiance, yet on second thoughts the junkie's mirth might as well be caused by the pure and simple fact of our presence down there, his gleeful surprise at catching us in a place where really we are not expected to be. What are we doing in this quasi-subterranean part of town? With whom might we have agreed to meet here so furtively? What 'subcultural', shady or shameful business – apart from mere voyeurist bystanderism – might we be in pursuit of?

CHAPTER SEVEN

Welsh and the Theatre

Adrienne Scullion

In his introduction to *You'll Have Had Your Hole* Irvine Welsh proposes that 'the good news for any novelist considering writing a play is that it should be well within [his or her] capabilities'.[1] Despite his breezily confident approach to the craft of the playwright, however, it remains as a novelist that Welsh's vivid imagined worlds and bold literary soundscapes have had the greatest impact on the wider culture, as well as on theatre-makers and audiences. It is the adaptations of his novels rather than his original plays that connect Welsh with the story of British theatre. Specifically, it is the adaptation of *Trainspotting* by Harry Gibson that achieved huge popularity and significant presence on the stage in the UK as well as internationally. In contrast, Welsh's own work for the theatre – *Headstate* (in collaboration with boiler-house theatre company, 1994), *You'll Have Had Your Hole* (1998), *Blackpool* (co-authored with Gibson, 2002) and *Babylon Heights* (co-authored with Dean Cavanagh, 2006), as well as Gibson's later adaptations of *Marabou Stork Nightmares* (1996), *Filth* (1999) and *Glue* (2001) – have had less critical success and impact despite often enjoying high-profile productions and attracting significant media interest. That said, there has always been a whiff of the showman about Welsh, be it his emboldened public persona expressed in self-reflexive performances for press interviews and poses in photographs, or the demotic dialogue and black-comedic edge of his prose. At each stage of his career Welsh has had some kind of professional engagement with the theatre and, at their best, these engagements have not only attracted new audiences, but also brought artists from other walks of life (club culture and punk music in particular) into theatre-making.

Robert Morace and Aaron Kelly both date the beginning of Welsh's publishing career back to 1991 when, in suitably performative style, Welsh created a stir with a brief correspondence in *The Scotsman*.[2] In what Kelly identifies as a wittily staged epistolary set-piece, Welsh rails against the capital's narrow-minded bourgeoisie. Welsh and '(Mrs) E. M. Bogie' – seemingly Welsh's *alter ego* – assume rather different critical perspectives on a production of Trevor Griffiths' *Comedians* at the Royal Lyceum Theatre in Edinburgh:

Sir, – Last Saturday, I attended a matinee performance of the Trevor Griffith plays *Comedians* [. . .] The play itself was performed to mesmerizing perfection by a highly talented cast. Unfortunately, my enjoyment of this production was marred by the constant whinging of other members of the audience, a large number of whom created further disturbance by leaving during the play. While I accept that some narrow-minded people will be upset by explicit language, it is unfortunate that such people cannot suspend their prejudices for a few hours.

Sir, – Why did your drama critic fail to warn readers that the play *Comedians* [. . .] was not only a rather dull and boring play but one in which the characters used foul, obscene and profane language throughout? Some of the sentiments expressed in the play were also insulting, to Jews, black people and the Irish. Surely an ordinary audience could only have a feeling of shame that such a degrading play could be produced and supported by so many illustrious bodies representing Edinburgh.[3]

The dialogue concluded the following week with Welsh affirming the political purpose of Griffiths' work and setting the scene for some of the criticism that his own work would soon attract:

> Sir, – Mrs E. M. Bogie [. . .] manages to illustrate the points I made about the knee-jerk reaction of the narrow-minded to explicit language. More importantly, she displays a great misunderstanding of the message and the sentiment of the brilliant play [which is] an attack on the ugly racism and sexism which underpin mainstream British humour, and the collusion of the audience with such racist and sexist attitudes [. . .] For a play such as this to work it requires an audience with a level of sophistication which enables them to see the evils of racism and sexism without colluding in them, but at the same time not reacting to the explicit language, which is used for illustrative and authenticity purposes. The Royal Lyceum may have to examine its publicity for events such as this, if only to encourage the moaners to stay away [. . .].[4]

The exchange is an appropriate curtain-raiser for Welsh's own forays into the theatre, and his characteristic exasperation with and baiting of the same bourgeois theatre institutions and audiences, in respect not just of his deployment of 'explicit language', but also the stories and representational modes – 'the message and the sentiment' – of his theatre.

Whatever its technical weaknesses – often tied up with limited character development and unconvincing plotting – Welsh's theatre has always been challenging in terms of its story, representation, language and action. All his plays feature the heightened idiomatic demotic of his prose and turn on acts of physical violence, often of the most appalling kind. 'Strong language' apart, the physical representation of such actions (drug-taking, physical abuse and rape) on stage tends to impact on audiences much more immediately, by materialising and confronting their own willingness to enter Welsh's imagined worlds, than the same scenarios might on the reading public. Certainly, his plays have been criticised for a titillating and even pornographic approach to the depiction of violence. Despite their production in contexts highly attuned to complex, difficult and challenging work neither *Headstate*, *You'll Have Had Your Hole*, *Blackpool* nor *Babylon Heights* has achieved that balance of 'message and sentiment', merging dramaturgical craft and theatrical efficacy, that Welsh celebrates in Griffiths's work and that was arguably achieved in Gibson's adaptation of *Trainspotting*.

'Welsh theatre' begins in 1994 with the first production of Gibson's *Trainspotting*, directed by Ian Brown, then artistic director of Edinburgh's Traverse Theatre, in a production for the Glasgow Arts Festival, Mayfest. The play was initially staged in one of the small studio spaces at the Citizens' Theatre before moving on to the Traverse. *Trainspotting* was staged again a year later in March 1995 at the Citizens', directed by Gibson himself. Brown's production transferred to London's Bush Theatre in April 1995 – another small, intimate theatre with a risk-taking penchant for new writing – while Gibson's production was taken up by the Ambassadors Theatre in London's West End before transferring to the Whitehall Theatre and then embarking on a main-stage national tour in 1995 and 1996, attracting new audiences in the bounce created by Danny Boyle's film. The twin appeal of *Trainspotting* not only to the theatre-literate, new writing-focused communities of the Bush and the Traverse but also to the wider, arguably more 'popular' and commercial audiences of the West End constitutes a distinctive feature of Welsh's theatre in general and the *Trainspotting* phenomenon in particular. The increasing popular momentum of the play led to its winning the *Sunday Times* Regional Theatre Award for best new play. (Interestingly, Morace speculates that the success of *Trainspotting* inspired 'a flurry of stage adaptations of Welsh's works and of other Scottish novels, including [Iain] Banks's *The Bridge*, [Janice] Galloway's *The Trick is to Keep Breathing*, and [Alasdair] Gray's *Lanark*',[5] though it would probably be overstating the case to argue that Welsh and Gibson were the chief key drivers behind this new trend of adapting contemporary Scottish novels for the stage.)

The play version of *Trainspotting* exists in several variations, including a somewhat sanitised one used in an off-Broadway production in 1998, which had been stripped of all representations of the actual bodily squalor and nastiness of drug injection. What the variations share is Gibson's robust editing. Gibson reduced the novel's forty-three scenes to just twenty and deployed four actors to play the twelve characters. Maintaining the novel's favouring of interior monologue via soliloquy and direct address, he stripped away some of the novel's heady black humour to reveal lives of self-destructive futility, signalled effectively at the end of the play, which does not show Mark Renton 'liberated' from Edinburgh or the UK, but concludes with a claustrophobic scene at Leith Central Station. Gibson's decision to limit the number of performers on stage to just four, all of whom play multiple roles, stands as a key element in the play's distinctive and successful dramaturgy. The play's sense of risk and experimentation, intimacy and confession – particularly in its presentation in smaller studio spaces such as the Citizens' Studio – also captured something of the ethos of Welsh's prose and worldview. *Trainspotting* was theatre honed down to its basic building blocks, showing bold characters in clear settings telling extraordinary stories to a closely engaged audience. However, as the *Trainspotting* phenomenon grew, specifically after the release of Boyle's film, the experience of watching the stage play changed. Tours began to take the play to larger theatre spaces – main stages and commercially operated venues – which created a very different atmosphere. Audiences, now largely composed of younger people drawn from the clubbing and popular music scenes, were offered a celebration of 'Cool Britannia' and the Welsh brand rather than a sense of experiential intimacy, dramaturgical risk and artistic experimentation.

With an eye to these new audiences and intent on continuing with what had developed into a successful creative journey, the Citizens' Theatre kept faith with Welsh's and Gibson's growing body of work and – following the adaptation of *Marabou Stork Nightmares*, which premièred in March 1996 in a large-scale, main-stage production, with an ambitious performance by *Trainspotting* veteran James Cunningham as Roy Strang at its centre – commissioned a further adaptation. The dramatic version of Welsh's third novel, *Filth*, premièred at the Citizens' in September 1999. Similarly pared back as the original *Trainspotting* production, *Filth* was adapted as a one-man monologue, featuring a bold and brilliant performance by Tam Dean Burn. It was played with minimal set and dressings in a tiny studio which only seated around sixty. As with the first production of *Trainspotting*, the physical proximity the audience had with the performer heightened the poignancy of the character's 'confession' to create a live experience that added significantly to the impact of Welsh's narrative. But although audiences in both Glasgow and at London's Bush Theatre recognised and celebrated Burn's performance as Bruce Roberson as something special, there was no subsequent production and the play never galvanised theatre-goers in the way *Trainspotting* had done. Nevertheless, with support from the Citizens' Gibson went on to produce a dramatic adaptation of *Glue*, staged under his own direction as a studio production in December 2001. But the impact of Gibson's versions of *Filth* and *Glue* – like that of Keith Wyatt's 1999 dramatisation of 'The

Undefeated' from *Ecstasy* and John Paul McGroarty's adaptation of *Porno*, which was produced as part of the Leith Festival in 2006 – was limited both commercially and critically, suggesting that by the late 1990s the moment for adapting Welsh for the stage had passed, not least also because the theatre culture within which it had originally found a place was evolving beyond the first shock of the so-called 'in-yer-face' phenomenon.

Certainly, one way to contextualise the success of Gibson's *Trainspotting* is by reference to the wider British theatre culture of the mid-1990s and its fascination with all things violent. British theatre in the 1990s was centred on new writers, new writing and a new set of representational means and voices, broadly and evocatively referred to as 'in-yer-face', an expression that the publication of Aleks Sierz's study would soon turn into a critical term describing a specific generic category.[6] Welsh's theatre, led by *Trainspotting*, was readily accommodated within this busy marketplace associated with high-profile new writing by Mark Ravenhill (b. 1967), Anthony Neilson (b. 1967), Sarah Kane (1971–99) and others. But in contrast to Welsh's plays, the core repertoire of in-yer-face theatre – Ravenhill's *Shopping and Fucking* (1996), Neilson's *Penetrator* (1993) and *The Censor* (1999), Kane's *Blasted* (1995) and *Cleansed* (1998) – was as formally daring as its content was shocking. These were plays attacking social and cultural conservatism with dramaturgical and theatrical insight. Ravenhill, Neilson and above all Kane understood dramaturgical convention – for example, the representational work of violence on the British stage from Shakespeare, Webster and Kyd to Pinter, Bond and Barker – and they used that understanding and craft awareness to dismantle convention from within. While Welsh was able to achieve similar effects with his prose, neither the adaptations of his work nor his original plays were informed by or directed towards theatrical innovation, formal experimentation or dramaturgical daring.

Both his plays and the adaptations of his novels were certainly part of the cultural context of in-yer-face drama, but they were never at the forefront of it in terms of possessing or carrying out a formally distinct representational agenda. Indeed, Welsh's plays – and *Trainspotting* in particular – seem more readily concerned with an awareness of the market, as well as the desire of a range of theatre-makers and producers to align production interests and audience-development goals with the rising star of Welsh and an immediately contemporary cultural repertoire. Not only must what success they had largely be ascribed to fashion and shrewd marketing, but often the main motivation behind commissioning and producing them was to do with finding a 'new' audience for the theatre, a crossover audience that had read the novels (or at least heard about them) and, later, seen the film. Welsh's achievement in drawing that 'new' audience into the theatre should not be underestimated, but its expectations must also be acknowledged: what this audience wanted from the theatre was for the world of the novel or the film to be represented more or less 'faithfully' on stage.

Of a different order from the novel adaptations and potentially rather closer to Welsh's own vision for the theatre, even hinting at theatrical innovation, was *Headstate* (1994), a collaboration between Welsh and the Scottish theatre company boilerhouse. The project was to create a kind of theatre that captured the risk and originality Welsh had achieved formally in his fictional representation of the so-called E-generation's high-energy, countercultural youth culture and music scene. Devised as 'a piece of physical theatre' recreating the atmosphere of 'a pre-club night',[7] *Headstate* saw realisation as a large-scale promenade performance, produced in Glasgow's post-industrial Tramway, drawing explicitly on the paraphernalia of the acid-house club culture of the time by using huge theatre curtains, video projections, moving platforms and its own soundtrack composed by Graham Cunnington, a member of the post-punk performance company Test Department. The rather sketchy script – fractured and impressionistic, in turns banal and savage – was put together collectively by the company but remained a somewhat elusive part of the performance. Indeed, the script of *Headstate* was never intended to stand alone as an authoritative play text; rather, it was conceived as part of the general sensory overload offered by the performance and contributing to the event's rather contradictory impression of 'a tightly controlled rave'.[8] The performers – not really characters in any narratively focused way – slip in and out of the audience's attention. Snatches of dialogue are overheard and relationships momentarily revealed. The main 'character' explored by the piece is the rave itself, experienced through the soundtrack's steadily growing musical beats as well as overheard snippets of dialogue which concern the clubbers' expectations of the rave, its potential for physical and emotional excess, and as escapist fantasy. The climax of the performance is not narratively driven or verbally signalled, but marked by the soundtrack and embodied by the performers who, joined by the promenade audience, dance through the space. The dénouement is the 'post-rave' chill-out, incorporated by the deflated clubbers engaging in fractured and incomplete dialogue. The concept, as well as its collaborative realisation, was timely and potentially very strong, but the script seemed too specific and ultimately distracting. Throughout the performance the audience strained to hear the dialogue, paying too much attention to knitting together a play from the fragments on offer and thereby missing out on the physicality of the experience.

Albeit flawed and contradictory, *Headstate* did succeed in connecting Welsh's multiple audiences – the clubbers and kids of the music and drug scenes, on the one hand, with the bourgeois readers and middle-class theatregoers, on the other. Both groups were not only excited by Welsh's imagined world, and even by his politics, but also by the new kinds of large-scale, even epic theatrical spaces opened up by venues such as Glasgow's Tramway and made the most of by contemporary companies such as boilerhouse, Test Department, nva and others. The collaborative, discursive and even experimental mode of *Headstate*'s creation was a distinctive outlet for Welsh's creativity, one that endures perhaps as the most interesting moment among Welsh's forays into theatre. Indeed, in interview Welsh frequently identifies collaboration as the most distinctive and rewarding feature of theatrical production, often framed in stark contrast to the solitary process of novel-writing.

At the Citizens' Theatre the artistic director, Giles Havergal, had promoted all of the previous Welsh/Gibson adaptations when, in light of their success, he commissioned the novelist and playwright to create an original text for his theatre. However, as Welsh and Gibson's new work developed and its sprawling cast grew, it began to exceed the resources of the Citizens' Theatre. In the end *Blackpool*, a musical – or perhaps simply a new play with songs – was developed for production with a cohort of final-year students of Queen Margaret University College, Edinburgh, where it premièred in 2002. Taking their idea to a drama school context allowed Gibson and Welsh not only to develop their characters and stories over a longer period of time, but also to indulge in personnel-heavy, yet essential, musical elements such as the chorus line. While working with students allowed for a more densely populated stage than most subsidised theatres could manage, the project also brought on board another new collaborator for Welsh, as he commissioned music and songs from punk pioneer Vic Godard, formerly of the band Subway Sect. From the initial proposal by Havergal to the main writing process with Gibson, through the workshop development with the students to the music created by Godard, *Blackpool* was a production demonstrably predicated on collaboration and partnership, but it was also strongly marked by some of Welsh's most characteristic tropes. The disaffected Edinburgh youths of his novels, inhabiting a music and/or drug scene harbouring barely concealed undercurrents of threat and menace that can at any moment explode into shocking violence, return here in another distinctive evocation of place, featuring the traditional English seaside resort now taken over by stag parties and raves. As with *Headstate*, what is truly exciting about Welsh's approach to the theatre at this time is his capacity for introducing to the theatre-making process entirely new voices and talents. In the case of *Blackpool* this was the discovery of a non-traditional musician whose punk attitude fitted Welsh and Gibson's vision of Blackpool's excess and decline, once again showing great potential for widening contemporary theatre's target demographic.

At the heart of *Blackpool*'s chaotic and rather vague story are two Edinburgh teenagers who run away to the seaside resort, where they find themselves part of a quixotic group including a Scottish goalkeeper and two prostitutes. Fifteen years later the group are reunited in Blackpool and must face up to the consequences of their wild, youthful escapades. Joyce McMillan detects in *Blackpool* some of the common problems of character, plot and storytelling that compound Welsh's plays, but she also recognises the energy and even the vision at its heart:

> Its storytelling is vague to the point of confusion, its characters barely develop, its songs are wistful and rambling rather than catchy, and so far as pace is concerned, it often seems to drift off into a kind of limbo where nothing much is happening at all. And yet somehow, behind and beyond all that, this show has a smell of the real and theatrical future about it that creates its own strange crackle of slow-burning excitement.[9]

McMillan's point is that, while Welsh's theatrical potential is tangible, theatre-craft eludes him. In other words, it is his lack of dramaturgical skills that weakens the play's overall impact: this is a problem that, arguably, affects all of Welsh's original work for the theatre.

Directed by Brown in his post-Traverse role as director of the West Yorkshire Playhouse, *You'll Have Had Your Hole* – really Welsh's only single-authored play – attracted high-profile media interest when it premièred in Leeds in 1998. The production coincided with the height of Welsh's popular success and is generally seen as belonging to the in-yer-face sub-genre of contemporary British theatre. A reflection of the *zeitgeist*, *You'll Have Had Your Hole* is also clearly a one-off, one-hit wonder, and a hotly contested and equivocal hit at that. Despite the fact that the production was something of a popular success and (reportedly) audiences were for the most part fully positive in their responses, the play's critical reception was damning. 'Horrible scenes are horrible to watch', exclaimed one critic, while another described *You'll Have Had Your Hole* as 'the saddest, sickest, most vile play I have ever sat through'.[10] The outrage, however, was not just – not really even – moral. Most reviewers did see and acknowledge the contemporary parallels with Kane, Ravenhill and the other in-yer-face playwrights; some even drew historical parallels with Jacobean revenge tragedy. Most consistently, however, the play was criticised for being poorly written.

In *You'll Have Had Your Hole* two petty gangsters, Docksey and Jinks, kidnap and, with increasingly explicit violence, torture their former collaborator, Dex, who spends the whole play tied up, most of the time suspended by chains from the ceiling of a disused, soundproofed recording studio, which provides the main setting of the play. In an unexpected and unconvincing romantic subplot Docksey also seduces Dex's girlfriend, Laney. Fuelled by drink and drugs Docksey and Jinks' revenge on the entirety of Dex's life and body is motivated by a heady combination of paranoia, fear, hysteria, fun, boredom and perhaps even a darkly skewed sense of justice:

> Jinks *pulls* Dex's *head back by the hair, and* Docksey *stuffs a ball-gag into his mouth. They secure it with straps from the back.*
>
> **Docksey** Look, Dex, don't be making nay long-term plans, because we're going to be here for a while. It's going to be quite a miserable time, in fact it's going to be the worst. We can't guarantee that we won't torture you at any time. The truth is that we might just torture you for fun, even if you do co-operate.
>
> Jinks *has produced a pair of long-nosed pliers and is holding them menacingly.*
>
> **Jinks** . . . but it won't be personal, if we're just doing it for fun, it'll simply be because of the pleasure it gives us, rather than cause of anything you've done wrong. It might no really sound it, angel heart, but that's far better than us doing it because you've annoyed us. There's a nastier edge to it then [. . .].[11]

By the end of the play Dex has been tortured, drugged, raped by Jinks ('whoa ya fuckin sexy piece of meat . . . here comes the choo-choo . . . inter-shitty bum express train'[12]) and finally murdered. Jinks then turns on Docksey who is chained up as Dex had been at the start of the play.

The play's physical and verbal violence is certainly unrelenting and at times the impact is inescapably visceral, yet ultimately the effect of all this is banal. The storytelling is fractured and the character development remains minimal. Violence is not deployed to develop characterisation or action but, seemingly, merely for voyeuristic effect. Crude and aggressive, if sometimes bleakly witty word-play, combined with hands-on torture in the first scenes, establish the familiar Welsh world, but move the drama on very little indeed. Verbal set pieces, such as the scene in which Docksey forces Dex to relive an earlier murder they had committed of an unfortunate debtor, do not deliver the punch they should, simply because so much else in the play is based on retelling rather than action. The play does not work as a play because it does not tell its story or reveal its characters by using the tools of the stage.

Critical opinion was more or less unanimous in deriding the play's nastiness, with critics most notably united in attacking Welsh's lack of dramaturgical craft. In the play Welsh's 'imagination and [. . .] dramatic skills [were said to be] pitifully exposed'. The play still felt 'as if it [was] at workshop stage' and, as another critic saw it, 'it's just so badly written'.[13] In agreement with much of the criticism, Michael Billington made a further shrewd assessment. Comparing Welsh's stagecraft unfavourably with his novels and short stories, he concluded that 'the play is stronger on sensation than argument and leaves one pining for Welsh's vivid prose'.[14] The critical reaction to *You'll Have Had Your Hole* was thus damning. A defence might possibly be launched by suggesting that it was the victim of its own high-profile publicity, so that expectations were simply overstocked for a first-time playwright. The critical reaction could also be read as an early indication that the in-yer-face bubble had burst, or that Welsh's cheekily bravura claim that writing a play hardly poses a great challenge to a novelist had riled the theatre establishment. But above all it was the failings of the play as a play – in other words, the failings of Welsh's craft as a playwright – that were really to blame. Unsurprisingly it was to be several years before Welsh would return to the stage, this time with a play developed not within the British theatre system, but in Dublin and California.

Welsh's most recent dramatic work is *Babylon Heights*, which he co-authored with Dean Cavanagh. The play premièred in San Francisco in 2006 and had an early production in Dublin, too. Set in Hollywood in the mid-1930s during the filming of Victor Fleming's *The Wizard of Oz*, the play focuses on the actors and extras employed to play the film's Munchkins. Its point of departure is the urban myth that one of the Munchkins committed suicide by hanging himself on set during the filming and that, allegedly, his body can be seen hanging from one of the fantastic trees in a key scene featuring Dorothy and the Tin Man. Mobilising a somewhat amoral fantasy, the play speculates on how and why it might have come about that such a suicidal act was committed.

The actors Bert Kowalski, Charles Merryweather, Raymond Benedict-Porter and Philomena Kinsella have nothing in common except that they are all of restricted growth and have been employed by MGM to play the Munchkins. They are billeted – along with the rest of the Munchkin performers – in a shabby hotel in Culver City. A mix-up means that Philomena has to share a bedroom with the three men, and the play is mostly set in this single room. Between them the four characters, who are drug addicts, sex addicts, drunks, thieves, fantasists and liars, embody, enact or are victims of a number of sins of excess. Indeed, one of the challenges of the play is that none of the characters is presented as in any way sympathetic to the audience while the action of the play effects very little by way of character development or evolution of the plot. While the first act is an all-too-wordy exercise in crude humour seemingly focused on shocking the audience (the first word uttered on stage is 'Cocksucker!'), the second act switches with absurd haste to unconcealed depravity, violence and tragedy. Despite this, the play is devoid of surprises. Audience members expect the bullying drunk Kowalski to be equipped with a heart of gold, just as they also expect the seemingly innocent Irish lass, Philomena, to be not quite as innocent as she appears. Merryweather is flagged as a victim from the very beginning, finding himself at the receiving end of Philomena's thieving fingers as well as being variously abused, even raped, by Benedict-Porter. Eventually, at a plot-turning moment of clear inevitability but dramaturgical confusion, which irreparably skews the play's imagined topography and timeline beyond coherence and logic, Merryweather commits suicide.

The play is an allegory of the Hollywood dream – the American Dream even – proceeding like a Dorothean journey between hope and reality. The metaphor of the victimised 'little guy' of Depression-era America is revisited in the *faux* flamboyance of the Munchkins and their battle not only with the Wicked Witch in Oz, but also the film producers in Hollywood. However, while this metaphor works on that first level, the amorality of the characters and their general lack of dramaturgical exposition and development limit the further, deeper impact of both their literal journey to Oz/Hollywood and their metaphorical journey once they are there. In the imagined world of the play, not only does the 'normal-sized' world corral and exploit the Munchkins, sequestering them in a cheap hotel and paying them below-standard wages. As it transpires, the small people are just as adept at exploiting and victimising each other. But the play is also about being small in a more literal and phenomenological sense. As requested by the authors, the roles are not to be played by reduced-growth actors. Rather, 'in order to maximize audience empathy with the "trapped" dwarves, the four actors who play the Munchkins will be of "regular" size [while] stage equipment – beds, doors, table, etc – will be outsized'. As Welsh and Cavanagh specify, 'the only reference to the outside world is the booming offstage voice of the "normal people", which should be intrusive and threatening'.[15] This a clear and committed theatrical choice and, as interviews with Welsh at the time of the production demonstrate, it was made after careful deliberation and in full cognisance of its political ramifications. Of course, it was a choice that did attract comment and indeed opposition from some disability groups, thereby adding to the 'shock value' that the other aspects of the narrative and its language encourage.

The American critic Chloe Veltman has speculated that there might be another metaphor at work in *Babylon Heights* to do with the writers' own struggle within contemporary (British) theatre and (British and American) film culture. To elucidate her point, Veltman quotes Welsh from an interview the morning after the play's première:

> 'There's such a fucking horrible theater culture in the western world. It's all luvvies, darlings, and sweethearts. It's a closed shop,' said the soft-spoken Welsh with uncharacteristic vehemence [. . .] [Welsh and Cavanagh] then discussed Welsh's abortive experiences in Hollywood, 'doing lunch' with producers for two months till both sides got bored. 'Maybe *Babylon Heights* is about all these ways of fighting against the system, says Cavanagh [. . .] Welsh nodded in

> agreement: 'Right. Success teaches you fuck all. Failure's the best and only way you can learn.' [16]

So far Welsh has had what can at best only be described as an equivocal relationship with the theatre, ranging from the huge success when he handed over the adaptation of *Trainspotting* to Gibson at one end to the critical mauling of *You'll Have Had Your Hole* at the other. From his early letter-writing in *The Scotsman* to a piece in *The Stage* entitled 'Why I Hate Theatre'[17] Welsh has worried at and about theatre, pursuing some brave experiments in the process. From the large-scale collaboration of *Headstate* to the provocative staging choices of *Babylon Heights* he has created theatre that might not have delivered dramaturgically, but that was never boring or safe in its failure.

CHAPTER EIGHT

Welsh and Identity Politics

Gavin Miller

There is a view of contemporary Scottish literature in which the value of Irvine Welsh's work is in its contribution to the cultural diversity of the Scottish canon. 'Voice' is a keyword in the jargon of this critical approach: Welsh's writing matters because it gives a voice to a subordinated social group – the urban working class – and this voice 'speaks' in Welsh's work without belittlement. The term 'voice' functions in this kind of criticism as a synecdoche for 'values', 'culture' or 'ethos': the linguistic difference of Welsh's protagonists stands for the whole of their ethical and cultural difference. By extension, the preservation of their linguistic voices in a non-standard orthography – a spelling free from the disparaging apparatus of apostrophes that mark supposed elisions and deviations – stands for respect and celebration, rather than misrecognition and depreciation, of their cultural difference. The *locus classicus* for this kind of account of contemporary Scottish fiction can be found in Cairns Craig's *The Modern Scottish Novel*, where it is argued (with regard to James Kelman's work) that representation of 'voice' in this way – particularly when it extends to the narratorial voice – marks a linguistic and textual subversion of social hierarchies, and a claim to the equality of working-class language, culture and experience.[1]

But does Welsh's fiction really represent, dignify and celebrate the difference of his favoured identity group? Is Welsh really part of the great 'identity bard' scheme promoted by contemporary Scottish literary criticism? Even at first glance, the evidence is equivocal. Certainly, in *Glue* (2001) Duncan Ewart spells out to his son, Carl, the 'ten rules' of their working-class Edinburgh community, and later – on his deathbed – enjoins Carl to preserve and continue this moral code: 'Mind the ten rules, he wheezed at his son, squeezing his hand' (G, 454). The storyline of *Glue*, however, casts doubt on the value of these commandments, one of which is 'Nivir shop anybody tae the polis [. . .] neither friend nor foe' (G, 23). This prohibition destroys Carl's friend Gally, who refuses to tell the police who is really the perpetrator of a vicious knife attack of which he stands accused. As a result, Gally is wrongly convicted and his life begins a downward spiral which ends in suicide. Tempting as it may be to see *Glue* as the manifesto for a 'preservationist ethic',[2] and Duncan Ewart as its authorised spokesman, the text itself challenges such an interpretation.

Indeed, leaving aside the questionable value of the decalogue which is passed down to Carl and his friends, a more fundamental criticism may be made of the preservationist ethic seemingly promoted by Duncan Ewart. The problem is that, in the words of Anthony Appiah, 'without some racialized conception of a group, one's culture could only be whatever it was that one actually practiced, and couldn't be lost or retrieved or preserved or betrayed'.[3] We can only think of Carl, or Gally, as honouring or betraying their culture by thinking of their culture as the property of their bloodline. After all, if Carl decided to modify his father's ten commandments by, for instance, informing to the police, then this modified decalogue would be as much Carl's culture as the unmodified ten rules. Such a modification counts as betrayal only if we think of Carl's culture not as belonging to him, but as an inheritance passed down from his forefathers, an inheritance that can be cherished or despoiled according to his actions. Such latent connections between descent and culture illuminate the main tendencies in Welsh's exploration of identity. Welsh's fiction represents 'blood' – descent, heredity and, more broadly, 'race' – as the usual stuff of identity, lurking within seemingly more innocent ideas such as 'memory' and 'trauma'. Even the concept of social class, as Welsh represents it, has been reworked in this way, so that a specious 'working-class identity' is passed down to the sons and daughters of the working class.

To find issues of 'blood' identity in Welsh's work is relatively straightforward: his writing frequently and pointedly deals with race, racial identity and racism. The most conspicuous engagement is perhaps in *Marabou Stork Nightmares* (1995), where the protagonist makes a contentious comparison between Scottish class structures and South African apartheid. There is much to be learned, though, from Welsh's interrogations of racism where the 'races' in question are other than the familiar colonial racial taxonomies ('Caucasoid', 'Negroid', 'Mongoloid') and are also cloaked in the seemingly innocuous garb of 'culture'. A variety of racism that equally concerns Welsh is found in so-called Scottish 'sectarianism' – in the hostility and tension that may exist in certain places and social strata between Scottish 'Catholics' and Scottish 'Protestants'. As Steve Bruce and his co-authors explain, Scottish sectarianism has, since the late nineteenth century, been a latently racial phenomenon in which religious practice is taken as an indication of descent. Modern Scottish sectarianism begins in the Victorian era with the economically motivated hostility of a largely Protestant Scottish population to the arrival of predominantly Catholic Irish immigrants.[4] The use of religion as a metonymy for race continues in contemporary sectarian identifications and hostilities, for 'when we talk of Protestants and Catholics, few of the people so designated are those things in the strict confessional sense'.[5] The more precise description of the objects of so-called 'anti-Catholic' discrimination in Scotland would really be 'Catholics descended from Irish migrant forebears':[6] in Scottish sectarianism 'Catholic' is a codeword for Irish ancestry and 'Protestant' a codeword for Scottish ancestry. It would be unwise to equate the extent, intensity and longevity of Scottish sectarianism with, for instance, the Jim Crow laws of the United States or South African apartheid: for most demographic groups, 'changes in the Scottish economy, polity and society since the late 1930s have reduced the importance of religious and ethnic identity to a point of irrelevance'.[7] But its prevalence notwithstanding, modern Scottish sectarianism is really one particular mode of Scottish racial identification: the interest in religious observance is in its supposed utility as an index of 'blood'.

Glue shares and extends such scepticism towards the supposed religious credentials of Scottish sectarianism. In *Glue* the essential significance of religious allegiance is as a mode of race, and this applies beyond even the supposed sectarian races of 'Catholic' and 'Protestant'. Topsy, workmate to the teenage Carl Ewart, sees, for instance, no contradiction in the idea of a 'Jewish' Protestant. He insists to Carl that even though their boss is an elder in the Scottish Kirk, this is an attempt to disguise a Jewish ethnicity that would more usually be expressed in religious observance. 'If the likes ay Jewmen just went tae the synagogue,' explains Topsy, 'they wid stand oot a mile. Aw this sneakin intae the proddy church is jist tae make it less obvious. Eh wants ye tae think eh's one ay us but eh isnae' (G, 123). Newman, their boss, is – in Topsy's mind, at least – a racial Jew who is trying to pass as a racial Protestant (or indigenous Scot) by adopting the stereotypical cultural forms of the latter. This racial logic of passing as a different 'sect' can also be found in an incident where the young protagonists of *Glue* bluff their way into a football match in which the Glaswegian 'Protestant' team, Rangers, are playing the Edinburgh 'Catholic' team, Hibernian. In order to infiltrate the areas allocated to Rangers fans, the Edinburgh youths perform through accent and regalia their supposed Protestant ethnicity as so-called 'Huns':

> Youse Rangers supporters, boys? A big cop asked us.
>
> – Course wi are, big man, Dozo said in a soapdodger accent, and we walked across the fifty yards ay no-man's land passin through the other cordon tae merge wi the Huns crowd and tae git intae the Dunbar end. Carl had taken oot the Rid Hand ay Ulster flag n drapped it roon ehs shoodirs. (G, 86)

The point of this incident, of course, is not that Welsh thinks his characters really are passing as another race. Rather, it is to expose the overwhelmingly performed nature of the 'Protestant' and 'Catholic' races. Irrespective of the actual descent groups of these Scottish Protestants and Catholics – that is, no matter whether their ancestors were from Kilmarnock or Kilkenny – they are, *en masse*, phenotypically indistinguishable. They lack even those superficial distinctions in 'the visible morphology – skin colour, hair type, facial features' that once legitimated the now scientifically discredited taxonomical distinction between Caucasian and Negro.[8] It is trivially easy for 'white' Scots to pass between 'Catholic' and 'Protestant' so long as they can obscure their immediate descent.

Even as Welsh's writing exposes and mocks Scottish sectarian racial identity, it also uses the same subject matter to challenge the idea of an intergenerationally transmitted cultural or psychological inheritance – the kind of inheritance, that is to say, which might substitute for the idea of racial descent, or 'blood' in contemporary discourse. Spud in *Porno* (2002), for instance, feels himself to be the object of a racial gaze as he enters Edinburgh's Central Library under the wary eye of a security guard: 'Ah could jist sortay tell thit this boy kens what ah am: tea leaf, junky, schemie, ghetto child, third-generation bog-wog, gyppo' (*P*, 145). It is his Irish racial identity as a 'bog-wog' (that is, as an 'Irish nigger') that Spud believes is somehow visible to the guard, rather than the more obvious marks of his poverty and addiction. Spud, however, also finds solace in this (probably imagined) racial discrimination. Such racism, he believes, can in part explain his troubled life:

> N the first thing ah noticed whin ah goat up here wis this pub acroas the road fae the Central Library called Scruffy Murphy's. [. . .] Lookin at it made ays go aw tense n ashamed inside but. In a just world these cats that run that bar should pay the likes ay me compensation for emotional damage incurred, man. Ah mean, that wis aw ah goat whin ah wis at the school, it wis 'Scruffy Murphy, Scruffy Murphy'. (*P*, 145)

Spud's dream of reparations towards the Irish-Scots (aka the 'Catholics') means that, sympathetic though he may be, he is not so different from those whom Sick Boy in the same novel identifies as the victims of the 'Celtic–Rangers FC thing', 'the best scam ever invented' and 'a licence to fleece morons [. . .] their children and their children's children' (*P*, 333). Spud has, in effect, decided to prolong the categories of Scottish sectarianism. Even though he may not inherit his race, he claims to inherit a history of trauma that has arisen because *others* believe in the existence of an Irish race, and it is this cultural-cum-psychological inheritance that identifies his supposed non-biological descent group – namely, 'Irish-Scottish'.

A similar, latently racial claim to a history of suffering is perceived elsewhere in *Porno*, as Edinburgh University student Nikki speculates on the motivations of a visiting American undergraduate who is a member of her Scottish history class: 'Ross, "the American Scat" in front of us, is probably hard as a rock in his Levi's as he scribbles, filling pages with tales of English cruelty and injustice' (*P*, 26). Nikki's speculations do of course suggest a particular criticism that could be made of Ross's quest for his ancestral roots – that he may well be competing with African-Americans in the acquisition of historical injustice. But a more fundamental question may be posed: can one really inherit the victimhood, or indeed the villainy, of one's ancestors? Or is this just the same poisonous old racial wine in new bottles? Welsh's answer is indicated by the moral disintegration of Samantha in the short story 'Fortune's Always Hiding: *A Corporate Drug Romance*' in *Ecstasy* (1996). Because of her mother's consumption of a licensed pharmaceutical, Tenazadrine, Samantha has been born without arms; from her shoulders sprout two short, flipper-like appendages. Aggrieved by her disability, and by its destructive effect on her parents, Samantha embarks on a programme of revenge, killing those whom she identifies as responsible for marketing the drug. Among her victims is Gunter Emmerich, the German research scientist who facilitated Tenazadrine's franchise in the United Kingdom. Samantha and her fellow Tenazadrine victim, Andreas, take revenge on Emmerich by kidnapping his infant son, Dieter, and then sawing off the boy's arms, killing him in the process. They send the child's severed limbs to Gunter, who receives in the post a package containing 'two small blue, puffy, chubby arms' (*E*, 77–8). The logic implicit in the mutilation and killing of Emmerich's child is clear. Dieter is an appropriate object of retribution because he has 'inherited' his father's sins; what Gunter Emmerich inflicted on Samantha may therefore be justly inflicted on Dieter in return.

Samantha's actions may seem insane, particularly as Welsh's narrative descends into scenes of mounting *grand guignol*. But her attribution of intergenerational culpability is in many ways part of mainstream historical discourse. In the years after Dieter's murder, Samantha reflects that 'the blood of the child' was the 'bitter communion wine' of her 'warped relationship' with Andreas (*E*, 142). The theological allusions are clear: rather than 'remember' the putative freeing of mankind from the burden of hereditary sin, Samantha chooses to perpetuate guilt and retribution across the generations. Her programme of revenge is thus an inverted New Covenant by which the burden of original sin is restored to humankind, or to some small part of it at least. The anamnesis and communion between Andreas and Samantha ('this do in remembrance of me' [Luke 22: 19]) binds them together in a miniature 'community of victims' confronted by a 'community of perpetrators' that persists through descent or 'blood'.

There is a fashionable term for a collective anamnesis of sins and suffering that binds together a descent community: the term is 'memory'. Had Dieter Emmerich lived to adulthood and learned something of his father's actions (whether by his father's testimony, or the testimony of others, or from documentary sources), what he would have acquired – in contemporary jargon – would not be historical knowledge, but collective 'memory'. We live, as Kerwin Lee Klein explains, in a 'new age in which archives remember and statues forget':

> Freed from the constraints of individual psychic states, memory becomes a subject in its own right, free to range back and forth across time, and even the most rigorous scholar is free to speak of the memory of events that happened hundreds of years distant or to speak of the memory of an ethnic, religious, or racial group.[9]

In Dominick LaCapra's psychoanalytic historiography, for instance, history is entirely reconceived as a derivative form of memory, particularly of traumatic memory. It is so-called 'secondary memory' that 'the historian attempts to impart to others who have not themselves lived through the experience or events in question. This procedure may require a muted or diminished transmission of the traumatic nature of the event but not a full reliving or acting out of it.' [10] Furthermore, although LaCapra insists that there is no such thing, for instance, as a 'German guilt that is visited on each and every German', his theory also maintains that there can be an intergenerational, psychoanalytically explicable transmission of guilt as well as trauma: 'Those born later at times may unjustifiably feel guilty about the past or bear within themselves an unresolved, phantomlike residue of the past acquired through unconscious, transferential processes of identification with loved ones and their encrypted experiences.' [11] Psychoanalytic mechanisms substitute for 'blood': both victimhood (as 'trauma') and guilt may be passed down the generations, constituting a supposed form of historical 'memory'.

As Welsh's representation of Samantha suggests, his work is highly sceptical of transpersonal historical memory and of its supposed role in the delineation of identities. The logic of memory-based communities of vicariously traumatised victims and secondarily guilty perpetrators is tested ruthlessly in *Filth* (1998), where it is applied to the novel's psychotic protagonist, Detective Sergeant Bruce Robertson. As well as believing himself to be interrogated by the voice of a tapeworm that inhabits his innards, Bruce also lives out a part-time cross-dressed existence in which he holds to the delusion that he is his own estranged wife, Carole. Bruce's psychology is a means by which Welsh explores, extrapolates and explodes the memory which supposedly assigns our intergenerational identities. Towards the end of *Filth*, Bruce's inner dialogue with his tapeworm begins to reveal the history of his family life and his troubled upbringing. Bruce's biological father is a rapist who conceived Bruce through one of his random sexual assaults. Rather than terminate her pregnancy, Bruce's mother heeded the advice of her Catholic priest and reared Bruce under the shaky pretence that he was the offspring of her own husband.

Bruce's adoptive father, and the wider community, though, were aware of Bruce's descent and far from convinced of the primacy of nurture over nature. In one significant childhood incident Bruce was forced by his adoptive father to eat coal: 'Ah've been fuckin diggin this shite aw day for you! Eat! But you still couldn't eat the food. Then he'd pick up a lump of coal and make you eat it. – Eat, he'd say' (*F*, 292). The tapeworm continues its recollections on Bruce's behalf: 'He started doing the things to you. With the coal. Making you taste the coal, taste the filth. You could understand none of it. What had you done? Why was he doing this? What had you done to deserve this?' (*F*, 315). The symbolism of the incident is clear. By forcing Bruce to ingest the coal, Ian Robertson is trying to make him manifest externally the hereditary 'filth' that he believes is invisible, hidden in Bruce's 'blood'. This blackness later emerges (symbolically) in Bruce's subconsciously intentional role in the death of his younger brother, who is buried by an avalanche of coal as they are raiding a coal bing: 'It seems to fill your lungs, that thick, black dust, but you scream STEVIE! The night watchman comes as you emerge blackened from that pile of coal' (*F*, 354). Still later in Bruce's alienated and guilty life, he understands this same inner darkness as the explanation for his ultimate filthiness, his adoption of the black uniform of the police during the British miners' strike of 1984–5.

Although Ian Robertson's mistreatment of his adoptive son is rationalised by a belief in heredity, it is of course a covert attempt to punish Bruce for the sins of his rapist father, 'The Beast'. What is really at issue is the community's demand that Bruce recognise his intergenerational memory or guilt as the child of a perpetrator. When Ian Robertson declares to his adoptive son, 'You're filth!' (*F*, 355), he is ultimately making the same kind of intergenerational ascription of guilt as that made by Samantha in 'Fortune's Always Hiding'. The community's prophecy eventually becomes self-fulfilling: by ostracising and reviling Bruce as the son of a 'beast', they create, through various psychological mechanisms, precisely the kind of person that they believe Bruce already to be. Indeed, there are further absurdities in 'memory' as it appears in *Filth*. Whether Bruce's community thinks of him as inheriting the biological essence of a rapist, or – with less self-deception, if no less injustice – as inheriting the guilt of his biological father's rape, it is important to note that in either case the community entirely neglects Bruce's descent from his mother. Bruce is somehow only related to 'The Beast', as if the latter's sperm had implanted a homunculus, a beast-in-miniature, in his mother's womb. This neglected matrilineal descent is vitally significant, for it conceals a paradox that results from consistent application of the logic of 'memory'. The paradox is this: Bruce should strictly speaking inherit both his father's guilt and his mother's victimhood (or 'trauma'). As a child conceived through rape, 'his' history is at once a history of paternal rapacity and maternal violation; he is a member of both a 'community of perpetrators' and a 'community of victims'.

Bruce's transgendered dissociative personality, his double-life as 'Bruce' and 'Carole', may thus be even more significant than it first appears. In terms of the novel's psychological realism, this psychopathology may be regarded as Bruce conjuring up an imaginary other to substitute for the real Carole. However, in broader symbolic terms, Bruce's feminine identity may be regarded as a claim to his maternal victimhood. This is why, in these latter terms, Bruce as 'Carole' allows himself to be abused and assaulted: 'It's strange, but we never thought of reacting: resisting or running off, although we had time to do both. This seems the right way' (*F*, 342). Acquiescence in this sexual assault also allows Bruce as 'Carole' to have revenge on a male assailant and thus to achieve displaced retribution for his mother's suffering: as he is sexually assaulted by 'Ghostie' Gorman, Bruce manages to bite off his attacker's tongue and then push him through a window to his death. *Filth* therefore partly deploys the psychology of dissociative personality in order to stage a solution to the paradox of Bruce's moral inheritance. This solution is of course sarcastic: only a madman can properly carry through the logic of 'memory' carried in Bruce's 'blood'. Historical memory leads almost inevitably to ethical absurdity. The same individual can lay claim to multiple 'memories' as victim or perpetrator, sometimes even (as in Bruce's case) with regard to the same crime. With a little work, practically anyone can conjure up some morally conflicting memories. As Walter Benn Michaels remarks with regard to US identity politics:

> It isn't just African Americans and Jews who are the descendants of injustice. What about Native Americans? What about Appalachian coal miners and poor white sharecroppers? Once you start looking for past injustice, you don't have a hard time finding it. And, by the same token, you may well find it where you don't really feel you need it.[12]

The problem of the ubiquity of memories of victimhood (particularly economic victimhood) is tackled by Welsh in *Marabou Stork Nightmares*. Roy Strang, the protagonist, moves as a child to South Africa, where he has expatriate Scottish relatives, but is forced by events to return to Edinburgh. The following provocative (and much criticised) reflections ensue:

> Edinburgh to me represented serfdom. I realised that it was exactly the same situation as Johannesburg; the only difference was that the Kaffirs were white and called schemies or draftpaks. Back in Edinburgh, we would be Kaffirs; condemned to live out our lives in townships like Muirhouse or So-Wester-Hailes-To or Niddrie, self-contained camps with fuck all in them, miles fae the toon. (*MSN*, 80)

Strang's obviously contentious claim that 'schemies' are in the same position as 'Kaffirs' is undermined by the novel's story-line, which eventually reveals that he is guilty of the rape of a female acquaintance. Although Strang's adult sexual violence may perhaps be mitigated by his childhood sexual abuse at the hands of his South African uncle, his retrospective declaration of solidarity with the racially oppressed is far less convincing. It seems little more than a conscience-salving claim that he is as much a victim as the woman he has raped. If the acme of 'white maleness' in Scotland is to be working-class, and the working class live under *de facto* apartheid, then, Strang seems to be saying, 'white maleness' is really akin to 'black maleness' and is at least partly an identity of the oppressed. Carole Jones argues that Strang's claim to be in effect a 'black male' is therefore a way of accruing the socio-political capital that is so vital to contemporary identity politics: as a male, Strang may be identified as an aggressor, but as a 'black', he is the victim of injustice. Jones regards Strang's unreliable claim 'to kinship in oppression' as 'an illustration, an alert even, of the appropriation of victimhood as one trend in contemporary culture [. . .] that puts the white man back at the centre of the discourses of power as a victim'.[13]

Although Jones's argument is powerful, it does not quite capture the ultimate target of Welsh's criticism of identity politics. Part of the inspiration for Jones's article is Sally Robinson's *Marked Men: White Masculinity in Crisis* (2000), according to which it is 'whiteness' and 'masculinity' that are in crisis: 'For white masculinity to negotiate its position within the field of identity politics, white men must claim a symbolic disenfranchisement, must compete with various others for cultural authority bestowed upon the authentically disempowered, the visibly wounded.' [14] It may indeed be tempting to think of Strang's musings on Scotland's apartheid as a way of resignifying his 'white masculinity' in order to appropriate the position of victim rather than perpetrator. But if we understand Strang as a perpetrator by virtue of his identity, then we have misunderstood *Marabou Stork Nightmares*. Strang is not guilty of rape by virtue of his membership of, as it were, the 'male community'. He is guilty of rape because he is in fact a rapist. Nor is Strang guilty of racial oppression by virtue of his 'whiteness'. Rather, he has very directly benefited from the South African regime under which he and his family lived. Strang's guilt is his own, rather than that supposedly attributable to his identity group. He is morally suspect because he is seeking to deny his individual guilt as a rapist and to present his working-class origins as a moral counterweight to the privileged status he enjoyed in South Africa.

The crucial point about Strang's hypocrisy is not, I think, that he attempts to resignify white masculinity via a racial analogy grounded in his working-class identity. Rather, it is his assumption that he actually has a working-class 'identity'. In Strang's mind, socio-economic class is reconfigured as an intergenerational community of victimhood and trauma – class is in effect racialised. Apartheid politics amalgamated race and class: members of the 'black' race did the dirty, menial, poorly paid jobs. Strang's fantasy is that this exceptional situation is the norm, that being 'working-class' is essentially the same as claiming a 'racial' identity, and that working-class 'identity' can be maintained through individual and collective memory of working-class experience. So, although Strang works as an IT specialist for a finance company, he still perceives himself as essentially working-class and hence distinct from his colleagues, who are 'drab, middle-class twats'. Such individuals 'are the cunts we should be hurtin, no the boys wi knock fuck oot ay at the fitba, no the birds wi fuck aboot, no oor ain Ma n Dad, oor ain brothers n sisters, oor ain neighboors, oor ain mates. These cunts' (*MSN*, 200–1). This is another of Strang's unreliable perceptions. As a well-paid white-collar worker, he is precisely one of the 'cunts' whom he claims to despise. The discrepancy between Strang's objective class position and his cultural performance indicates that his accent and actions work in the same way as the football colours displayed elsewhere in Welsh's writing by 'Catholics' and 'Protestants'. Strang reflects that he is 'leading a compartmentalised life': at 'the weekends it was clubs and fitba with the boys', while 'at work I was getting on alright, doing well in my day release in computer studies at Napier College' (*MSN*, 136). Just as football colours supposedly indicate the ethnic origins of their wearers, so Strang's accent, dialect and weekend leisure activities are a putative expression and authentication of his working-class experience and ancestry. According to this quasi-racial mythology, Strang's weekday life, his economic role, is that of a 'working-class' male passing as 'middle-class'.

Strang is of course mistaken in his belief that he is a member of the working class even while doing the most middle-class of jobs. As Michaels explains, class identities are not inherited, nor do they remain constant in the individual: 'The *garçon de café* who saves his tips and buys the café is not a member of the proletariat passing as a member of the petit bourgeoisie – he *is* petit bourgeois.' Class identities are, as Michaels puts it, wholly performative: 'The identity that is identical to action is not really an identity – it's just the name of the action: worker, capitalist.' [15] It is what one does in a particular economic system that determines one's class position, not what one's ancestors did, not what one once did, nor even the cultural and linguistic systems that one habitually employs. What the character of Roy Strang exposes is the effort to use the concept of 'memory' to turn social class into collective, descent-based 'identity'.

There is, then, something quite radical that can be gleaned from Welsh's interrogation of contemporary identity politics. His writing traces sceptically the disavowed racial or genealogical essentialism, the persistence of 'blood', in such contemporary identity discourses as Scottish sectarianism, the supposed historical memory of guilt and trauma, and the curious transformation of economic class into cultural identity. As indicated at the beginning of this chapter, there is a temptation to think of Welsh's writing as a declaration and defence of working-class identity. Yet, in fact, his work treats the categories of identity with scepticism, lest they prove simply a way of 'visiting the iniquity of the fathers upon the children, and upon the children's children' (Exodus 34:7). In this respect, Samantha's blood feud in 'Fortune's Always Hiding' is perhaps the kernel of Welsh's ideas on identity. Furthermore, when the flawed and covertly racial categories of collective 'memory', 'guilt' and 'trauma' encounter the discourse of socio-economic class in Welsh's writing, then their absurdity multiplies. In the delusions of a neoliberal bourgeois subject such as Roy Strang, to be working-class is to speak with a 'working-class voice' acquired through descent or upbringing, rather than to perform a particular (disadvantaged and exploited) role in a capitalist economic system. If Scottish literary criticism were to overlook Welsh's satire on this resignification of class, then it would fall into the same trap as much contemporary US literary studies:

> The minute you start reading literature by poor people in the same way that you read ethnic literatures, you've arrived in something like inequality heaven. Where you used to just distract yourself from economic difference by focusing on cultural difference, now you can celebrate economic difference by pretending that it *is* cultural difference.[16]

The fallacious conclusion follows, as Michaels clearly implies, that the right thing to do is to recognise, respect and celebrate economic difference (or 'poverty', as it was once quaintly known) – a course of action that ultimately works only to perpetuate inequality. For precisely this reason, Scottish literary criticism must refuse the neoliberal invitation to regard Welsh's work as a writing that celebrates the difference of the working class.

CHAPTER NINE

Welsh and Edinburgh

Peter Clandfield and Christian Lloyd

The maps and guides dispensed by the Edinburgh Tourist Information Centre on Princes Street touch on remarkably few of the sites where Irvine Welsh's fiction is located, despite his work's huge commercial success and considerable role in attracting visitors to the city. The streets of Leith, the main setting of *Trainspotting* and *Porno*, are not covered by maps provided in freebies such as PRM Marketing's *Edinburgh Inspiring Capital: City Centre Pocket Map*, on which an arrow signposting the 'Way to the Royal Yacht Britannia' obscures Leith Walk in the very corner of the sheet. Meanwhile, Landmark's *Welcome to Edinburgh: Free Guide with Detailed City Maps* offers the unexpected suggestion 'Visit Leith, Edinburgh's port, for great seafood', adding that 'within easy reach of the city centre are larger shopping malls such as Ocean Terminal in Leith'.[1] However, characterising Leith as a centre of royalism, gastronomy and consumerism obscures the port's deeper history. An advert for the *Britannia* in *Welcome to Edinburgh* pictures middle-aged tourists on the yacht enjoying their audio-guides – a staged photograph which, like others in the advert, is taken facing the water so nothing of Leith itself can be seen. In such productions, much of Welsh's Edinburgh remains literally and figuratively off the map.

Countering such longstanding biases, in 1993 Welsh himself, together with Kevin Williamson, published *A Visitor's Guide to Edinburgh*. Aimed ostensibly at visitors to the Edinburgh Festival, this short pamphlet, with predictable cover illustration of Greyfriars Bobby, purports to offer 'a compact little guide book' detailing sites of interest 'to be gleaned from Edinburgh if one steps out of the centre and into [. . .] wonderful places such as Leith, Warriston and Crewe Toll'. On a closer look, though, *A Visitor's Guide to Edinburgh* is anything but an extension of the usual tourist guides: it delivers a survey of non-tourist Edinburgh, aimed at heavy drinkers, massage parlour frequenters and 'normal partakers of the harmless but illegal drug ecstasy'. The guide covers these street cultures ironically in the familiar flat idiom and staged photographs of the guidebook, while mocking tourist board attempts to refigure Edinburgh as an 'inspiring [cultural] capital' for the middle-class visitor. The disjuncture between subject matter and style peaks with the *Guide*'s take on Leith's Newkirkgate shopping centre, in reality a parade of tatty chain stores, but here, absurdly, 'a place to sample that unique Parisian Left Bank atmosphere' while 'relaxing with a coffee and perhaps a tasty snack of chips and ketchup'.[2] A second look at the blurry cover image shows that Greyfriars Bobby has a hypodermic needle in his foreleg: the legend of the dog's futile wait for its dead owner becomes a gruesome joke about waiting for the man.

The largest irony of *A Visitor's Guide to Edinburgh* is that having thus mocked the genre of the guidebook, Welsh will go on in his novels, screenplays and short stories to fulfil its prefatory promise to concentrate on 'Real people. Doing real things. Among real buildings' – though this is not to suggest that he necessarily adheres to a mode of realism or aspires to monologic authority. The strategy adopted in this chapter is to consider Welsh's fictions as supplementary guides to Edinburgh, which both point to and partly make up for blind spots in mainstream cultural and spatial representations of the city. It relies implicitly on Jacques Derrida's notion of the supplement in order to characterise the way Welsh's fictions explore the interdependence of Edinburgh's different quarters by upsetting binary oppositions between celebrated places and areas supposedly insignificant or toxic.[3] One of Edinburgh's noted attractions is its New Town, whose architectural neatness is widely cited as manifesting eighteenth-century principles of rationality and order. Without rejecting all possibilities for genuine progress, the supplementary approach of Welsh's work troubles the aspiration to neat completeness associated with both the New Town and more recent improvement schemes in Edinburgh, such as the modernist public housing of early postwar decades and the redevelopment of many areas throughout the 1990s and 2000s. Most specifically, the chapter investigates the function of Leith in Welsh's fiction as a dangerous supplement, a territory that unsettles and encroaches on the assumed integrity and self-sufficiency of tourist-friendly, governmentally groomed Edinburgh as both signifier and signified of Scottish culture.

Trainspotting's close attention to the geographies and histories of Leith, and to links between class and space in Edinburgh, was obscured initially by the novel's provocatively unapologetic treatment of hard drug use and aggressively unconventional style and structure. Yet as Tim Bell demonstrates in his detailed tours of its many specific locations, the novel's vignettes of its characters' chaotic lives are linked by specific references to their urban environments.[4] The novel's opening immediately connects urban geography and social hierarchy. Mark Renton and Simon 'Sick Boy' Williamson, suffering from heroin withdrawal, attempt to get to a dealer but find no taxis in Leith because, in Sick Boy's words, they are all 'up cruising fat, rich festival cunts' (*T*, 4). According to Renton, Sick Boy speaks 'deliriously and breathlessly'

(*T*, 5), which underlines that his perception is hardly objective, but the incident still suggests how the tourist presence in Edinburgh helps to isolate Welsh's characters in Leith, and the passage inaugurates a running commentary in Welsh's fiction on the irritations of the tourist industry for locals.[5] Indeed, the shortage of transportation is especially ironic since Leith, as Edinburgh's port, has historically provided transport connections essential to the city's prosperity. Robert Morace points out that Welsh's Edinburgh, in *Trainspotting* particularly, is distinctively 'traversed on foot and by bus and taxi rather than [. . .] private car'.[6] Reliance on slow transportation not only underlines the characters' marginal status, but also allows, in *Trainspotting* and in Welsh's other fictions, time for observation on the details of urban environments.

Trainspotting targets Edinburgh's tourist colonisation using both characters' voices, as in Sick Boy's rant, and third-person narration, which notes, for example, the pretentious décor of a Royal Mile pub which 'aim[s] at an American theme-bar effect, but not too accurately' (*T*, 62). Such third-person passages are important not only as comments on cultural inauthenticity infiltrating even richly historic areas, but also because they take the novel's critique of the city's development beyond the views of individual characters. A particularly memorable statement comes from Renton when he is coerced by Frank Begbie into visiting a much-marketed area of the New Town: 'Only arseholes, wankers and tourists set fit in Rose Street' (*T*, 76). Adapting this passage into the title for a recent article, Lewis MacLeod suggests that *Trainspotting* 'posits a categorical distinction between Leith and Edinburgh as central to almost every character's sense of self'.[7] The text indeed associates Edinburgh with forces of consumer capitalism and Leith with residual resistance to these forces; arguably, though, its view of the city is more complex than a simple binary opposition of Leith and Edinburgh would allow. Welsh's fictions do not simply set Leith and its people against overweening forces associated with Edinburgh's privilege and power; rather, they explore and sometimes connect many peripheral and neglected places in and around Edinburgh, implying possibilities for a more equitable future. Nor do Welsh's texts set up any one character, or type of character, as a reliable guide to the city. As Aaron Kelly notes, Welsh's Bakhtinian rendering of multiple voices – notably including Edinburgh working-class voices – challenges the power of any 'singular authoritative discourse to fix itself in language'.[8] Reckoning with Welsh's view of the city thus involves comparing and holding in tension multiple perspectives.

In one of the more unusual critical accounts of *Trainspotting*, Dominic Head argues that despite the novel's challenge to Enlightenment assumptions, key passages, where even dysfunctional characters evince moral concern and mutual understanding, create 'a disguised lament for a simpler and more human world [based upon] the stereotypical home and hearth values of the pre-war working classes'.[9] Head's assessment points to the novel's attention to home places both as psychological factors in characters' lives and as subjects of social debate. The early section 'Growing up in Public' has Nina, Renton's teenage Goth cousin, attending the wake of her Uncle Andy. Initially disdainful of her relatives' observance of the rituals of the occasion, she eventually finds herself crying cathartically in the arms of her Aunt Cathy, Renton's mother, and experiencing 'memories of Andy and Alice, and the happiness and love that once lived here, in the home of her auntie and uncle' (*T*, 40). The funeral of HIV casualty Matty Connell occasions another passage about homes and families: Matty's daughter, Wee Lisa, thinks about her father: 'It would be good to go to heaven, to play with him, like they used to when she was really wee. He'd be well again in heaven. Heaven would be different from Wester Hailes' (*T*, 295). Taken out of context, such passages could seem sentimental, but the pointed reference to Wester Hailes hints at the shortcomings of this suburban housing scheme and at the critique of such failed utopias that Welsh will develop more forcefully in later works. Lisa's thoughts, like Nina's burst of nostalgia, also indicate Welsh's concern not just with extreme experiences of addiction, but with lives of ordinary people affected by underlying social dysfunctions. Such passages where peripheral characters become temporarily central show how, as Morace has written, 'minor characters [. . .] weave their way through the novel to create a sense of local community'.[10]

Despite Renton's rejection of ambitions and loyalties in some of the text's best-known passages, other moments convey his and his family's persistent concern with the ordinary difficulties and possibilities of living in Edinburgh. Renton's surname punningly marks his ambivalence about staying in Leith, Edinburgh and Scotland. In 'House Arrest', having nearly died from an overdose, Renton finds himself back in the bedroom of his youth. He feels imprisoned by his parents' determination to oversee his rehabilitation, and the section features some of his harshest words on Leith and on Scotland as 'a place ay dispossessed white trash in a country fill ay dispossessed white trash'. Yet just prior to this he reflects sympathetically on his mother's experiences with his disabled brother and judgemental neighbours who 'think thit her n ma faither used Davie's profound handicap tae git oot ay the Fort n git this nice Housing Association flat by the river' (*T*, 190). As Bell points out during his tour, the 'Fort' is Fort House, part of one of Leith's modernist housing schemes. The Fort scheme's two large tower blocks were demolished in 1997, and Fort House itself is reportedly scheduled for the same fate. Renton's thoughts imply the shortcomings of the Fort itself to be well known, but also acknowledge that Leith is not wholly a wasteland. Later, ill-at-ease with his parents in the Leith Dockers' Club, Renton is nevertheless moved by this spell of proximity to acknowledge his feelings for them, albeit in (as

Bell points out) characteristically perverse terms: 'Ah love the fuck oot ay the bastards, if the truth be telt' (*T*, 203). Moreover, it is through the elder Rentons that *Trainspotting* conveys detailed information about the drug problem in Edinburgh, as a semi-delirious Renton watches a TV game show while overhearing his father relaying news reports to his mother: 'Said here that Scotland's goat eight per cent o the UK population but sixteen per cent o the UK HIV cases . . . *What's the scores, Miss Ford?* . . . Embra's goat eight per cent o the Scottish population but ower sixty per cent o the Scottish HIV infection, by far the highest rate in Britain [. . .] they say thit they discovered this blood-testin punters in Muirhoose fir summit else' (*T*, 193). The statistics add to Renton's immediate stress, but also register a daunting situation in Muirhouse (the large housing scheme in Edinburgh's northern suburbs where Welsh himself grew up after his family's move from Leith) and in the city at large. Renton senior's information about the spread of HIV corresponds closely to accounts such as John Sturrock's 1988 *Granta* photo-essay. Sturrock makes a point of attending to the everyday home lives, as well as the addictions, of the people he depicts, but also expresses concern that 'we have no way of receiving these pictures'[11] without resorting to simplistic judgements. *Trainspotting*'s own allusions to the problems of Muirhouse do not explicitly venture solutions. However, by detailing 'the scale o the problem' through the idiomatic voice of Renton's father (Glaswegian though he is originally) rather than through journalistic, medical, sociological or criminological discourse, Welsh implies that remediation of these problems is within the purview not only of experts but also of ordinary people.

Similarly, Renton's post-heroin resolution to 'git oot ay Leith, oot ay Scotland. For good' (*T*, 201) should not be read as the novel writing off Edinburgh's future. A better indication of Welsh's approach to the city can be found in Renton's reflection that 'they say you have to live in a place to know it, but you have to come fresh tae it tae really see it' (*T*, 228). Though this is a cliché, it also points to the pattern of departure and return that has been followed by many of Welsh's characters as well as by Welsh himself, and that is key to Welsh's ability to bridge outsiders' and insiders' perspectives on the city. Renton expresses his and Spud's disdain for Princes Street as 'deadened by tourists and shoppers, the twin curses ay modern capitalism', yet then notes that 'when ye come back oot ay Waverley Station eftir bein away fir a bit, ye think: Hi, this isnae bad' (*T*, 228). And in his descriptions of late 1980s London, Renton's outsider's approach reflects both a perverse pride in his home city and a prescient view of the pitfalls of property: 'Ah've known scheme junkies in Edinburgh wi a healthier asset-tae-debt ratio thin some two-waged, heavily-mortgaged couples doon here' (*T*, 230). Here, what seems to be Renton's particular distaste for Edinburgh widens into general contempt for ill-conceived urban development.

'Home', *Trainspotting*'s penultimate section, centres on the episode 'Trainspotting at Leith Central Station', which reiterates at once Renton's strange sense of belonging to Edinburgh's margins and his impulse to abandon the city. Walking from Waverley into Leith, he reflects, 'perversely, ah feel safer the further doon ah git. It's Leith. Ah suppose that means hame' (*T*, 306). Renton bumps into Begbie, validating his thoughts about both the familiarity and the incipient violence of the place. After the inevitable pub session, they 'go fir a pish in the auld Central Station at the Fit ay the Walk'. Renton, thinking of the long-disused building's impending demolition, reminds Begbie of its better days, but Begbie responds: 'If it still hud fuckin trains, ah'd be oan one oot ay this fuckin dive' (*T*, 308–9). Bell notes that the station's condition parallels Renton's and Begbie's bleak prospects, and that Begbie's estranged father, who suddenly appears out of nowhere, might be 'the ghost of a generation of unemployed Leith men';[12] the scene thus underscores how long-standing are the area's problems. Kelly notes that 'the characters have no *station*' in a social sense either, 'since the former working-class identity which structured Leith and North Edinburgh has collapsed',[13] the past offers no guidance for the present, and unproductive activities like trainspotting or drug-taking seem fitting. Meanwhile, the more literal point that trainspotting is especially futile at Leith Central because 'there aren't any trains'[14] takes up the novel's opening attention to the logistics of Edinburgh's social and geographical inequities. This attention is one means by which Welsh's fiction, in Kelly's apt terms, works 'to try to reconvene a sense of [. . .] social reality' in Edinburgh and the linked larger world.[15]

A sense of entrapment in Leith, exacerbated by the presence of the likes of Begbie, spurs Renton's apparently final decision to detach himself. But the 'Home' section also finds Renton voicing informed opinions about causes of Edinburgh's inequities. Noting the bad state of council housing in West Granton, just east of Muirhouse, where his friend Tommy is living with HIV in 'one ay the varicose-vein flats, called so because ay the plastered cracks all over its facing', he alludes to the Thatcher regime's 'Right to Buy' legislation: 'It's no really the council's fault; the Government made them sell off all the good hooses.' He continues: 'There's nae votes for the Government doon here, so why bother daein anything fir people whae urnae gaunnae support ye? Morally, it's another thing. What's morality goat tae dae with politics, but? It's aw aboot poppy' (T, 315).[16] These reflections ironise Renton's own subsequent sellout of his friends in a London deal which is 'aboot poppy' – both money and opiates. Neither of the views of Edinburgh most explicitly foregrounded in *Trainspotting* – tourist attraction or toxic place to flee – is presented as adequate. Welsh's fictions repeatedly set up such oppositions between one oversimplified view of Edinburgh and another, and thus imply the need – and the responsibility for readers – to find sustainable positions in the spaces between such polarities. The strategic juxtaposition of skewed views of Edinburgh is particularly striking in the relation between Welsh's next two novels, *Marabou Stork Nightmares* (1995) and *Filth* (1998).

Having grown up in Muirhouse, Roy Strang, the narrator of *Marabou Stork Nightmares*, calls himself a 'schemie'. Strang concisely evokes the failure of the modernist ideals behind Muirhouse: 'It was a systems built, 1960s maisonette block of flats, five storeys high, with long landings which were jokingly referred to as "streets in the sky" but which had no shops or pubs or churches or post offices on them' (*MSN*, 19).[17] This ill-engineered environment, Strang implies, motivates his violent self-assertion in the wider world and influences his excesses as a football 'casual' and a vicious abuser of women. By contrast, for Detective Sergeant Bruce Robertson, the narrator of *Filth*, Edinburgh proper is territory to be protected from subhuman schemies rightly relegated to peripheral areas: 'Zero tolerance of crime in the city centre; total laissez-faire in the schemie hinterlands' (*F*, 273). Driving past Salisbury Crags, Robertson declares: 'This city of ours is truly beautiful and we like this part where there is not a scheme in sight. Why could we not simply move all the scum to the middle of nowhere, like Glasgow [. . .]? Come to think of it, that's exactly what we did do, when we built the schemes' (*F*, 327).

Despite their opposed social roles, Strang and Robertson resort to the same trope. Recalling his family's brief emigration to apartheid South Africa, Strang parallels the latter's racial segregation with his home city's geographical division: 'Back in Edinburgh, we would be kaffirs; condemned to live out our lives in townships like Muirhouse or So-Wester-Hailes-To or Niddrie' (*MSN*, 80). Less subtly still, in the climactic scene of *Filth*, Robertson screams: 'WE HATE NIGGERS! ESPECIALLY THE WHITE ONES THEY CALL SCHEMIES' (*F*, 350). As the novel's remaining pages reveal, Robertson's outburst is a confession: his pathological behaviour has driven away his wife, Carole, and her relationship with a black man has impelled him to murder another black man, whose death he has (supposedly) been investigating. Roy Strang comes to diagnose his violence as an expression of self-hatred, while Robertson's lethal contempt for schemies and other Others is equally revealed to express self-loathing. The fact that these two very distinct characters use the same trope for Edinburgh's schemes suggests that Welsh might be endorsing the notion that the city is indeed divided by class segregation amounting to apartheid. However, by drawing attention to the uneven benefits of Edinburgh's development and redevelopment schemes, both novels implicitly warn against such simplistic views of the resulting injustices. Notably, therefore, in *Glue* (2001) and *Porno* (2002), the oppositions between competing views of Edinburgh are represented as far less extreme.

'Windows '70', the opening chapter of the first of *Glue*'s four main sections, expands Welsh's exploration of living spaces in Edinburgh by addressing the prospect of progress the city's housing schemes represented in their heyday between roughly 1960 and 1970. Davie Galloway, looking out from his family's new flat, feels 'like a newly crowned emperor surveying his fiefdom', suggesting that the place represents a reinvention of the city itself: 'Bright, clean, airy and warm, that was what was needed. He remembered the chilly, dark tenement in Gorgie; covered with soot and grime for generations when the city had earned its "Auld Reekie" nickname' (G, 3). Two other men, Duncan Ewart and Wullie Birrell, share Davie's initial enthusiasm for the scheme's amenities, but when their extra expense hits home, the moment stands metonymically for how quickly the new buildings will lose promise: 'As winter set in and the first bills came through the post, the central-heating systems in the scheme clicked off; synchronized to such a degree it was almost like they were operated by one master switch' (G, 27). Each of the three subsequent main sections, spaced roughly at ten-year intervals, begins with a 'Windows' chapter reiterating the opening emphasis on housing conditions as indicators of the state of the city. Following a period in prison Davie Galloway re-emerges in 'Windows '00' as a security officer in a large housing scheme, noting the latter's ironic parallels with prison as well as its disorder, with surveillance cameras disused and vandalised. Alongside 'Windows '70' the chapter underlines the gap between the design and the reality of the schemes, their juxtaposition highlighting the poignancy of their unfulfilled promise.[18]

Welsh's next novel, *Porno*, continues to use narrative structures to reinforce his commentary on urban environments. Redeveloping the diffuse narrative of *Trainspotting* into something more schematic, *Porno* is built around two contrasting Leith projects: Sick Boy's bid to reinvent himself as an urban entrepreneur and Spud's effort to write and publish a history of the place. The novel's opening echoes that of *Trainspotting*, with Sick Boy laboriously on the move. This time, though, he is in London, surveying his shabby new Hackney flat, and it is his friend Croxy doing the actual heavy lifting and 'sweating from exertion rather than from drug abuse' (*P*, 3). This repetition-with-a-difference sets up Sick Boy's aggressively entrepreneurial return to Leith as revenge for the abjection of his earlier experiences there. Significantly, he refers to his practice of mailing gay pornography anonymously to the imprisoned Begbie as 'part of my little war against my home city' (*P*, 24). More subtly suggestive is another early key passage where Sick Boy, restive in 'this bedsit that estate agents love to call a studio flat', reflects: 'That's the English for you: ridiculously pompous to the last. Who else would be grandiosely deluded enough to call a scheme an estate? I'm huntin, fishin, shootin Simon David Williamson from Leith's Banana Flats Estate' (*P*, 33). The disdain for English pretension implies a warped Scottish nationalism and residual Leith pride, and the remark is, for Sick Boy, uncharacteristically straightforward, acknowledging his youthful home – the early 1960s Leith flat block officially known as Cables Wynd House – by the local nickname its curved shape inspired. Sick Boy's debunking of the term 'estate' evokes the frequent gap between aim and reality in modernist public housing.[19] In a different vein of irony, though, the passage also introduces the landlordly posture that Sick Boy will shortly strike upon returning to Leith and launching his own scheme to rebrand his Aunt Paula's traditional pub, the Port Sunshine, as an upscale establishment. This project meshes with his parallel scheme to become a player in the porn industry: 'Leith's been a grand old lady far too long [. . .] I want to reinvent her as a sexy, hot young bitch and pimp that dirty wee hoor oot for aw she's fuckin worth' (*P*, 60–1). Indicating the dubious ethics of gentrification, such schemes do pay off, at least in the short run. Counterpointing them in the novel, however, is Spud's very different take on the reinvention of Leith.

Spud's immersion in Leith both inspires his project and impedes its success. He cannot get away from Leith's addictive temptations, and particularly from the malevolent presence of Begbie. Interrupting Spud's revision of his research notes, Begbie responds with belligerent incomprehension to Spud's efforts to articulate his critique of the 'embourgeoisement' of working-class districts:

> Ah but, very soon, Franco, auld Leith will be gone. Look at Tollcross, man, it's a finance centre now. Look at the South Side: a student village. Stockbridge's been yuppiesville for donks, auld Stockeree. Us and Gorgie-Dalry'll soon be the only places left in the inner city for working-class cats, man [. . .]
>
> Ah'm no fuckin workin class, eh says pointin at ehsel, – ah'm a fuckin businessman, eh goes, raisin ehs voice. (*P*, 261)

Passages like this one, whose account of the city's redevelopment elaborates earlier allusions in *Filth* and *Glue* (*F*, 273; *G*, 465), show that Spud hopes to complicate official narratives of progress. Caroline Gottschalk-Druschke points out that Welsh's own project parallels Spud's, arguing convincingly that *Porno* is Welsh's 'own oppositional history of Leith'.[20] Yet the novel does not actually incorporate sections from Spud's manuscript, which seems odd given Welsh's usual readiness to render a wide range of idioms and discourses. This omission leaves open the possibility that Spud's work does somewhat resemble the 'badly written celebration of yob culture' (*P*, 380) Welsh's fictional publisher Alan Johnson-Hogg dismisses it as, even though Spud is easily the most sympathetic main character in both *Trainspotting* and *Porno*, while Johnson-Hogg's ethical unreliability is indicated by the fact that his firm's directors include Conrad Donaldson QC, Roy Strang's ruthless lawyer in *Marabou Stork Nightmares* (*MSN*, 208–12). Gottschalk-Druschke ascribes Spud's failure to his lack of rhetorical skills, but the most crucial difference between character and author is certainly that, unlike Spud, Welsh possesses the capacity to distance himself from his material and to consider a range of perspectives upon it.

The linked mobility and ambivalence that inform Welsh's views of Edinburgh surface most evocatively in Paul McGuigan's under-appreciated film version of *The Acid House* (1998), which imaginatively documents the state of particular parts of Edinburgh at a particular time, achieving a local specificity that Danny Boyle's *Trainspotting* notably does not.[21] Welsh plays the put-upon parkie in the football sequence which opens 'The Granton Star Cause', the first of the three stories the film adapts from Welsh's 1994 collection. The cameo role locates Welsh within the film's version of Edinburgh and also attests that the film's stories are grounded in Welsh's own experience. Shot on location, the film version of 'Granton Star' is Welsh's tribute to Muirhouse, offering a specific figure for the flexibility of Welsh's relation to Edinburgh. In the film hapless Boab Coyle meets a jaded God who mocks him for his failures and gleefully turns him into a fly. Boab's Kafkaesque metamorphosis literalises the supposed insignificance of schemies. However, it also enables him to move around Muirhouse and other areas – a freedom the film exploits in several sequences that adopt the fly's aerial perspective. These sequences illuminate Welsh's own relation to Edinburgh: materially grounded (the fly is a pest interested in shit) yet mobile, able to see the environment from new heights and unconventional angles, unbound by conventions of decorum or realism. The first and longest of the fly's-eye sequences, lasting more than a minute of screen time – with swooping camera and grainy, oversaturated colour, plus soundtrack cover of the nostalgic 1960s song 'Summer Wind' – temporarily reveals Muirhouse's potential beauty, revealing the geometric neatness of its design and hinting at lost utopian hopes. Thus the film expands on the defamiliarisation achieved in several of the original collection's stories. In 'Where the Debris Meets the Sea' Madonna, Kylie Minogue, and other stars read magazines such as *Scheme Scene* and daydream wistfully (in Edinburgh accents) about one day taking the 'hoaliday ay a lifetime' in Leith (*AH*, 91–2). 'Snowman Building Parts for Rico the Squirrel' juxtaposes an idealised American TV family with a disastrous Scottish one, but in the story's world, the happy American family is real and the Scottish one the subject of a TV programme, *The Skatch Femilee Rabirtsin*, which the American children watch in fascination. In these stories, as in the film, and in many of his other takes on Edinburgh, Welsh moves beyond a realist-documentary mode while always remaining in touch with material conditions.

Welsh's most recent Edinburgh-based novel, *The Bedroom Secrets of the Master Chefs* (2006), continues both his exploration of local conditions and his satirical campaign against the shams and inanities of the city's self-promotion. The novel's dual-identity trope, whereby the physical after-effects of the debauchery of one protagonist, Danny Skinner, are visited on his prudish counterpart, Brian Kibby, may be a laboured plot device, but the opposition between the two characters develops into an antisyzygy which draws out linked strains in Welsh's view of Edinburgh. Skinner, as a restless streetwise Leith boy, has obvious things in common with his author, but Kibby too has affinities with Welsh: as a model railway enthusiast (a kind of trainspotter) he has constructed his own virtual city composed of 'tenements, tower blocks, bungalows, everything he could think of as his town sprawled across the attic, mirroring the development of the west of Edinburgh where he grew up' (*BS*, 30). The papier-mâché hills of 'Kibbytown' – built for Kibby by his father, Keith – prove to hide a crucial diary which reveals that, having been one of Skinner's mother's lovers in 1980, Keith may be Skinner's father as well as Kibby's. The discovery of the diary in the model city dramatises the idea that idealised versions of Edinburgh contain their own supplements that will not remain hidden permanently. The diary's revelations also resonate with Skinner's sceptical view of a new Edinburgh landmark – 'our toytown parliament: like looking for a father and being presented with a guardian from the social work department' (*BS*, 340). The toytown analogy articulates another deft swipe at grandiose programmes for the future of city and nation while hinting that Skinner may indeed be biologically related to Kibby. In evoking uncanny links between seemingly opposed views of the city – bland middle-class utopia and night-townish zone of temptation and mystery – the Skinner–Kibby relationship is perhaps Welsh's strongest acknowledgement of the complex challenges of representing Edinburgh. The novel also underlines, through Skinner's perception of the city in autumn, Welsh's concern with its quotidian aspects: 'He felt that the city was more at ease with itself at this time than at any other. Freed from external definitions dubbing it the "arts capital of the world" (festival) or "the party capital of Europe" (Hogmanay), its populace were simply allowed to get on with the prosaic but remarkable business of everyday life in a North European city' (*BS*, 281).

In *Edinburgh: A Cultural and Literary History* Donald Campbell faults Welsh for undue emphasis on Edinburgh's 'ugliness and vulgarity'. At the same time, somewhat inconsistently, Campbell asserts that 'there is little of Edinburgh in [Welsh's] writing', and it is true that Welsh's more upbeat fictions often involve characters escaping the city, physically and/or chemically. But whether or not Campbell is right to assert that 'Welsh's stories might easily be taking place in any British or, indeed, American city',[22] his observation hints at Welsh's constructive contribution to international debates on contemporary urban development. Welsh's attention to the questionable benefits of Edinburgh's renewal schemes not only links his writings to the work of urban theorists such as David Harvey.[23] His explorations of the intersection of drugs and inequitable urban development also set up potential comparisons with recent film and television texts such as, for example, the HBO series *The Wire* (2002–8), set in Baltimore, the Canadian drama *Da Vinci's Inquest* (1998–2005), set in Vancouver's less salubrious areas, and Mathieu Kassovitz's *La Haine* (1995), whose restive characters in Paris's isolated suburbs have a lot in common with Welsh's 'schemies'.

Welsh currently lives in Dublin and in Miami, the latter of which also provides the main setting for his most recent novel, *Crime*. Yet since May 2009 he has also been a visible, everyday presence in Leith, as his face, along with those of other local luminaries like The Proclaimers, appears on banners carrying the phrase 'I ♥ LEITH' which adorn lamp-posts on Leith Walk. Meanwhile, parts of the Walk itself, like parts of Princes Street in the city centre, are blocked for construction of Edinburgh's new tram system, due to open in 2011. The system will run from Turnhouse airport in the northwest through the city centre, then into 'Edinburgh North' via Leith Walk and Constitution Street, and on to Ocean Terminal and Newhaven. Redesignation as part of 'Edinburgh North' might be seen as another instance of Leith's subordination to plans originating elsewhere, and the factsheets promoting the tram cite potential benefits – more visitors, higher property values – that favour Sick Boy's priorities over Spud's. Welsh's involvement in the 'I ♥ LEITH' campaign might be seen as epitomising his conversion from iconoclast to icon, indicating his co-option by the same forces of civic self-aggrandisement that he has often mocked: the banners bear (in small print) the marketing slogan 'Inspiring Capital', with the address for the City Council's website *Edinburgh Shopper*, which nervously touts the 'quirky individuality of Leith' as a consumer attraction.

However, the fact that Welsh's image on the banners appears almost to be supervising the construction work – tramspotting, so to speak – can also be regarded as a fitting evocation of his enduring concern with the community. Welsh's quizzical, chin-stroking pose suggests reserved judgement on the surrounding developments and their potential to bring social improvement through technological modernisation and aesthetic upgrading. We may recall that such was also the promise, but less often the achievement, of the housing schemes where many of Welsh's characters carry on their everyday struggles. And while its promotion may be glib and its construction inconvenient, the tram scheme represents the possibility of a more effective and equitable connection between Edinburgh and Leith, one capable of reducing the social and economic as well as geographical distance between the city's privileged and less privileged areas. The transport link will be further material recognition of Leith's supplementarity to tourist Edinburgh with all that this implies; it will also usefully replace the literalised metaphor that was Leith's derelict Central Station. Morace emphasises that Leith has changed greatly since the 1980s and suggests that '*Trainspotting* and the Irvine Welsh phenomenon it set in motion'[24] now belong less to the present than to history. It seems likely, nevertheless, that Welsh's ongoing interest in questions of living space and equitable urban development, in Edinburgh and elsewhere, will prove one of the most constructive and durable features of his work.

CHAPTER TEN

Welsh in Translation

Katherine Ashley

Since the publication of *Trainspotting* in 1993, Irvine Welsh's reputation has steadily grown. If not a household name, his books are nonetheless available in over twenty-five languages – proof that his appeal is broad and his writing resonates with readers from diverse cultural backgrounds. When *Trainspotting* first appeared, it shocked for two reasons: its subject matter and its language. In presenting Welsh's books to the world, however, publishers have tended to focus on the former and have sought to establish common literary ground across national and linguistic boundaries, stressing the global aspects of his work and situating him in relation to other well-known twentieth-century authors. At the same time, it has been argued that Welsh's initial commercial and critical success is attributable to his vibrant language.[1] This underscores an inherent contradiction in the reception of his work abroad. While his novels and short story collections deal with subjects that cross national lines – for example, youth and drug culture, class, gender, sexuality, consumerism and colonialism – these topics are addressed in an unmistakably local vernacular: Welsh's voice, which is aggressively, sometimes uncompromisingly, Scottish, is precisely what cannot be conveyed in translation. Consequently, the minority–majority language tensions at the heart of novels like *Trainspotting*, and the challenges that Welsh's language presents to textual norms, remain within Scottish borders. Translating Welsh reinforces the global character of his subject matter, but minimises the deliberately provocative qualities of his language.

Aaron Kelly believes that it is 'misleading to confuse the success of Danny Boyle's 1995 film version of *Trainspotting* with the early reception of Welsh's work',[2] but this is untrue as far as his reception abroad is concerned. The film played a pivotal role in bringing Welsh's writing to non-English speakers, and its seductive heroin-chic imagery and its (non-Scottish) soundtrack took hold in countries around the world. The American edition of the novel was published shortly before the film appeared in cinemas, but as Table 10.1 illustrates, no translations were published before the film's global release. Eleven translations were published in 1996, and virtually all early foreign

Table 10.1 Translations of *Trainspotting* (1993)

1996	Croatian, Dutch, Finnish, French, German, Italian, Japanese, Norwegian, Portuguese (Portugal), Spanish, Swedish
1997	Czech, Hebrew, Korean, Polish, Serbian, Slovenian
1998	Hungarian, Lithuanian
1999	Greek
2001	Turkish
2003	Russian
2004	Portuguese (Brazil)
2005	Latvian
2006	Romanian

editions have film tie-in covers, proof that the film played a key role in exporting Welsh.[3] Further evidence of the film's influence in selling Welsh internationally is the different role that *The Acid House* (1994) played in the UK and abroad. In Britain, sales of *The Acid House* positively affected the reception of *Trainspotting*; the reverse is true abroad, where only the Croatian edition of the short story collection was published before 1997, when it was translated into Dutch, Italian and Spanish. Foreign-language publishers were clearly banking on the success of both the film and the original novel to make Welsh palatable abroad. The film adaptation allowed a writer who wrote about marginalised characters in a marginalised dialect to reach global audiences and situated Welsh's writing in relation to international youth culture.

Welsh's success abroad can be linked to the 1990s craze for all things British, from the Spice Girls to *Mr. Bean*. While Welsh's books problematise notions of Britishness, they also participated in 'New' Labour's 'Cool Britannia' branding of British culture. Welsh became an icon abroad, a 'Great Scot', a writer of 'cult status', 'the enfant terrible of recent British fiction';[4] he was placed on a top-100 list by Asian booksellers Kinokuniya and was called upon to teach creative writing in the United States and judge a literary award in Mauritius.[5] Indeed, Michael Gardiner has demonstrated that many of the dangers associated with Welsh's writing were mitigated by his 'Cool Britannia' associations. According to Gardiner, *Trainspotting*'s status as 'combative literature'[6] was negated abroad because Welsh's writing was assimilated within a government-sponsored, UK-wide but London-centred cultural phenomenon. This framework affected the reception of other books as well: just as Welsh's first novel lost its combativeness, his second, *Marabou Stork Nightmares* (1995), morphed into a 'Brit Pop Novel' in Japan, despite the horrifying gang rape at its centre.[7] Perhaps for the very reason that it rests uneasily with the 'Brit Pop' moment, *Marabou Stork Nightmares*, with its complex structure, Scottish and South African settings, psychotic-fantasy plot and dissection of masculinity, nationalism and colonialism, is Welsh's least translated text (see Table 10.2). Even though it is one of his better received novels in the UK, it has been translated into only six languages, whereas *Ecstasy*, which was poorly received in the UK, is available in thirteen, *Filth* in sixteen, *Glue* in thirteen and *Porno* in seventeen.

Since the release of *Trainspotting*, a certain international idea of Welsh has emerged, apparent in the covers of his books. Book covers usually vary considerably from country to country, but the domestic and foreign covers of Welsh's books project a more or less homogeneous image that crosses national and linguistic boundaries and is designed to appeal to the so-called 'chemical generation'. The 'tawdry' design and lurid colours depict the books as 'provocative' challenges to mainstream culture.[8] *Porno*, for instance, was marketed in much the same way at home and abroad: the French, German, Italian and Spanish editions bear the image of the same deflated plastic sex doll that appears on the original Jonathan Cape edition. Rather than focus on any distinctively Scottish aspect of Welsh's writing, marketing departments have established common ground through design similarities. This is especially true of *Trainspotting, Filth, Ecstasy* and *Porno*, but even recent publications like *The Bedroom Secrets of the Master Chefs* and *If You Liked School, You'll Love Work* have similar covers in the United Kingdom, Germany and Spain (a checked tablecloth and a Subbuteo figure respectively). Branding makes Welsh recognisable worldwide, but also diminishes the implied shock value of his books because of the familiar imagery.

The tension between the mainstream and the marginal is also manifest in the series in which Welsh's texts are published abroad. The fact that he has been translated at all suggests a level of recognition (or tolerance) and that he is a secure investment for foreign publishers. Nonetheless, many of them situate him in relation to the margins and focus on his avant-garde credentials when placing him on their lists. In France, he has been published in Editions de l'Olivier's 'Marges' ('Margins') series. In Russia, his works appear in a collection called 'Al'ternativa' ('Alternative'), while in the Czech Republic his books are found in the 'Cesty tam a zase zpátky' (which translates, loosely, as 'Roundtrip') series, with an emphasis, no doubt, on the return to safety after reading his books. Most revealing, however, is Spanish publisher Editorial Anagrama's decision to include *Trainspotting, The Acid House, Ecstasy* and *Filth* in its 'Contraseñas' ('Password') collection, which is devoted to 'so-called outlawed literature' ('Las Colecciones'). This positions Welsh relative to other roguish *agents provocateurs* in the collection, like fellow Scot Alexander Trocchi (1925–84), as well as William Burroughs (1914–97), Charles Bukowski (1920–94) and Armisted Maupin (b. 1944), authors who openly and unabashedly treat hitherto taboo subjects such as sexual excess, alcohol addiction and homosexuality.

Table 10.2 Translations of Welsh

	Train. (1993)	*AH* (1994)	*MSN* (1995)	*Ecs.* (1996)	*Filth* (1998)	*Glue* (2001)	*Porno* (2002)	*BSMC* (2006)
Croatian	1996	1996			2004	2004	2002	
Czech	1997	1999	2003	2000	2001	2003	2004	
Danish				1998	2001			
Dutch	1996	1997			1999	2002	2003	
Estonian					2003			
Finnish	1996				2000	2002	2004	
French	1996			1999	2000	2009	2008	2008
German	1996	1999		1997	1999	2003	2004	2008
Greek	1999			1997		2002		
Hebrew	1997			1998				
Hungarian	1998	1999					2004	
Italian	1996	1997	2001	1997	1999	2002	2003	2006
Japanese	1996	1999	1997	1997	1999		2003	
Korean	1997							
Latvian	2005							
Lithuanian	1998							
Norwegian	1996				2000	2002	2004	
Polish	1997				2003	2004	2006	
Portuguese	1996			1997	2003	2004	2003	
Romanian	2006				2006		2008	
Russian	2003	2003	2002	2001	2005			
Serbian	1997	2000		2000				
Slovenian	1997						2005	
Spanish	1996	1997	1997	1998	2000	2003	2005	2007
Swedish	1996					2003	2004	
Turkish	2001			2003			2002	

While Welsh has been marketed as a radical author, there are indications that he is increasingly accepted as a canonical contemporary writer, if such a thing can be said to exist. In Italy, where he has sold over half a million books and been described as a shining figure in international literature,[9] his publisher, Guanda, includes his texts in its 'Narratori de Fenice' collection. 'Fenice' means phoenix: hence Welsh is seen to participate in a literary renaissance. There are further examples that suggest a shift towards Literature (with a capital L): publishers like Romania's Polirom categorise *Trainspotting*, *Filth* and *Porno* as 'literatura engleza' or 'literatura universala'; the same books that were released in Olivier's 'Marges' series are now published by one of France's big three publishers, Seuil. What is more, Editorial Anagrama has published Welsh's latest books, including *Glue*, *Porno* and *The Bedroom Secrets of the Master Chefs*, in its 'Panorama de narrativas' collection rather than in the 'Contraseñas' collection. 'Panorama de narrativas' is devoted to 'la más interesante narrativa internacional contemporánea' ('the most interesting international contemporary fiction') and includes in its pantheon virtually all award-winning contemporary authors, from Louise Welsh, Nick Hornby, Graham Swift and Ian McEwan to Paul Auster and Amélie Nothomb, proof of Welsh's mainstream status. In Spain, Welsh is now regarded as a major figure in the literary establishment, and his novels are 'posibles clásicos del futuro' (they might come to be considered literary classics in the future) in 'Las Colecciones'. Welsh is no longer being marketed as marginal, which mirrors his own recent attempts to situate himself in relation to canonical authors like Scott, Austen, Waugh and Eliot, and his characters in relation to Jekyll and Hyde and Dorian Gray.

Welsh has been marketed as a 'hip', countercultural and anti-establishment author, but he is also considered a littérateur who appeals to the intelligentsia. Despite branding him as a junkie novelist and the frequent reminders in the foreign press of his working-class credentials,[10] Welsh's readership is broad and he straddles both high and low culture. The very fact that this analysis of his global reception and translation forms part of a volume published by a university press attests to Welsh's acceptability as a subject of intellectual inquiry. His Dutch-language readers come from the same demographic as his English-language audience: he has 'een verscheiden publiek: van halve analfabeten tot hooggeleerde academici'[11] (a diverse audience that ranges from the semi-literate to highly learned academics). In the United States, Welsh is published by W. W. Norton, which is described by his American editor as a 'formerly conservative publishing house'.[12] In academic circles, Norton is principally known for its canon-forming Norton Anthologies, in which Welsh is almost certain not to appear. As declared in the 'About W. W. Norton' section of the publisher's website, its mandate is to 'publish books not for a single season, but for the years'. The fact that Norton had to be dared to publish Welsh suggests that for them he initially fitted into the former rather than the latter category.[13]

Welsh is undoubtedly part of a global cultural phenomenon, but analysing his work from the perspective of translation and reception underscores the fact that he writes against cultural neutrality and that language is one of his primary concerns. Above all, he seems to react to a comment made by Jenny, one of his own characters in 'The Acid House', who lives in Edinburgh, that she and her friends 'were located in an eighties English-speaking strata where culture and accent are homogenous and nationality is a largely irrelevant construct' (*AH*, 162). Welsh's experimentation, particularly with respect to language and form, makes his texts homogeneous neither in terms of culture nor in terms of accent. Through their subject matter, but particularly through their distinctive use of language, they participate in a reconfiguration of Scottish literary identity. Unlike many commercially successful authors, Welsh's writing is experimental with respect to layout, typography and voice. His books incorporate song lyrics, contain references to highbrow and popular culture, make playful use of the visual and graphic possibilities of print, and brim with linguistic creativity. This is indicative of heterogeneity rather than homogeneity, and impacts on how he is read abroad.

Reception and translation are 'dependent on the relations within a certain cultural system', and one of the biggest challenges translators face is reproducing 'the dominant textual relations of the original'.[14] With regard to Welsh, these relations concern both structure and language and affect his reception in English and in translation. Welsh produces superimposed narratives (*Filth*, 'The Acid House'), simultaneous narratives ('Across the Hall' [*AH*, 103–5]), and narratives like *Marabou Stork Nightmares*, in which font changes show how the unconscious flow of Roy Strang's thoughts is interrupted by memories, hallucinations and overheard conversations. These narrative practices reinforce the oral qualities of Welsh's language and destabilise the texts by presenting multiple voices which struggle to be heard. Cairns Craig maintains that typographical experimentation is related to 'overthrow[ing] the rule of type', which is 'synonymous with overthrowing the type of rule under which the culture has struggled for self-expression'.[15] When this experimentation is transferred to another culture, or to another language through translation, the struggle is transferred to a different cultural and linguistic context, challenging a foreign rule of type. By the time this transfer occurs, the texts themselves are no longer marginal; transferring them to another culture assimilates them into a new context, and, most likely, the new 'rule of type' that is being overthrown will belong to a dominant culture/language that does not – and may not want to – contain the same political, cultural or linguistic tensions as does Scotland. Indeed, this could account for the fact that there are relatively few translations of *Marabou Stork Nightmares*, Welsh's most unstable text.

According to Antoine Berman, 'translation can occur only between "cultivated" languages'.[16] Welsh's language is not 'cultivated': it has no standard written norms, it is not taught, it is not global. It is, on the contrary, 'weird English', a 'conscious appropriation of hybridity'.[17] In Scotland, local linguistic realities need to be weighed against the historical imperative to write in English, which is a 'cultivated' language. Since Welsh's books are classified and sold as English-language literature in English-speaking countries, it is not uncommon to hear complaints from Anglophone critics about Welsh's vernacular. The 'brogue' in *Filth* is considered annoying and potentially 'off-putting to Indian readers'. Begbie in *Porno* is 'nearly incomprehensible'. Reviews of *The Bedroom Secrets of the Master Chefs* comment on Welsh's 'penchant for phoneticising Scottish dialect' and state that 'Scottish dialect will slow down American readers'. *If You Liked School, You'll Love Work* (2007), in which only one story takes place in Scotland, is reported to feature 'semi-intelligible Scots dialect'.[18] Yet, of course, the purpose of dialect is not to frustrate readers but to mark the texts as 'other'. Dialect is a means of resisting the linguistic and textual norms that codify (and have colonised) Scottish literature. This is confirmed by Welsh's refusal to include a glossary in the UK edition of *Trainspotting* because he did not want 'all these fuckers up in Charlotte Square putting on the vernacular as a stage managed thing'.[19] For Welsh, the vernacular is a statement of independence from the political, cultural and literary power symbolised by Edinburgh's Charlotte Square, which is associated with the pro-Union and pro-English-language sentiments of the Scottish Enlightenment. Significantly, Charlotte Square is not only the locus of the headquarters of the National Trust for Scotland and also, until 1990, that of the Scottish Arts Council, it is also the home of the Edinburgh International Book Festival.

Intentionally estranging the text from Standard English provides direct access to characters who would otherwise remain voiceless, but can also close the text to non-Scots. Robert Crawford asserts that Welsh's dialect 'is close enough to English to be comprehensible to an international audience',[20] but *Trainspotting* contains passages that suggest that the opposite effect is sought (if not necessarily achieved). One of the biggest barriers to reading Welsh abroad is that his language is already 'foreign' to many native English speakers, a fact that crystallises when Begbie attempts to engage two Toronto tourists in a discussion on the train to London:

> – Pardon? it sais tae us, sortay soundin likes, 'par-dawn' ken?
> – Whair's it yis come fae then?

> – Sorry, I can't really understand you . . . These foreign cunts've goat trouble wi the Queen's fuckin English, ken. Ye huv tae speak louder, slower, n likesay mair posh, fir the cunts tae understand ye.
> – WHERE . . . DO . . . YOU . . . COME . . . FROM?
> . . .
> – Ehm . . . we're from Toronto, Canada.
> – Tirawnto. That wis the Lone Ranger's mate, wis it no? ah sais. The burds jist look it us. Some punters dinnae fuckin understand the Scottish sense ay humour. (*T*, 114–5)

This scene speaks volumes about reading *Trainspotting* abroad: just as Begbie's idiom eludes the Torontonians, Welsh's dialect has the potential to escape his Anglophone readers.[21] For Begbie, the issue is class: he needs to speak 'mair posh'. For foreign readers, the issue is slowing down: they need to read with increased vigilance.

As spokesperson for Norton, Gerald Howard states that 'when we signed up Irvine Welsh's first novel, *Trainspotting*, I joked that it was going to be Norton's first foreign-language publication'.[22] Howard is, as he points out, joking, and the novel was not marketed as a 'foreign-language publication' in America; even so, Norton was aware of the interpretive difficulties it might cause. Comprehension, not identity politics, is the issue when reading Welsh beyond Scotland's borders: despite Welsh's strident opposition to including a glossary in the British edition of the novel, the American edition contained one, which was also printed in the *Paris Review*. In addition, the film adaptations of *Trainspotting* and *The Acid House* contain subtitles and/or dubbing, which (sometimes humorously) reinforce the oral status of dialect. An act of translation takes place every time English speakers read Welsh's work, but while the source texts' difference is recognised, it is rarely analysed because emphasis is put on Welsh's subject matter rather than his language.

Linguistic marginalisation is difficult to export. The decision not to write in Standard English is both a literary and a political act, intimately connected to recasting Scottish literary identity in a way that is not generally recognised, or recognisable, in translation. Although France's *Le Monde* describes modern Scottish literary language as 'un acte révolutionnaire, une forme de protestation politique' (a revolutionary act, a form of political protest) and acknowledges that Welsh's language startles English speakers,[23] it is difficult to transplant the debates surrounding majority and minority languages in Scotland into French or any other national language. This is obvious from the first sentence of the novel. Whereas the Standard English prepositions 'off of' are functional grammatical units, in *Trainspotting* the unit becomes 'oafay', which has the same denotation, but acquires additional connotation because it is no longer culturally neutral. Translations of the first line are, however, comparatively neutral. They convey powerful images, but in no way recreate the linguistic difference of the preposition 'oafay'. In Spanish 'Sick Boy sudaba a chorros'[24] (Welsh 1999: 11) (that is, he 'sweated/was sweating buckets') is colloquial, as is Eduardo Barros-Grela's more emphatic 'Sick Boy estaba sudando a chorros', but there is no linguistic defamiliarisation. The French 'Sick Boy avait ses fuites'[25] (that is, he 'was leaking') is more creative, but still well within the realm of grammatically acceptable standard French. There is a sense of Sick Boy's drug-induced panic, but not of Renton's Scottish voice.

As this example shows, translation can blur the relationship between the margins and the centre, between minority and majority languages, and between language and identity because the target language may have no means of expressing source-text concepts, much less the source text's linguistic 'difference'. Gardiner provides a fascinating example of the former when he points out that in Japanese the distinction between 'England' and 'Britain' is blurred. When Renton explains that he feels neither British nor Scottish in the chapter 'London Crawling', and when the skinheads parade their 'Ulster is British' shirts in 'NaNa and other Nazis', these subtle and not-so-subtle assertions of national and personal identity are all but meaningless, because there is no way to convey these concepts.[26] If the Japanese language cannot render the idea of British as opposed to English national identity as these notions are expressed in Standard English, conveying the linguistic difference that drives the novel as a whole will be doubly difficult. For this reason, texts like *Trainspotting*, which address language issues, are inevitably read differently abroad than they are in Scotland.

In *Trainspotting*, perhaps more than in Welsh's other texts, the Scottish voice is affirmed and linguistic difference is championed. Many voices coexist in the novel; no single voice dominates. The struggle for self-expression is particularly acute because the characters' identities – and ultimately their fates – are articulated via their linguistic (in)competence. Whether the characters rise above their situation depends to a large extent on their linguistic adaptability: Renton and Sick Boy, for example, are inveterate code-switchers, moving from dialect to Scottish Standard English with aplomb, mimicking others and manoeuvring between different social milieux like chameleons. There is no doubt that this facilitates their exit from Leith, as Renton flees to Amsterdam and Sick Boy spends time in France. Spud and Begbie are less adaptable, have difficulty negotiating register changes and therefore have more limited access to the world beyond Edinburgh. Both are at times literally imprisoned in the city. Yet while linguistic adaptability impacts upon Renton's social and geographical mobility, he is not fully aware of how language shapes him. As Sick Boy says to him, 'the fact that you use the term "cunt" in the same breath as "sexist", shows that ye display the same muddled, fucked-up thinking oan this issue as you do oan everything else' (*T*, 28). Language represents both freedom and imprisonment for the characters. For readers, the problem lies elsewhere: if translation denies the possibility of distinguishing between 'oafay' and 'off of', or 'I' and 'Ah', or if the relationship between language and freedom, and dialect and neutral English, is not made clear in the target language, then scenes like 'Courting Disaster', 'The Glass', 'Speedy Recruitment' or even the contentious return to omniscient Scottish Standard English in 'Station to Station', become all but empty as commentaries on language, power and identity in Scotland.

The chapter 'Inter Shitty', already mentioned in the context of the alienating effect of dialect on English speakers, clearly illustrates the minority–majority language tensions of the source text: Begbie speaks in dialect while the Canadians' speech is represented in Standard English, except when Begbie comments on their pronunciation. While Begbie, as narrator, is in the position of authority, his vernacular is not neutral because of the humorous way in which it is presented, and because it contains phoneticised spellings like 'ah', 'sais' and 'mair'. This is not the case in the French translation, in which Begbie's speech is peppered with expletives and obviously colloquial in its syntax, but remains unmistakably standard French. The tourists' French, on the other hand, is represented phonetically even where Begbie has not commented on their pronunciation in the original, and as a result their Canadian French is conferred the same status as Begbie's speech is in the source text. Whereas there is no minority–majority language tension between Scotland and Canada, there is between metropolitan and Canadian French, so the dynamic changes quite fundamentally.[27] In the example below, the standard written French is in square brackets:

> – Je vous demande pardon? qu'elle me fait et ça sonne genre « démainde pairdon ».
> – Attends, toi, tu viens d'où?
> – Je rgraitte [regrette], je ne vous comprin [comprend] pas bien . . . Les cons qui viennent d'ailleurs ont de vrais problèmes avec notre putain d'anglais anglais. Pour que ces cons prennent, il faut leur parler fort, lentement, et surtout façon je ne suce que des virgules épluchées avec des gants.
> – PUIS-JE . . . SAVOIR . . . D'OÙ . . . TU . . . VIENS . . .?
> . . .
> – Ehm . . . Nous sommes de Trointo, Canédé. [Toronto, Canada]
> – Tonto. C'était le pote du Lone Ranger, non? je fais. [28]

The French unwittingly reverses the power relation between the languages: the Canadians' speech is represented phonetically, giving more authority to Begbie because his (admittedly urban) French is presented non-phonetically in a standard written form.

Language is never neutral in *Trainspotting*, and the smallest details anchor it firmly in Edinburgh. Words like 'likesay' – translated as 'genre', 'quoi', 'si t'aimes bien' and 'si tu veux' in French, and 'sabes', 'y eso', 'cómo te digo', 'digamos' and 'y tal' in Spanish – might be semantically and grammatically meaningless discourse markers, but are nevertheless specific to certain populations in Edinburgh. Spud uses it incessantly, Davie and Gavin rarely. 'Genre, mec, tu vois', on the other hand, could just as easily translate 'dude, like, you know' or 'you see, mate'. Sick Boy's Sean Connery tic is one of the few that can be adequately translated into French and Spanish because it involves phonologically altering common English vocabulary: phrases like 'pre*sh*ishly *Sh*imon' become 'ab*ch*olument *C*himon' and 'pre*sh*i*sh*amente, *Sh*imon'.[29] These verbal tics establish how socially, regionally and individually identifiable the characters' voices are, and they also allow readers to distinguish between them. This is crucial because there are eight different first-person narrators in *Trainspotting*, in addition to third-person narration in which the point of view shifts from one chapter to the next. Moreover, the characters frequently assume different voices, further fragmenting the text in a way that is dulled in translation: although the novel's language is referred to as 'torturée à l'excès' ('tortured in the extreme'),[30] in French there is little difference between Renton's language in 'Courting Disaster' and in his numerous junkie dilemmas.[31]

Swearing is also regionally and socially marked in *Trainspotting*, and much of it is sexual in nature. In German, by contrast, scatology is the norm and expletives are, generally speaking, less regular than in English.[32] In Canadian French and Spanish swearing frequently draws on religious imagery. Martin Bowman notes that a monologue of Begbie's in his Québécois version of Harry Gibson's play contains almost seventy 'cunts' and 'fuckins'; in translation these are replaced by 'câlisse' (chalice), 'tabarnac' (tabernacle) and 'hostie' (host).[33] Replacing *Trainspotting*'s expletives with religious or scatological obscenities (or eliminating them altogether, as Barros-Grela contends happens in Spanish) necessarily affects characterisation and the tone of the text, and anchors the story in a different cultural milieu. While it can be reasoned, as Bowman has done, that the religious expletives in Québécois 'affir[m] the Catholicism of Welsh's characters', in the novel Welsh does not distinguish between creeds when it comes to cursing: Renton's Glaswegian uncle Charlie, an Orangeman, uses the same obscenities as the Catholic trainspotters. Obscenities serve a largely rhythmical function in Welsh's dialogues, but are apt to acquire semantic meaning in translation. Even where an equivalent term can be used, it may not have the same force: there is a difference in degree of acceptability between 'sexist cunt' and 'con sexiste', and the standard French does not necessarily reflect the same linguistic confusion as the original.

Translations tend to render Welsh's vernacular using inner-city speech patterns that convey education and social status without being regionally marked. Class differences therefore supplant language differences and focus attention on thematic rather than linguistic concerns. As in the German translation of *Trainspotting*, for which Peter Torberg chose not to use 'regional or dialectical forms',[34] the French translation is colloquial, but not regionally specific. Negations are deleted, while abbreviations, unstressed e's and reduced forms are used ('z'avez', 'jme'). There are borrowings from other languages and phonetic renderings, but the phonological system itself is not different, nor is the syntax indicative of dialectical or 'weird', hybrid French. These inner-city idioms could translate any regional, colloquial or spoken variety of English, but nevertheless allow for switching between non-standard and standard language. Foreign readers will clearly understand that the characters are using 'un langage de la rue'[35] (a street language) that corresponds to Welsh's subject matter, but what this signifies for a Scottish text operating within a British literary context will not be apparent.

If self-expression, place and linguistic difference are considered major themes in *Trainspotting*, it is reasonable to attempt to convey this by translating into an equivalent target-language dialect or sociolect, if only to avoid what Berman refers to as the 'effacement of the superimposition of languages'.[36] Translating into a target-language sociolect rather than a standard language could potentially better accentuate code-switching, register changes and linguistic difference by accounting for majority–minority language tensions. Thus, when translating the play *Trainspotting* into French in Canada, Québécois *joual* (working-class Montréal French) stood in for the language of Leith. This approach works because theatre is a spoken medium, and Welsh's characters' idiom is both distinctly oral and lacking a standardised written form. The advantage of this method is also its pitfall: *joual*, like any sociolect, is indelibly rooted in a particular place and spoken by a particular group of people. Consequently, a *joual*-ised *Trainspotting* risks shifting the reference points beyond the Scottish culture of origin and thereby negating any political, cultural or linguistic message inherent in the source language. In an oral context, however, rendition in *joual* produces an excellent translation because, as Bowman has explained, the characters 'speak language, not a language', and because *joual* lends itself to code-switching. Still, although the characters on stage 'speak language', readers read 'a language'. The point is that the novel endorses dialect as a means of written expression: it self-reflexively comments on minority–majority language relations and on linguistic and textual norms in Scotland, and makes a case for the vernacular having a rich life in print.

Welsh is widely translated abroad, but since his vernacular is not 'cultivated', it is almost inevitable that his texts will be standardised in translation (back-translating them would probably result in a standard English text).[37] In one sense, this negates the significance of the linguistic tensions within novels like *Trainspotting* and suggests that asserting the primacy of dialect is to deny that same dialect access to the world. In this sense, translation is a tool in cultural globalisation, on a par with the production of homogeneous book covers that create a Welsh brand. On the other hand, and perhaps more appropriately for an author like Welsh, this textual taming adds a layer of meaning. It allows foreign readers to see his work from a global perspective rather than a Scottish one, directing attention to shared themes – class, education, drug culture, sexuality, capitalism, and the like. Welsh explained to an Italian interviewer that the only way he could remain true to Edinburgh was through distance: 'La distanza aiuta a essere obiettivi e veritieri' ('distance leads to truth and objectivity').[38] At least theoretically, normalisation through translation also reinforces the theme of distance as exclusion, which finds expression in the excluded, absent dialect itself. This is not necessarily negative: considering translation as an act of exclusion brings us back to the way Welsh has been marketed abroad. While we may rage against a publishing machine that stresses uniformity and turns authors into brands, when it comes to translating Welsh, this is apposite because it underlines the fact that novels like *Trainspotting* are just as trapped in their own linguistic situation as some of its characters. Translation therefore allows Welsh's writing to work on two levels: in the original, *Trainspotting* is heteroglossic, 'breaks' English and engages with debates surrounding dominant and minority discourses, whereas in translation it engages with themes that resonate across linguistic and national boundaries and thus at once participates in and agitates against cultural hegemony. Depending on one's perspective, this is either liberating or alienating. It acknowledges the chameleon nature of Welsh's texts, which implicitly grants dialect the majority status that it has hitherto been denied in Scotland while letting foreign readers read Welsh as an author rather than purely as a *Scottish* author. It also accounts for Welsh's continuing success in Scotland and also abroad.

Endnotes

Introduction – Schoene

1. Hamish White and Janice Galloway, quoted in Robert Morace, *Irvine Welsh's* Trainspotting: *A Reader's Guide* (New York and London: Continuum, 2001), p. 21.
2. Craig Beveridge and Ronald Turnbull, *The Eclipse of Scottish Culture* (Edinburgh: Polygon, 1989), p. 112.
3. See Gavin Wallace and Randall Stevenson (eds), *The Scottish Novel Since the Seventies: New Visions, Old Dreams* (Edinburgh: Edinburgh University Press, 1993).
4. Robin Spittal, '*Trainspotting*: A New Scottish Icon?', *Etudes Ecossaises* 5 (1998), p. 205.
5. Gavin Wallace, 'Voices in Empty Houses: The Novel of Damaged Identity', in Wallace and Stevenson, *The Scottish Novel Since the Seventies*, p. 231.
6. Derek Paget, 'Speaking Out: The Transformations of *Trainspotting*', in Deborah Cartmell and Imelda Whelehan (eds), *Adaptations: From Text to Screen, Screen to Text* (London and New York: Routledge, 1999), p. 140.
7. Jenifer Berman, 'Irvine Welsh', *Bomb* (Summer 1996), p. 57.
8. Alan Freeman, 'Ourselves as Others: *Marabou Stork Nightmares*', *Edinburgh Review* 95 (1996), p. 135.
9. Patricia Horton, '*Trainspotting*: A Topography of the Masculine Abject', *English* 50: 198 (2001), p. 231.
10. Fiona Oliver, 'The Self-Debasement of Scotland's Post-Colonial Bodies,' *SPAN* 42/43 (April and October 1996), p. 120.
11. Berman, 'Irvine Welsh', p. 57.
12. Willy Maley, 'Subversion and Squirrility in Irvine Welsh's Shorter Fiction', in Dermot Cavanagh and Tim Kirk (eds), *Subversion and Scurrility: Popular Discourse in Europe from 1500 to the Present* (Aldershot: Ashgate, 2000), p. 193.
13. Berman, 'Irvine Welsh', p. 61.
14. Willy Maley, 'You'll Have Had Your Theatre', *Spike Magazine* (1998), www.spikemagazine.com/0199welshplay.com.

15. Berman, 'Irvine Welsh', p. 61.
16. Maley, 'Subversion and Squirrility in Irvine Welsh's Shorter Fiction', p. 196.
17. Paget, 'Speaking Out: The Transformations of *Trainspotting*', p. 133.
18. Drew Milne, 'The Fiction of James Kelman and Irvine Welsh: Accents, Speech and Writing', in Richard J. Lane, Rod Mengham and Philip Tew (eds), *Contemporary British Fiction* (Cambridge: Polity, 2003), pp. 158 and 160.
19. Cairns Craig, *The Modern Scottish Novel: Narrative and the National Imagination* (Edinburgh: Edinburgh University Press, 1999), p. 98.
20. Irvine Welsh, *'Trainspotting' and 'Headstate'* (London: Minerva, 1996), p. 83.
21. Morace, *Irvine Welsh's Trainspotting*, p. 46.
22. Welsh, *'Trainspotting' and 'Headstate'*, p. 83.
23. Robert Morace, *Irvine Welsh* (Basingstoke: Palgrave Macmillan, 2007), p. 147.
24. Ibid., pp. 145–6.

Chapter 1 – Ferrebe

1. Kurt Wittig, *The Scottish Tradition in Literature* (Edinburgh: Mercat Press, 1978 [1958]), p. 4.
2. 'Cristie Leigh March and A. L. Kennedy', *Edinburgh Review* 101 (1999), p. 106, and Tobias Jones, 'Alan Warner: The Wild Man of Letters', *Independent* (24 May 1998), p. 2.
3. Quoted in John Walsh, 'The Not-So-Shady Past of Irvine Welsh', *Independent*, Weekend Section (15 April 1995), p. 25. Walsh notes that Welsh uses the term 'classics' 'with faint distaste, as one might say "the Government"'.
4. Alexander Trocchi, *Cain's Book* (London: Jupiter, 1966 [1960]), p. 184.
5. *The Story of the Novel*, Channel 4, July 2003.
6. Aaron Kelly, 'Irvine Welsh in Conversation with Aaron Kelly', *Edinburgh Review* 113 (2004), p. 8.
7. T. F. Henderson, *Scottish Vernacular Literature: A Succinct History* (Edinburgh: John Grant, 1910 [1898]), pp. vi–vii.
8. Craig, *The Modern Scottish Novel*, p. 98.
9. Alan Riach, *Representing Scotland in Literature, Popular Culture and Iconography: The Masks of the Modern Nation* (Basingstoke: Palgrave Macmillan, 2005), p. 14.
10. Alan Sinfield, *Literature, Politics and Culture in Postwar Britain* (London: Continuum, 1997), p. xxvii.
11. Quoted in Sinfield, *Literature, Politics and Culture in Postwar Britain*, p. xxvii.

12. Bonnie Blackwell, 'The Society for the Prevention of Cruelty to Narrative', *College Literature* 31 (Winter 2004), p. 2.
13. Irvine Welsh, 'A Scottish George Best of Literature', in Allan Campbell and Tim Neil (eds), *A Life in Pieces: Reflections on Alexander Trocchi* (Edinburgh: Rebel Inc, 1997), p. 18.
14. Craig, *The Modern Scottish Novel*, p. 19.
15. Morace, *Irvine Welsh*, p. 16.
16. Catherine Hall, 'Histories, Empires and the Post-Colonial Moment', in Iain Chambers and Lidia Curti (eds), *The Post-Colonial Question: Common Skies, Divided Horizons* (London: Routledge, 1996), p. 67.
17. Gerard Carruthers, David Goldie and Alastair Renfrew (eds), *Beyond Scotland: New Contexts for Twentieth-Century Scottish Literature* (Amsterdam: Rodopi, 2004), pp. 14–15.
18. Maley, 'Subversion and Squirrility', p. 192.
19. Harold Bloom, *The Anxiety of Influence* (New York: Oxford University Press, 1973), p. 5.
20. Riach, *Representing Scotland in Literature, Popular Culture and Iconography*, pp. 21–2.
21. See Alan Bold, *MacDiarmid – Christopher Murray Grieve: A Critical Biography* (London: Paladin, 1990), p. 157.
22. Seamus Heaney, 'A Torchlight Procession of One: On Hugh MacDiarmid', *The Redress of Poetry: Oxford Lectures* (London: Faber and Faber, 1996), p. 104.
23. *BBC Home*, Editor's review of Alan Warner's *The Man Who Walked*, 'Collective' (2 August 2002), www.bbc.co.uk/dna/collective/A819308.
24. Gareth Evans, 'Niall Griffiths: Between the Rocks and Hard Places', *Independent* (2 March 2002), www.independent.co.uk/arts-entertainment/books/features/niall-griffiths-between-the-rocks-and-hard-places-653746.html, and Katy Guest, 'Sex and the City of Liverpool' (9 April 2002), www.independent.co.uk/arts-entertainment/books/reviews/brass-by-helen-walsh-559341.html.
25. Aaron Kelly, *Irvine Welsh* (Manchester: Manchester University Press, 2005), p. 19.
26. Craig, *The Modern Scottish Novel*, p. 98.
27. Milne, 'The Fiction of James Kelman and Irvine Welsh', p. 158, and Morace, *Irvine Welsh*, pp. 20–1.
28. Quoted in Kirsty MacNeill, 'Interview with James Kelman', *Chapman*, 57 (Summer 1989), pp. 4–5.
29. Morace, *Irvine Welsh*, p. 21.
30. Kelly, *Irvine Welsh*, p. 196.
31. Elspeth Findlay, 'The Bourgeois Values of Irvine Welsh', *Cencrastus* 71 (2002), p. 5.
32. Terry Eagleton, *The Idea of Culture* (Oxford: Blackwell, 2000), p. 71.

33. Gregory Smith, *Scottish Literature: Character and Influences* (London: Macmillan, 1919).
34. Welsh, 'A Scottish George Best of Literature' (1997), p. 18.
35. Morace, *Irvine Welsh*, p. 139.
36. Robert Crawford, *Devolving English Literature* (Oxford: Clarendon Press, 2000 [1992]), p. 333.
37. Morace, *Irvine Welsh*, p. 124.
38. Paul Gilroy, *There Ain't No Black In the Union Jack: The Cultural Politics of Race and Nation* (London: Routledge, 1992 [1987]), p. xxiv.
39. See Alan Riach (ed.), *Selected Prose: Hugh MacDiarmid* (Manchester: Carcanet Press, 1992), p. 3.

Chapter 2 – McGuire

1. Morace, *Irvine Welsh*, p. 13.
2. Michael Brockington, 'Poisoned Haggis', *Vancouver Review* (Fall/Winter 1995), www.sfu.ca/brocking/writing/phaggis.html; Sarah Hemming, 'Grim Wit in a Drug Wasteland', *Financial Times* (21 December 1995), p. 11; Lucy Hughes-Hallet, 'Cruising for a Bruising', *Sunday Times* (15 August 1993), p. 6.
3. Quoted in Walsh, 'The Not-So-Shady Past of Irvine Welsh', p. 25.
4. Quoted in John Mulholland, 'Acid Wit', *Guardian* (30 March 1995), p. 8.
5. Liam McIlvanney, 'The Politics of Narrative in the Post-war Scottish Novel', in Zachery Leader (ed.), *On Modern British Fiction* (Oxford: Oxford University Press, 2002), pp. 181–202.
6. Maley, 'Subversion and Squirrility', p. 192.
7. Ian Watt, *The Rise of the Novel* (London: Pimlico, 2000 [1957]).
8. Morace, *Irvine Welsh*, p. 46.
9. Alan Freeman, 'Ourselves as Others', pp. 135–41; Ellen-Raïssa Jackson and Willy Maley, 'Birds of a Feather? A Postcolonial Reading of Irvine Welsh's *Marabou Stork Nightmares*', *Revista Canaria de Estudios Inglese*, 41 (2000), pp. 187–96.
10. James Kelman, 'Elitist Slurs Are Racism by Another Name', *Scotland on Sunday* (16 October 1994), p. 2.
11. Roddy Doyle, *The Barrytown Trilogy: The Commitments, The Snapper* and *The Van* (London: Minerva, 1993), p. 38.
12. See, for example, Stewart Hall, *The Hard Road to Renewal: Thatcherism and the Crisis of the Left* (London: Verso, 1988).
13. Findlay, 'The Bourgeois Values of Irvine Welsh', pp. 5–7.
14. See Berthold Schoene, 'The Dark Continent of Masculinity: Irvine Welsh's *Marabou Stork Nightmares*', *Writing Men: Literary Masculinities from Frankenstein to the New Man* (Edinburgh: Edinburgh University Press, 2000), pp. 155–6.

15. John Scaggs, *Crime Fiction* (London: Routledge, 2005), p. 60.
16. Kelly, *Irvine Welsh*, p. 153.
17. Ibid., p. 176.
18. Quoted in Kelly, 'Irvine Welsh in Conversation with Aaron Kelly', p. 10.

Chapter 3 – Borthwick

1. All quotations in this opening paragraph are from Frank O'Connor, *The Lonely Voice: A Study of the Short Story* (London: Macmillan, 1965), pp. 18 and 21.
2. Kelly, *Irvine Welsh*, p. 80.
3. Milne, 'The Fiction of James Kelman and Irvine Welsh', p. 159.
4. Kelly, *Irvine Welsh*, p. 15.
5. William Boyd, 'A Short History of the Short Story,' *Prospect* (Summer 2006), www.prospect-magazine.co.uk/article_details.php?id=7447.
6. Kelly, *Irvine Welsh*, p. 81.
7. Kevin Williamson, 'Introducing Rebel Inc.', www.canongate.net/News/RebelInc.
8. Duncan McLean, *Ahead of Its Time: A Clocktower Press Anthology* (London: Cape, 1997), p. x.
9. Morace, *Irvine Welsh*, p. 75.
10. Jürgen Neubauer, *Literature as Intervention: Struggles over Cultural Identity in Contemporary Scottish Fiction* (Marburg: Tectum, 1999), p. 207.
11. Morace, *Irvine Welsh*, p. 91.
12. Irvine Welsh, in a booklet enclosed in *Trainspotting: The Definitive Edition* (dir. Danny Boyle, 1996).
13. Zygmunt Bauman, 'Making and Unmaking of Strategies', in Peter Beilharz (ed.), *The Bauman Reader* (London: Blackwell, 2001), p. 207.
14. Zygmunt Bauman, *Liquid Life* (Cambridge: Polity, 2005), p. 1.
15. Ibid., p. 3.
16. Ibid.
17. Bauman, 'From the Word Ethic to the Ethic of Consumption', in Beilharz, *The Bauman Reader*, p. 318.
18. Bauman, *Liquid Life*, p. 7.
19. Alan Freeman, 'Ghosts in Sunny Leith: Irvine Welsh's *Trainspotting*', in Susanne Hagemann (ed.), *Studies in Scottish Fiction: 1945 to the Present* (Frankfurt: Lang, 1996), p. 257.
20. Alan Riach, 'The Unnatural Scene: The Fiction of Irvine Welsh', in James Acheson and Sarah C. E. Ross (eds), *The Contemporary British Novel* (Edinburgh: Edinburgh University Press, 2005), p. 36.
21. Ibid., p. 45.
22. Milne, 'The Fiction of James Kelman and Irvine Welsh', p. 165.
23. Kelly, *Irvine Welsh*, p. 85.

24. Gerard Carruthers, *Scottish Literature* (Edinburgh: Edinburgh University Press, 2009), p. 148.
25. Morace, *Irvine Welsh*, p. 90.
26. See also Ian Brown, 'Alternative Sensibilities: Devolutionary Comedy and Scottish Camp', in Berthold Schoene (ed.), *The Edinburgh Companion to Contemporary Scottish Literature* (Edinburgh: Edinburgh University Press, 2007), pp. 325–6.
27. Morace, *Irvine Welsh*, p. 91
28. Maley, 'Subversion and Squirrility', p. 192.
29. Kelly, *Irvine Welsh*, p. 87.

Chapter 4 – Petrie

1. For a detailed account of the emergence of a new Scottish cinema, see Duncan Petrie, *Screening Scotland* (London: BFI, 2000), and for a consideration of the links between Scottish literature and film over the last twenty-five years, see Duncan Petrie, *Contemporary Scottish Fictions: Cinema, Television and the Novel* (Edinburgh: Edinburgh University Press, 2004).
2. *Trainspotting* earned eighteen awards internationally, including the 1995 BAFTA for Best Adapted Screenplay, the 1996 Evening Standard Film Award for Best Screenplay, the 1997 Brit Award for Best Soundtrack, the 1997 BAFTA Scotland awards for Best Film and Best Actor (Ewan McGregor), the 1997 Empire Awards for Best Film, Best British Director, Best British Actor (McGregor) and Best Debut (Ewen Bremner). In addition to the Oscar nomination the film earned a further thirteen nominations, including the 1997 Writer's Guild of America Award for Best Adapted Screenplay.
3. Morace, *Irvine Welsh*, p. 65.
4. John Arlidge, 'Return of the Angry Young Men', *Observer* (23 June 1996), p. 24.
5. Murray Smith, *Trainspotting: BFI Modern Classics* (London: BFI, 2002), p. 84.
6. John Hodge, *Trainspotting and Shallow Grave* (London: Faber and Faber, 1996), p. x.
7. Irvine Welsh, quoted in Hodge, *Trainspotting and Shallow Grave*, pp. 118–19.
8. Danny Boyle, quoted in Geoffrey MacNab, 'The Boys Are Back in Town', *Sight and Sound*, 6:2 (February 1996), p. 10.
9. John Orr, *Contemporary Cinema* (Edinburgh: Edinburgh University Press, 1998), p. 15.
10. Smith, *Trainspotting*, p. 75.
11. Ibid., p. 33.
12. Ibid., p. 20.

13. For a detailed analysis of the US distribution of *Trainspotting*, see Sarah Street, *Transatlantic Crossings: British Feature Films in the USA* (London: Continuum, 2002).
14. Morace, *Irvine Welsh*, p. 60.
15. John Hill, 'British Cinema as National Cinema', in Robert Murphy (ed.), *The British Cinema Book*. second edition (London: BFI, 2001), p. 211.
16. Ibid.
17. Hodge, *Trainspotting and Shallow Grave*, p. x.
18. Irvine Welsh, quoted in Mark Salisbury, 'Great Scots', *Premiere*, 20:1 (September 2006), p. 92.
19. Bert Cardullo, 'Fiction into Film, or Bringing Welsh to a Boyle', *Literature/Film Quarterly*, 25:3 (1997), pp. 158–62.
20. Sinfield, *Literature, Politics and Culture in Postwar Britain*, pp. xxvi and xxiv.
21. Kelly, *Irvine Welsh*, p. 70.
22. Quoted in Laura McDonald, '100% Uncut Irvine Welsh on *The Acid House*' (4 August 1999), ttp://www.indiewire.com/people/int_Welsh_Irvine_990804.html.

Chapter 5 – Jones

1. Morace, *Irvine Welsh*, p. 128.
2. Stefan Herbrechter, 'From *Trainspotting* to *Filth* – Masculinity and Cultural Politics in Irvine Welsh's Writings', in Russell West and Frank Lay (eds), *Subverting Masculinity: Hegemonic and Alternative Versions of Masculinity in Contemporary Culture* (Amsterdam: Rodopi, 2000), p. 109.
3. Morace, *Irvine Welsh*, p. 27.
4. Riach, 'The Unnatural Scene', p. 45.
5. Morace, *Irvine Welsh*, p. 128.
6. See Kelly, *Irvine Welsh*, p. 121.
7. See Jackson and Maley, 'Birds of a Feather', pp. 187–96; Schoene, 'The Dark Continent of Masculinity', pp. 145–56.
8. Berthold Schoene, 'Nervous Men, Mobile Nation: Masculinity and Psychopathology in Irvine Welsh's *Filth* and *Glue*', in Eleanor Bell and Gavin Miller (eds), *Scotland in Theory* (Amsterdam: Rodopi, 2004), pp. 121–45.
9. James Campbell, 'Scratch and Sniff', *Guardian* (28 April 2001), p. 8.
10. Roderick Watson, 'Speaking in Tongues: Reflections after Bakhtin on the Scots Literary Tradition and Contemporary Writing', in Alastair Renfrew (ed.), *Exploiting Bakhtin*, Strathclyde Modern Language Studies, New Series No. 2 (University of Strathclyde: Department of Modern Languages, 1997), p. 5.
11. Kelly, *Irvine Welsh*, p. 25.
12. Riach, 'The Unnatural Scene', p. 41.
13. Lynne Pearce, *Reading Dialogics* (London: Edward Arnold, 1994), p. 54.

14. Morace, *Irvine Welsh*, p. 19.
15. Pearce, *Reading Dialogics*, p. 55.
16. Pam Morris, *Literature and Feminism* (Oxford: Blackwell, 1993), p. 155.
17. Mary Russo, 'Female Grotesques: Carnival and Theory', in Teresa de Lauretis (ed.), *Feminist Studies/Critical Studies* (Basingstoke: Macmillan, 1986), p. 219.
18. Kate Webb, 'Seriously Funny: *Wise Children*', in Lorna Sage (ed.), *Flesh and the Mirror: Essays on the Art of Angela Carter* (London: Virago, 1994), p. 301.
19. Watson, 'Speaking in Tongues', p. 13.
20. Webb, 'Seriously Funny', p. 305.
21. Ibid.
22. Jackson and Maley, 'Birds of a Feather', p. 193.
23. Riach, 'The Unnatural Scene', p. 40.
24. Kelly, *Irvine Welsh*, p. 53.
25. Ibid., p. 50.
26. Abigail Soloman-Godeau, 'Male Trouble', in Maurice Berger, Brian Wallis and Simon Watson (eds), *Constructing Masculinity* (New York: Routledge, 1995), p. 73.
27. Schoene, 'The Dark Continent', p. 156. See also Carole Jones, 'White Men on their Backs – From Objection to Abjection: The Representation of the White Male as Victim in William McIlvanney's *Docherty* and Irvine Welsh's *Marabou Stork Nightmares*', *International Journal of Scottish Literature*, 1 (2006), www.ijsl.stir.ac.uk/issue1/jones.htm.
28. Morace, *Irvine Welsh*, p. 92.
29. Kelly, *Irvine Welsh*, p. 165.
30. Schoene, 'Nervous Men, Mobile Nation', p. 140.
31. Kelly, *Irvine Welsh*, pp. 175–6.
32. Morace, *Irvine Welsh*, p. 124.
33. Robert Morace, 'Irvine Welsh: Parochialism, Pornography and Globalisation', in Berthold Schoene (ed.), *Edinburgh Companion to Contemporary Scottish Literature* (Edinburgh: Edinburgh University Press, 2007), p. 228.
34. Maria Pini, *Club Cultures and Female Subjectivity: The Move from Home to House* (Basingstoke: Palgrave Macmillan, 2001), p. 170.
35. Schoene, 'Nervous Men', pp. 140-1.
36. Morace, 'Irvine Welsh', p. 234, and Morace, *Irvine Welsh*, p. 124.
37. Webb, 'Seriously Funny', p. 305.
38. Claire Monk, 'Underbelly UK: the 1990s Underclass Film, Masculinity, and the Ideologies of "New Britannia"', in Justine Ashby and Andrew Higson (eds), *British Cinema: Past and Present* (London: Routledge, 2000), p. 285.
39. Schoene, 'Nervous Men', pp. 140–1.
40. Clair Wills, 'Upsetting the Public: Carnival, Hysteria and Women's Texts',

in Ken Hirschkop and David Shepherd (eds), *Bakhtin and Cultural Theory*. Second edition (Manchester: Manchester University Press, 2001 [1989]), p. 93.

Chapter 6 – Schoene

1. Cardullo, 'Fiction into Film, or Bringing Welsh to a Boyle', p. 159.
2. Patricia Horton, '*Trainspotting*: A Topography of the Masculine Abject', *English* 50:198, p. 223.
3. The site was demolished in 1989 and later redeveloped. It now houses a supermarket and the Leith Waterworld Leisure Centre.
4. Cardullo, 'Fiction into Film', p. 160.
5. Horton, '*Trainspotting*: A Topography of the Masculine Abject', p. 221.
6. Kevin McCarron, 'The Disenchanted Circle: Slave Narratives and Junk Narratives', *Dionysos* 8:1 (1998), p. 6.
7. Kevin Williamson, *Drugs and the Party Line* (Edinburgh: Rebel Inc, 1997), p. 113.
8. Neil McMillan, 'Junked Exiles, Exiled Junk: Irvine Welsh and Alexander Trocchi', in Glenda Norquay and Gerry Smyth (eds), *Space and Place: The Geographies of Literature* (Liverpool: Liverpool John Moores University Press, 1997), p. 241.
9. Ruth Helyer, '"It Was a Madhouse of Assorted Bric-à-Brac": Urban Intensification in Irvine Welsh's *Trainspotting*', in Philippe Leplace and Eric Tabuteau (eds), *Cities on the Margin/On the Margin of Cities: Representations of Urban Space in Contemporary British & Irish Fiction* (Besançon: Universitaires Franc-Comtoises Presses, 2003), p. 226.
10. McMillan, 'Junked Exiles, Exiled Junk', p. 243.
11. Ibid., p. 252.
12. Robert Morace, *Irvine Welsh's* Trainspotting*: A Reader's Guide* (London and New York: Continuum, 2001), p. 65.
13. Maley, 'Subversion and Squirrility', p. 199.
14. Karen Lury, 'Here and Then: Space, Place and Nostalgia in British Youth Cinema of the 1990s', in Robert Murphy (ed.), *British Cinema of the 90s* (London: BFI, 2000), p. 107.
15. Horton, '*Trainspotting*: A Topography of the Masculine Abject', p. 236.
16. Ian Haywood, *Working-Class Fiction from Chartism to Trainspotting* (Plymouth: Northcote House, 1997), p. 158.
17. Anthony Burgess, *A Clockwork Orange* (Harmondsworth: Penguin, 1972 [1962]), p. 34.
18. Berman, 'Irvine Welsh', p. 61.
19. Paget, 'Speaking Out', p. 139.
20. Welsh, 'Drugs and the Theatre, Darlings', in '*Trainspotting*' *and* '*Headstate*' (London: Minerva, 1996), p. 1.

21. Welsh, 'Drugs and the Theatre', p. 3.
22. Simon Reynolds, 'Rave Culture: Living Dream or Living Death?', in Steve Redhead (ed.), *The Clubcultures Reader: Readings in Popular Cultural Studies* (Oxford: Blackwell, 1997), p. 89.
23. Haywood, *Working-Class Fiction from Chartism to Trainspotting*, p. 158.
24. Reynolds, 'Rave Culture', p. 88.
25. Ibid., p. 90.
26. Tim Adams, 'Just Say No', *The Observer* (2 June 1996).
27. Irvine Welsh, 'Introduction', *You'll Have Had Your Hole* (London: Methuen, 1998), p. vii.
28. Ken Gelder, *Subcultures: Cultural Histories and Social Practice* (Abingdon: Routledge, 2007), pp. 3–4.
29. Sukhdev Sandhu, 'The Quest for Pure Feeling', *Daily Telegraph* (17 August, 2002).
30. John Walsh, 'Irvine Welsh: Upwardly Mobile', *Independent* (12 August 2002).

Chapter 7 – Scullion

1. Welsh, *You'll Have Had Your Hole*, p. v.
2. Kelly, *Irvine Welsh*, pp. 12-13, and Morace, *Irvine Welsh*, p. 145.
3. *The Scotsman* (18 October 1991), p. 14.
4. *The Scotsman* (25 October 1991), p. 16.
5. Morace, *Irvine Welsh*, p. 148.
6. See Aleks Sierz, *In-Yer-Face Theatre: British Drama Today* (London: Faber, 2001).
7. Morace, *Irvine Welsh*, p. 149.
8. Ibid.
9. Joyce McMillan, 'Theatre Review: Irvine Welsh's *Blackpool*', *Scotsman* (27 February 2002), http://thescotsman.scotsman.com/ViewArticle.aspx?articleid=2305940.
10. See reviews of *You'll Have Had Your Hole* by Robert Butler, *Independent on Sunday*, and by Robert Gore-Langton, *Express on Sunday* (both 1 March 1998), reprinted in *London Theatre Record* 18.4 (1998), pp. 221–5.
11. *You'll Have Had Your Hole*, p. 8.
12. Ibid., p. 50.
13. See reviews of the play by Charles Spencer (*Daily Telegraph* [26 February 1998], reprinted in the *London Theatre Record* 18.4 [1998], p. 222), Andrew Aldridge (*The Stage* [11 February 1999], p. 1), and Robert Gore-Langton (*Express on Sunday* [1 March 1998], reprinted in the *London Theatre Record* 18.4 [1998], p. 222).
14. See review of the play by Michael Billington, *Guardian* (25 February 1998), reprinted in the *London Theatre Record* 18.4 (1998), p. 223.

15. Irvine Welsh and Dean Cavanagh, *Babylon Heights* (London: Vintage, 2006), p. 4.
16. Chloe Veltman, 'Oz-mosis', *SF Weekly*, http://www.sffringe.org/media/babylon3.html.
17. Irvine Welsh, 'Why I Hate Theatre', *The Stage* (4 February 1999), p. 4.

Chapter 8 – Miller

1. Craig, *The Modern Scottish Novel*, pp. 100–3.
2. Kwame Anthony Appiah, *The Ethics of Identity* (Princeton, NJ: Princeton University Press, 2005), p. 131.
3. Appiah, *The Ethics of Identity*, p. 137.
4. Steve Bruce, Tony Glendinning, Iain Paterson and Michael Rosie, *Sectarianism in Scotland* (Edinburgh: Edinburgh University Press, 2004), p. 13.
5. Bruce, *Sectarianism in Scotland*, p. 65.
6. Ibid., p. 5.
7. Ibid., pp. 172–3.
8. Kwame Anthony Appiah, *In My Father's House: Africa in the Philosophy of Culture* (London: Methuen, 1992), p. 59.
9. Kerwin Lee Klein, 'On the Emergence of Memory in Historical Discourse', *Representations*, 69 (2000), p. 136.
10. Dominick LaCapra, *History and Memory after Auschwitz* (New York: Cornell University Press, 1998), p. 21.
11. LaCapra, *History and Memory after Auschwitz*, p. 64.
12. Walter Benn Michaels, *The Trouble with Diversity: How We Learned to Love Identity and Ignore Inequality* (New York: Metropolitan, 2006), p. 131.
13. Jones, 'White Men on Their Backs – From Objection to Abjection', p. 10.
14. Sally Robinson, *Marked Men: White Masculinity in Crisis* (New York: Columbia University Press, 2000), p. 12.
15. Walter Benn Michaels, 'Autobiography of an Ex-white Man', *Transition*, 73 (1997), pp. 140, 142.
16. Benn Michaels, *The Trouble with Diversity*, p. 201.

Chapter 9 – Clandfield and Lloyd

1. *Welcome to Edinburgh: Free Guide with Detailed City Maps* (Carrbridge: Landmark Press, 2009), pp. 4 and 26.
2. Irvine Welsh and Kevin Williamson, *A Visitor's Guide to Edinburgh* (Edinburgh: Rebel Inc., 1993), pp. 3 and 8.
3. We understand 'supplement' as referring to how a supposedly finished text – from a sentence to a building – carries traces of alternative or additional meanings. Derrida develops the theory of the supplement in *Of Grammatology* (tr.

G. C. Spivak [Baltimore, MD: Johns Hopkins University Press, 1997 (1967)], see especially pp. 144–5, 157–8). Also noteworthy is Derrida's *Spectres of Marx*, which evokes the way 'great unifying projects' of modern Europe continue to be haunted by spectres of excluded interests or incompletely-fulfilled promises (tr. P. Kamuf [New York: Routledge, 1994 (1993)], p. 3).

4. This chapter is indebted to the sharp commentary Bell provides during his tours and in his writings about Leith and Welsh's work. For further information, see www.leithwalks.co.uk.
5. In *Glue*, the no-taxis vignette is reprised from a different viewpoint: Carl Ewart, hurrying to see his dying father, is stranded at Edinburgh's west-end Haymarket Station: 'The rank was empty. No taxi had its sign up. The Festival' ([London: Vintage, 2002 (2001)], p. 525). The laconic phrasing casts the Festival as an annual plague which locals submit to stoically.
6. Morace, *Irvine Welsh*, p. 40.
7. Lewis MacLeod, 'Life among the Leith Plebs: Of Arseholes, Wankers, and Tourists in Irvine Welsh's *Trainspotting*', *Studies in the Literary Imagination* 41:1 (2008), p. 90.
8. Kelly, *Irvine Welsh*, p. 19.
9. Dominic Head, *The Cambridge Introduction to Modern British Fiction, 1950–2000* (Cambridge: Cambridge University Press, 2002), p. 45.
10. Morace, *Irvine Welsh*, p. 54.
11. John Sturrock, 'Muirhouse', *Granta* 25 (1988), pp. 229–48, p. 246.
12. Tim Bell, 'Leith Central Station', in Scottish Publishers' Association, *A Sense of Place: A Collection of New Scottish Writing* (New Lanark: Waverley Books, 2005), pp. 99–100.
13. Kelly, *Irvine Welsh*, p. 47.
14. MacLeod, 'Life among the Leith Plebs', p. 103.
15. Kelly, *Irvine Welsh*, p. 48.
16. As Joe Moran explains, the Thatcher government's '1980 Housing Act gave millions of council tenants [across the UK] the right to buy their homes at huge discounts, partly in the expectation that these new homeowners would be more likely to vote Conservative'. Moran terms this one of Thatcherism's most 'socially divisive' measures, and links it to the era's wider 'credit and mortgage booms', whose dangers are now increasingly clear (*Reading the Everyday* [London: Routledge, 2005], pp. 129–30).
17. 'Streets in the sky' seems to have originated as a sincere and literal description of modernist architects' visions for public housing, so Strang's description of the phrase as a joke comments pointedly on the limits of such visions.
18. See also Peter Clandfield and Christian Lloyd, 'Redevelopment Fiction: Architecture, Town-planning and "Unhomeliness"', in Berthold Schoene (ed.), *The Edinburgh Companion to Contemporary Scottish Literature* (Edinburgh: Edinburgh University Press, 2007), pp. 124–31.
19. The common Scottish usage 'scheme' is a more aptly nuanced term

than 'estate', evoking at least three relevant meanings: detailed architectural and social designs, grandly unfeasible dreams, and underhand shady dealings.

20. Caroline Gottschalk-Druschke, 'Irvine Welsh's Rhetoric of Liminal Space: "A History of Leith Fae the Merger tae the Present"', North East Modern Language Association Roundtable on Scottish Fiction, Boston, MA (1 April 2005), unpublished typescript, p. 6.
21. John Hodge, screenwriter of *Trainspotting*, has contended that controlled location shooting on a housing estate is 'no closer to the real experience' of everyday life in such environments than is using 'stylized or fantastical elements' like those of the *Trainspotting* film, but what Welsh and director Paul McGuigan achieve in *The Acid House* is a strong hybrid of the real/documentary and the stylised/fantastic. On the *Trainspotting* film's marked detachment from the novel's local grounding, see also Kelly, *Irvine Welsh*, p. 68, and Bell, 'Leith Central Station', p. 100.
22. Donald Campbell, *Edinburgh: A Cultural and Literary History* (New York: Interlink, 2004), pp. 205 and 191–2.
23. See David Harvey, *Spaces of Capital: Towards a Critical Geography* (New York: Routledge, 2001).
24. Morace, *Irvine Welsh*, p. 152.

Chapter 10 – Ashley

1. Ricarda Weißenberger, *The Search for a National Identity in the Scottish Literary Tradition and the Use of Language in Irvine Welsh's 'Trainspotting'* (Berlin: Dreisen Edition Wissenschaft, 2006), p. 381.
2. Kelly, *Irvine Welsh*, p. 36.
3. The fact that the film poster does not grace the covers of all more recent translations, like the Russian, Latvian and Greek editions, reinforces its importance in exporting Welsh in the 1990s. (The 2006 Romanian cover does refer to the film.)
4. Gerald Howard, 'Hanging with the Scottish Homeboys: Adventures in Literature with James Kelman, Duncan McLean, and Irvine Welsh', 1997, www.wwnorton.com/catalog/featured/irvinewelsh/scots.htm; Bert Bultinck, 'Kant of kont?', *De Morgen* (8 October 2003), in *Factiva*, http://global.factiva.com; and Keith McPhalen, 'Going for the Jugular of Conventionality', *The Daily Yomiuri/Yomiuri Shimbun* (28 March 1999), in *Factiva*, http://global.factiva.com.
5. Welsh taught at Columbia College, Chicago and served as a judge for the 'Prix Prince Maurice du roman d'amour', an award for romance novels.
6. Michael Gardiner, 'British Territory: Irvine Welsh in English and Japanese', *Textual Practice*, 17:1 (2003), p. 106.
7. Ibid., p. 112.

8. Anon., 'The Bedroom Secrets of the Master Chefs', *The Nation* (Thailand) (16 October 2007), in *Factiva*, http://global.factiva.com; Simonetta Fiori, 'Cibo, sesso e viaggi – in bozze', *La Repubblica* (14 October 2006), in *Factiva*, http://global.factiva.com.
9. Emilia Ippolito, 'Gli amori proibitii i Welsh', *L'Espresso* (2 August 2008), in *Factiva*, http://global.factiva.com.
10. Eduardo Barros-Grela analyses the theoretical implications of socio-economic differences between Welsh and his translators, and provides an alternate Spanish translation of the beginning of *Trainspotting* ('El tratamiento de lexicografía ficticia en la traducción de narrativa. Una perspectiva prosódico-discursiva en torno a la idiosincrasia sociocultural del traductor', *Espéculo: Revista de estudios literarios*, 23 (12 April 2003), www.ucm.es/info/especulo/numero23/traducci.html.
11. Jonas Mortier, 'Opgeraapt van de dansvloer', *De Standaard* (1 August 2002), in *Factiva*, http://global.factiva.com.
12. Howard, 'Hanging with the Scottish Homeboys'.
13. See Ibid.
14. Itamar Even-Zohar, 'The Position of Translated Literature within the Literary Polysystem', in Lawrence Venuti (ed.), *The Translation Studies Reader* (New York and London: Routledge, 2002), pp. 203–4.
15. Craig, *The Modern Scottish Novel*, p. 181.
16. Antoine Berman, 'Translation and the Trials of the Foreign' [tr. L. Venuti], in Venuti, *The Translation Studies Reader*, p. 286.
17. Evelyn Nien-Ming Ch'ien, *Weird English* (Cambridge, MA: Harvard University Press, 2004), pp. 5 and 12–14.
18. McPhalen, 'Going for the Jugular of Conventionality', n.p.; K. C. Nambiar, 'Scenes of Edinburgh', *The Hindu* (18 July 2000), in *Factiva*, http://global.factiva.com; Jeff Zaleski, '*Porno* (Book)', *Publishers Weekly*, 249:40 (7 October 2002), p. 54, in *Academic Search Premier*, http://search.ebscohost.com/; Anon., 'The Bedroom Secrets', and Bob Minzesheimer, 'The Bedroom Secrets of the Master Chefs', *USA Today* (31 August 2006), 'Life' section, p. 7d, in *Academic Search Premier*, http://search.ebscohost.com/; and Anon., 'If You Liked School, You'll Love Work', *Kirkus Reviews* (15 August 2007), 75:16, p. 825, in *Academic Search Premier*, http://search.ebscohost.com/.
19. Quoted in Morace, *Irvine Welsh's 'Trainspotting'*, p. 27.
20. Robert Crawford, *Scotland's Books: The Penguin History of Scottish Literature* (London: Penguin, 2007), p. 671.
21. See also Jeffrey Karnicky, 'Irvine Welsh's Novel Subjectivities', *Social Text*, 21:3 (2003), pp. 135–53.
22. Gerald Howard, 'A *Trainspotting* Glossary', *Paris Review*, 38:138 (1996), p. 348.
23. Christine Jordis, 'Gens de Glasgow', *Le Monde des Livres* (22 February 2008), p. 4, and Agnes-Catherine Poirier, '*Trainspotting* sera-t-il l'*Orange mécanique*

des années 90?', *Le Monde* (10 May 1996), both in *Factiva*, http://global.factiva.com.

24. Irvine Welsh, *Trainspotting*, tr. F. Corriente (Barcelona: Anagrama, 1999), p. 11.
25. Irvine Welsh, *Trainspotting*, tr. E. L. Fall (Paris: Editions de l'Olivier/Points, 2007), p. 11.
26. Gardiner, 'British Territory', pp. 108–9.
27. Québécois films are sometimes subtitled in France, just as *Trainspotting* was subtitled in North America. It should also be noted that the 'Inter Shitty' pun disappears in French where the chapter becomes 'Caca dedans', literally meaning 'shit inside'.
28. Welsh, *Trainspotting*, tr. E. L. Fall, pp. 135–6.
29. Ibid., p. 42, and *Trainspotting*, tr. F. Corriente, p. 37. Emphasis added.
30. Martine Silber, 'Littératures – Assis sur leurs rêves', *Le Monde* (3 April 1998), in *Factiva*, http://global.factiva.com.
31. Reproducing specific voices is problematic in some of Welsh's other works as well. Bultinck believes it adversely affected the Dutch translation of *Porno*, a novel in which dialect plays a less prominent role than in *Trainspotting* ('Kant of kont?'), while Mortier believes the same is true of the Dutch translation of *Glue* ('Opgeraapt van de dansvloer').
32. Martin Brüggemeier and Horst W. Drescher, 'A Subculture and its Characterization in Irvine Welsh's *Trainspotting*', *Anglistik & Englischunterricht*, 63 (2000), pp. 135–50.
33. Martin Bowman, '*Trainspotting* in Montreal: The Dramatic Version', *International Journal of Scottish Theatre*, 1:1 (2000), www.arts.gla.ac.uk/ScotLit/ASLS/ijost/Volume1_no1/M_Bowman.htm. The Québécois translation of the play has not been published, but the monologue appears to correspond to the chapter 'A Disappointment', for which the French translation of the novel uses 'putain', 'con', 'saloperie', 'foutu' and 'enculé' – words which are no less specific to France than 'câlisse' is to Québec.
34. Brüggemeier and Drescher, 'A Subculture and its Characterization', p. 146.
35. Anon., 'Irvine Welsh nous sert la suite de *Trainspotting*', *Ouest France* (3 January 2008), in *Factiva*, http://global.factiva.com.
36. Berman, 'Translation and the Trials of the Foreign', p. 280.
37. For example, 'Tirawnto. That wis the Lone Ranger's mate, wis it no?' → '*Tirawnto*. Ése era el socio del Llanero Solitario, ¿no es así?' (Trainspotting, tr. F. Corriente, p. 121) → Tirawnto. That was the Lone Ranger's sidekick, wasn't it?
38. Ippolito, 'Gli amori proibitii i Welsh'.

Further Reading

Works

4-Play: Trainspotting, Marabou Stork Nightmares, Ecstasy, Filth. (London: Vintage, 2001).
The Acid House. London: Vintage, 1995 [London: Cape, 1994].
The Acid House: A Screenplay. London: Methuen, 1999.
[with Dean Cavanagh] *Babylon Heights: A Play*. London: Vintage, 2006.
The Bedroom Secrets of the Master Chefs. London: Cape, 2006.
Crime. London: Cape, 2008.
Ecstasy: Three Tales of Chemical Romance. London: Cape, 1996.
Filth. London: Jonathan Cape, 1998.
Glue. London: Jonathan Cape, 2001.
If You Liked School, You'll Love Work. London: Cape, 2007.
The Irvine Welsh Omnibus. London: Secker & Warburg/Cape, 1997.
Marabou Stork Nightmares. London: Cape, 1995.
Porno. London: Cape, 2002.
Reheated Cabbage. London: Cape, 2009.
Trainspotting. London: Minerva, 1994 [London: Secker & Warburg, 1993].
'Trainspotting' and 'Headstate'. London: Minerva, 1996.
You'll Have Had Your Hole. London: Methuen, 1998.

Criticism

Berman, Jenifer (1996), 'Irvine Welsh', *Bomb Magazine*, 56-61.
Carruthers, Gerard (2009), *Scottish Literature*. Edinburgh: Edinburgh University Press.
Collin, Matthew (1997), *Altered State: The Story of Ecstasy Culture and Acid House*, London: Serpent's Tail.
Craig, Cairns (1999), *The Modern Scottish Novel: Narrative and the National Imagination*, Edinburgh: Edinburgh University Press.
Findlay, Elspeth (2002), 'The Bourgeois Values of Irvine Welsh', *Cencrastus* 71, 5–7.

Haywood, Ian (1997), *Working-Class Fiction from Chartism to Trainspotting*, Plymouth: Northcote House.
Horton, Patricia (2001), '*Trainspotting*: A Topography of the Masculine Abject', *English* 50:198, 219–34.
Jackson, Ellen-Raïssa and Willy Maley (2000), 'Birds of a Feather? A Postcolonial Reading of Irvine Welsh's *Marabou Stork Nightmares*', *Revista Canaria de Estudios Ingleses* 41, 187–96.
Kelly, Aaron (2005), *Irvine Welsh*, Manchester: Manchester University Press.
Maley, Willy (2000), 'Subversion and Squirrility in Irvine Welsh's Shorter Fiction', in Dermot Cavanagh and Tim Kirk (eds), *Subversion and Scurrility: Popular Discourse in Europe from 1500 to the Present*, Aldershot; Ashgate, pp. 190–204.
McGuire, Matt (2009), *Contemporary Scottish Literature: A Reader's Guide to Essential Criticism*, Basingstoke: Palgrave, Macmillan.
Morace, Robert (2001), *Irvine Welsh's* Trainspotting: *A Reader's Guide*. New York and London: Continuum.
Morace, Robert (2007), *Irvine Welsh*, Basingstoke: Palgrave Macmillan.
Neubauer, Jürgen (1999), *Literature as Intervention: Struggles over Cultural Identity in Contemporary Scottish Fiction*, Marburg: Tectum.
Paget, Derek (1999), 'Speaking Out: The Transformations of *Trainspotting*', in Deborah Cartmell and Imelda Whelehan (eds), *Adaptations: From Text to Screen, Screen to Text*, London and New York: Routledge, 128–40.
Petrie, Duncan (2004), *Contemporary Scottish Fictions: Film, Television and the Novel*, Edinburgh: Edinburgh University Press.
Schoene, Berthold (2000), *Writing Men: Literary Masculinities from Frankenstein to the New Man*, Edinburgh: Edinburgh University Press.
Schoene, Berthold (2004), 'Nervous Men, Mobile Nation: Masculinity and Psychopathology in Irvine Welsh's *Filth* and *Glue*', in Eleanor Bell and Gavin Miller (eds), *Scotland in Theory: Reflections on Culture and Literature*, Amsterdam: Rodopi, 121–45.
Schoene, Berthold (ed.) (2007), *The Edinburgh Companion to Contemporary Scottish Literature*. Edinburgh: Edinburgh University Press.
Smith, Murray (2002), *Trainspotting*, London: BFI.
Whyte, Christopher (1998), 'Masculinities in Contemporary Scottish Fiction', *Forum for Modern Language Studies* 34:3, 274–85.

Notes on Contributors

Katherine Ashley has a PhD in French from the University of Edinburgh and degrees in English, French and European Literature from Acadia, Rouen and Cambridge Universities. She has published on nineteenth- and twentieth-century French and Scottish literature.

David Borthwick teaches English and Scottish literature at the University of Glasgow's Dumfries Campus. His main interests include contemporary Scottish literature and ecocriticism. His most recent research centres on the poetry of John Burnside.

Peter Clandfield teaches in the Department of English Studies at Nipissing University, North Bay, Ontario. He is working on a book-length project about fictional representations of development, redevelopment and urban environments.

Alice Ferrebe is Senior Lecturer in English at Liverpool John Moores University. Her book *Masculinity in the Male-Authored Novel, 1950–2000* was published in 2005.

Carole Jones is Lecturer in English at the University of Edinburgh. Her research engages with issues of gender and sexuality in contemporary writing, and she has published widely on Scottish fiction. She is the author of *Disappearing Men: Gender Disorientation in Scottish Fiction, 1979–1999* (2009).

Christian Lloyd is Assistant Academic Director at Queen's University (Canada) International Study Centre at Herstmonceux Castle, East Sussex, where he also teaches literary studies and British studies.

Matt McGuire is Lecturer in the Department of Scottish Literature at the University of Glasgow. He is the author of *Contemporary Scottish Literature*

(2008) and co-editor of *The Edinburgh Companion to Contemporary Scottish Poetry* (2009).

Gavin Miller is Research Fellow in the English Research Institute at Manchester Metropolitan University. He is the author of *R. D. Laing* (2004) and *Alasdair Gray: the Fiction of Communion* (2005). His research interests include science fiction, Scottish literature, and the history of psychiatry.

Duncan Petrie is Professor of Film and Television at the University of York. His books include *Creativity and Constraint in the British Film Industry* (1991), *The British Cinematographer* (1996), *Screening Scotland* (2000), *Contemporary Scottish Fictions* (2004) and *Shot in New Zealand* (2007).

Berthold Schoene is Professor of English and Director of the English Research Institute at Manchester Metropolitan University. He is the author of *The Making of Orcadia* (1995), *Writing Men* (2000) and *The Cosmopolitan Novel* (2009) and editor of *Posting the Male* (2003) and *The Edinburgh Companion to Contemporary Scottish Literature* (2007).

Adrienne Scullion teaches in the Department of Theatre, Film and Television at the University of Glasgow where she is James Arnott Professor of Drama. Her research and teaching interests focus on Scottish theatre and drama from the eighteenth century to the post-devolution period.

Index

AIDS *see* HIV infection
apartheid, 24, 90–1, 96–8, 106
Appiah, Anthony, 90
autism, 72

Bacon, Francis, 46
Bakhtin, Mikhail, 55, 102; *see also* carnivalesque; heteroglossia
Bauman, Zygmunt, 36–8
Benn Michaels, Walter, 96–9
Berman, Jenifer, 3, 69–70
Betts, Leah, 71
Blairism *see* New Labour
Bloom, Harold, 13
Bowman, Martin, 123
Boyle, Danny, 2, 23, 42–53, 55–6, 65, 76
branding, 1, 14, 17, 30, 35, 37, 50, 52, 68–9, 80, 114–15, 125; *see also* commercialisation
BritArt, 50
Britpop, 47, 50, 114
Burgess, Anthony, 69
Burroughs, William, 10, 115

'Caledonian Antisyzygy', 17, 110; *see also* divided self
Cardullo, Bert, 50, 65, 66
carnivalesque, 40, 55–6, 58–9, 60–4; *see also* Bakhtin, Mikhail
Cavanagh, Dean, 86–7
Children of Albion Rovers, 33
club culture, 23, 38, 73–4, 80, 82; *see also* rave culture
cocaine, 23, 28, 29, 75
commercialisation, 12, 27, 75
commodity capitalism, 51–2, 68
'Cool Britannia', 50, 80, 114; *see also* New Labour
'Cool Caledonia', 52; *see also* New Labour
Craig, Cairns, 6, 10, 12, 15, 89, 118
cross-dressing, 58–9, 59, 96

Derrida, Jacques, 101, 136n
différance, 14–15, 18
divided self, 17, 28, 109–10
Doyle, Roddy, 24
drugs, 66–75; *see also* cocaine; ecstasy; heroin

Eagleton, Terry, 15, 16
ecstasy, 23, 38, 71–4, 100

femininity, 54–64, 72
feminism, 25, 56
Findlay, Elspeth, 16, 25
Freeman, Alan, 3, 24

Gardiner, Michael, 114, 121
Gelder, Ken, 74

Gemmill, Archie, 46, 49–50
gender, 54–64, 69–72; *see also* femininity; masculinity
gentrification, 27, 108
Gibson, Harry, 44, 77, 79–81, 83, 123
Gottschalk-Drutschke, Caroline, 108–9
Grassic Gibbon, Lewis, 10
Gray, Alasdair, 1, 10, 14, 21, 42
Griffiths, Niall, 14
Griffiths, Trevor, 77–9

hard man, 24, 44, 54, 57–8, 72; *see also* masculinity
Helyer, Ruth, 67
Henderson, T. F., 10
Herbrechter, Stefan, 54
heroin, 9, 20–3, 45, 65–72
heteroglossia, 55, 59, 125; *see also* Bakhtin, Mikhail
Hird, Laura, 14, 33
HIV infection, 20, 45, 68, 70, 104
Hodge, John, 42, 44, 50, 138n
homophobia, 25, 56, 70
homosexuality, 57–8
Horton, Patricia, 3, 65, 66, 69

'in-yer-face' theatre, 81, 84
inferiorism, 2

Jones, Carole, 97
junk narratives, 67

Kane, Sarah, 81, 84
Kelly, Aaron, 10, 15, 16, 26, 27, 31–2, 39, 51–2, 57, 77, 102, 105, 113
Kelman, James, 2, 5, 10, 14, 15–16, 21, 24, 42, 53, 89
Kennedy, A. L., 9
Kubrick, Stanley, 46

LaCapra, Dominick, 94
'ladlit', 54
language, Welsh's use of, 113
  and gender, 56–7
  and Scottishness, 118–25
  as demotic, 11, 14–15
  as political, 15–16
  as synthetic, 2–3, 11
  as vernacular, 10–11, 15–18, 55, 57, 59–60, 113, 119, 122, 124–5
  in relation to Standard English, 11, 16, 18, 56, 119–22, 124
Leith, 3, 27, 30, 100–12
lumpenproletariat, 37, 74; *see also* underclass
Lury, Karen, 68–9

McCann, Madeleine, 29
McCarron, Kevin, 66–7
MacDiarmid, Hugh, 2, 11–13, 14, 18
MacDonald, Andrew, 42, 45
McGuigan, Paul, 11, 52, 109, 138n
McIlvanney, Liam, 21
McIlvanney, William, 10, 21
McLean, Duncan, 32–3
McMillan, Neil, 67–8
Maley, Willy, 4, 5–6, 13, 22, 24, 40, 68
masculinity, 24–5, 54, 56–60, 62–4, 70, 72, 97
memory, 93–6
misogyny, 25–6, 54, 62, 64
Morace, Robert, 6, 7, 12, 16, 17, 34, 35, 40, 43, 49, 54, 58, 68, 77, 102, 103, 111–12
Muir, Edwin, 12–13, 18

Neilson, Anthony, 81
neoliberalism, 7, 50, 74, 99
Neubauer, Jürgen, 34
New Labour, 21, 43, 50–2

O'Connor, Frank, 31, 39, 41

paedophilia, 29, 75
Paget, Derek, 2, 70
Palahniuk, Chuck, 25
Pini, Maria, 59
pornography, 23, 27–8, 75
postcoloniality, 18, 23–4, 66
postmodernism, 14–15, 17

'queering', 59

Rab C. Nesbitt, 1
racism, 4, 23–6, 57, 58, 78, 90, 92; *see also* apartheid
rave culture, 32–4, 38, 59, 71–4, 82; *see also* club culture
Ravenhill, Mark, 81, 84
realism, 3, 4, 7, 10–11, 15, 21, 28, 31, 39–41, 45–6, 47, 55, 96, 101, 109
Reynolds, Simon, 71–3
Riach, Alan, 10, 13–14, 39
Russo, Mary, 55

Saadi, Suhayl, 14
sampling, 13, 39
Schoene, Berthold, 60, 64
Scottishness, 2–4, 7–8, 10, 13
  as a 'culture of erasure', 12, 18; *see also* language and Scottishness
sectarianism, 23, 90–2
sexism, 54–9, 78, 121–2, 123
Shallow Grave, 42, 43, 46, 47–8
short story, 31–2, 39, 41
Sierz, Aleks, 81
Sinfield, Alan, 10–11, 51
Smith, Murray, 43–4, 47
Standard English; *see* language
Sturrock, John, 104
subculture, 3, 63, 68–70, 72, 74–6
supplement, 101, 136n

Tarantino, Quentin, 25, 47
Thatcherism, 20, 33, 43, 51–2, 105, 137n
Theweleit, Klaus, 64
Trocchi, Alexander, 9–10, 12, 13, 33, 53, 115

underclass, 2, 4, 68, 74

Wallace, Gavin, 1–2
Warner, Alan, 9, 11, 14, 33
Webb, Kate, 56, 62
Welsh, Irvine
  The Acid House, 7, 11, 32, 33–7, 40–1, 52–3, 109, 114, 138n
  Babylon Heights, 77, 79, 86–8
  The Bedroom Secrets of the Master Chefs, 7, 11–12, 17, 28–9, 109–10
  Blackpool, 77, 79, 83–4
  Crime, 8, 29, 75–6, 111
  Ecstasy, 23, 32, 33, 38–9, 71, 73–4, 93
  'Eurotrash', 36
  Filth, 26, 58–9, 76, 80, 94–6, 106
  'Fortune's Always Hiding', 39, 93–4, 95, 99
  Glue, 16, 26–7, 59, 89–90, 91, 106–7
  'The Granton Star Cause', 40–1, 109
  Headstate, 6, 77, 79, 82–3
  'The House of John Deaf', 35
  If You Liked School, You'll Love Work, 7, 41
  Marabou Stork Nightmares, 23–5, 54, 62, 80, 90, 96–9, 106, 114–15
  Porno, 4, 27–8, 69, 72, 74–5, 92–3, 107–9, 115, 119
  Reheated Cabbage, 8
  'A Smart Cunt', 37

Welsh, Irvine (*cont.*)
Trainspotting, 1, 2 5, 19–23, 42–53, 55–6, 65–71, 76, 101–5, 113–14, 119–25
'The Undefeated', 37, 38, 73–4
Wedding Belles, 54, 60–4
'Where the Debris Meets the Sea', 34–5, 60, 109
You'll Have Had Your Hole, 77, 79, 84–6
Williamson, Kevin, 32–3, 40, 67, 100
The Wire, 111
Wittig, Kurt, 9, 17–18
working-class identity, 4, 15, 96–9; *see also* underclass

EU Authorised Representative:
Easy Access System Europe Mustamäe tee 50, 10621 Tallinn, Estonia
gpsr.requests@easproject.com

Printed and bound by CPI Group (UK) Ltd, Croydon, CR0 4YY
06/07/2026
02160605-0001